CRIMINOLOGY
A complete introduction

To my wife, Julie, and my daughters, Emmeline and Eleanor

Teach Yourself®

CRIMINOLOGY
A complete introduction

Peter Joyce

First published in Great Britain in 2012 by Hodder & Stoughton. An Hachette UK company.

First published in US in 2012 by The McGraw-Hill Companies, Inc.

This edition published 2012

Copyright © Peter Joyce 2012

The right of Peter Joyce to be identified as the Author of the Work has been asserted by him in accordance with the Copyright, Designs and Patents Act 1988.

Database right Hodder & Stoughton (makers)

The *Teach Yourself* name is a registered trademark of Hachette UK.

British Library Cataloguing in Publication Data: a catalogue record for this title is available from the British Library.

Library of Congress Catalog Card Number: on file.

10 9 8 7 6 5 4 3 2 1

The publisher has used its best endeavours to ensure that any website addresses referred to in this book are correct and active at the time of going to press. However, the publisher and the author have no responsibility for the websites and can make no guarantee that a site will remain live or that the content will remain relevant, decent or appropriate.

The publisher has made every effort to mark as such all words which it believes to be trademarks. The publisher should also like to make it clear that the presence of a word in the book, whether marked or unmarked, in no way affects its legal status as a trademark.

Every reasonable effort has been made by the publisher to trace the copyright holders of material in this book. Any errors or omissions should be notified in writing to the publisher, who will endeavour to rectify the situation for any reprints and future editions.

Cover image © mipan – Fotolia.

Typeset by Cenveo Publisher Services.

Printed in Great Britain by CPI Group (UK) Ltd, Croydon, CR0 4YY.

Hodder & Stoughton policy is to use papers that are natural, renewable and recyclable products and made from wood grown in sustainable forests. The logging and manufacturing processes are expected to conform to the environmental regulations of the country of origin.

Hodder & Stoughton Ltd

338 Euston Road

London NW1 3BH

www.hodder.co.uk

Contents

Preface

This book is designed as an introduction to the study of criminology and is written for those who have no existing knowledge of the subject area. It seeks to provide readers with an understanding of the very broad range of issues that are the concerns of criminology.

Much of the material is global in scope, covering subjects that have relevance to countries across the world. As criminal justice systems tend to be specific to individual countries, discussions related to this aspect of criminology focus on England and Wales but place this within an international context to enable similarities and comparisons to be drawn. In particular, aspects of the American criminal justice system are used in this context.

The chapters contain a number of common features. Each contains blocks of quotations from major texts that readers studying criminology in an academic setting can incorporate into their written work. One or two case studies are included to highlight general issues that are raised in each chapter. Readers are also invited to test their understanding of the content of the chapter in a multiple-choice test. The 'Dig deeper' section of the chapter is designed to enable readers to extend their knowledge of the material by consulting more specialized texts.

Peter Joyce

July 2012

1

What is crime?

Although most of us probably have an opinion as to what constitutes a crime, there is less agreement among criminologists as to what this term embraces. A particular issue is whose views determine whether an act is criminal or not – does crime reflect popular opinion concerning what is regarded as improper behaviour or is it defined by those who wield power in society who may use their position to outlaw actions that threaten their dominance? This chapter examines the main viewpoints regarding how crime might be defined and then discusses the manner in which various types of crime are classified.

Definitions of crime

Key idea

Crime is generally regarded as an act that breaks the law. However, criminology wishes to examine this issue further by explaining what determines whether an action is considered criminal or not.

An initial concern of criminology is to define the scope of what is studied. To argue that it entails studying criminal behaviour begs the question: *What is criminal behaviour?* Although the obvious answer to this question is *an act that breaks the law*, criminology needs to go beyond this and examine *what determines whether an act is criminal or not* – why are some actions subject to a process within society that results in them being criminalized.

The legalistic definition of crime views it as 'an intentional act in violation of the criminal law (statutory or case law) committed without defense or excuse and penalized by the state as a felony or misdemeanour' (Tappan, 1947: 100).

Tappan, P. (1947). 'Who is the Criminal?'.
American Sociological Review 12(10): 96–102.

Let us now consider four views that relate to what determines why certain actions are considered to be criminal.

POPULAR VIEWS OF RIGHT OR WRONG BEHAVIOUR

Key idea

One explanation of why some acts are defined as criminal is that they constitute actions which most members of society regard as wrong.

It might be argued that actions that are regarded to be criminal are those which are widely disapproved of by the general public. Most of us would regard killing a fellow human being as wrong and this action is thus defined as the crime of murder and severe consequences follow for those who commit it.

This suggests, therefore, that there exists agreement (or *consensus*) within society as to actions that should not be tolerated – a crime, therefore, consists of an act that most people regard as wrong. Criminals are thus a minority who fail to obey society's common standards of behaviour. Additionally, popular perceptions that certain acts are wrong are likely to be relatively stable over historical periods of time since this definition implies that some acts are inherently regarded as wrong.

There is, however, a major problem with this definition. This is the extent to which there is a consensus within society regarding actions that are acceptable and those that are not. On occasions, there may be widespread tolerance if not acceptance of an act that is commonly defined as criminal.

A female who kills her abusive male partner to protect herself and her children from violence may have technically committed murder. However, it is likely that many members of the general public, if acquainted with the full facts of the situation that drove her to carry out this action, would not condemn her for doing it.

A house owner whose use of self-defence results in the killing of an unarmed burglar who broke into his or her property may also have committed murder – but many members of society would not regard this action as wrong. This issue became the subject of public debate in England and Wales in 1999 in connection with a Norfolk farmer, Tony Martin, who was charged with murdering a 16-year-old burglar (who had been arrested on 26 previous occasions) who broke into his property. Although the farmer was convicted of murder (reduced the manslaughter on appeal), many felt the action was justified.

There are many other examples that might be cited in this context that include euthanasia for a person who is terminally ill. Some societies condone 'honour killings'. But what these examples imply for our definition of crime is that it does not necessarily reflect popular views of what constitutes right and wrong actions. There is fuzziness at the edges, even for the most serious of crimes, in which the circumstances under which the criminal act occurred affect public perceptions of whether the behaviour was right or wrong. And for actions that constitute less serious criminal offences, this consensus becomes even more problematic.

This therefore suggests that factors other than popular views regarding how actions are viewed shape the definition of an act as being criminal. It might alternatively be argued that the definition of a criminal act reflects the views of powerful members of society who are able to secure their adoption throughout society.

CRIME IS DEFINED BY THOSE WHO EXERCISE POWER IN SOCIETY

Key idea

A second explanation of what defines a criminal act focuses on the ability of powerful minorities to secure the adoption of their views throughout society as to what are right and wrong actions.

The view that a criminal act is one that conflicts with views that are widely held within society regarding right and wrong conduct are challenged by a view that defines a criminal act as one that is passed down by those who wield power within society. They are able to use their power to impose their views as to what constitutes unacceptable behaviour on the rest of society.

This explanation suggests that those who wield economic and/ or political power in society have the ability to secure the adoption of their views as to right and wrong behaviour on the remainder of society. They may do this because they regard their views as being in the best interests of society: their views may be enlightened and progressive and their intention is to improve the overall conditions of all members of the general public.

Alternatively, the actions of a powerful minority may be inspired by purely selfish motives. They may use their power to define acts as criminal in order to preserve their interests against any threat that might undermine them. Marxists would argue that the powerful in society are those who wield economic power (termed the *bourgeoisie*) and that the process of criminalization is typically directed against actions undertaken by members of the working class (the *proletariat*) who wish to challenge their economic dominance (and the exploitation that underpins it).

Seen in this light, crime may be viewed as a means to secure the redistribution of wealth throughout society, and the criminal assumes a romantic guise – a Robin Hood-type figure waging through crime a war in the interests of the majority against the tyranny of a latter-day Prince John and his supporters.

One other issue that derives from an explanation of a crime as an action that is defined as wrong in order to serve the interests of a powerful majority in society is how – in liberal democratic societies such as the UK and US – is this outcome achieved. One explanation (which we will consider more fully in Chapter 3) is the concept of a *moral panic*.

A final implication of this definition of criminal actions is that it implies that it alters in accordance with threats posed to those who exercise power within society. Unlike the definition that we considered above, crime is not a relatively permanent label applied to actions that are widely disapproved of by most members of society throughout history.

This definition (and the one that preceded it) suggests that the definition of crime is set by individual nations and thus is likely to differ from one country to another. The next definition of a crime that we shall consider in this chapter is international in scope and suggests that all societies should adhere to common standards regarding how they view right and wrong behaviour.

CRIME IS DEFINED BY THE INTERNATIONAL COMMUNITY'S VIEWS OF RIGHT AND WRONG BEHAVIOUR

Key idea

A third explanation of what constitutes a criminal act suggests that it entails a violation of standards of behaviour that all societies should adhere to. The international community thus defines criminal actions.

The next definition of crime that we shall consider concentrates on the international community rather than the nation state and places the protection of individual citizens centre stage.

According to this definition, crime is viewed as a violation of basic human rights and values that all societies should embrace. This definition embraces actions that are criminal and also those that are immoral rather than illegal, such as exploiting labour in developing nations by companies that operate in first world countries. It further suggests that criminal actions can be carried out by persons and institutions that wield political and economic power, such as governments and business corporations.

An important issue that relates to this view of what constitutes criminal behaviour concerns who is responsible for defining these values and how they are enforced.

> The view of crime as a violation of standards that should be adhered to in all countries implies the need for an international enforcement mechanism. The 1945 United Nations Charter is compatible with this objective. 'The United Nations Charter was the first treaty to make human rights a matter for global concern. By identifying violations as a danger to world peace and security, it provided a mechanism for international intervention, as a last resort, in the affairs of nation states. What it did not do was to impose any legal duty on member states to comply with human rights standards. [...] For this reason the Charter pledges on human rights were circumscribed: the duty spelled out in article 55(c) was to promote respect for and observance of human rights, not to guarantee them as a matter of law for all citizens' (Robertson, 2000: 25–6).
>
> Robertson, G. (2000). *Crimes against Humanity: The Struggle for Global Justice*. Harmondsworth: Penguin.

One development related to a universal definition of criminal actions is the European Convention on Human Rights which sets out a menu of entitlements that citizens in every country that has signed up to it can expect to exercise. It is enforced by the European Court of Human Rights.

Case study: The European Convention on Human Rights

The European Convention on Human Rights views crime as a violation of rights and liberties that citizens of all countries ought to enjoy.

The European Convention on Human Rights identified 15 basic rights (all of which were incorporated into the UK's 1998 Human Rights Act). These were:

1   the right to life (Article 2)

2   the prohibition of torture (Article 3)

3   the prohibition of slavery and forced labour (Article 4)

4   the right to life and security (Article 5)

5   the right to a fair trial (Article 6)

6   the right not to be punished save in accordance with the law (Article 7)

7   the right to respect for private and family life (Article 8)

8   freedom of thought, conscience and religion (Article 9)

9   freedom of expression (Article 10)

10   freedom of assembly and association (Article 11)

11   the right to marry (Article 12)

12   the prohibition of discrimination (Article 14)

13   the protection of property (Article 1 of Protocol 1)

14   the right to education (Article 2 of Protocol 1)

15   the right to free elections (Article 3 of Protocol 1).

However, these rights are not of equal standing under the act. Article 3 is absolute and can never be contravened. Articles 2, 4, 5, 6 and 7 are fundamental but may be restricted for specific reasons identified in the Convention. Articles 8, 9, 10 and 11 are qualified rights that may be limited in connection with certain circumstances or conditions that are laid down in the Convention, which require the interference to be justified and prescribed by law.

The procedure of opting out of the Convention on Human Rights is known as 'derogation'. In the latter case the state may be required to prove that its action is proportionate to the threat posed to the general wellbeing of society.

There are other initiatives that seek to define crime in terms of standards of behaviour which have international application and which are capable of being enforced on the world stage. One of these affects the manner in which armed conflict between and within nations should be waged.

Spotlight

The belief that certain standards of behaviour should apply to all countries underpinned the setting up of the International Criminal Court in 2002. Its role is to prosecute individuals for crimes against humanity, war crimes and genocide. However, a number of nations (including the US, Russia and China) have been critical of this body and the US is not a member and participates in its operations only as an observer.

Attempts to define standards of behaviour in these situations were first attempted in the Hague Conventions of 1899 and 1907. Contravention of these standards constituted a *war crime* which was subsequently developed to include actions that constituted a *crime against humanity*. The prosecution of persons whose actions are alleged to be in breach of these standards are currently conducted by a permanent body, the International Criminal Court, which was set up in 2002 and is based in The Hague in the Netherlands.

CRIME IS DEFINED BY REACTION TO BEHAVIOUR

In this section, we shall extend our discussion of crime by considering the concept of deviance.

Key idea

Deviance does not have the same meaning as crime. It refers to behaviour that contravenes accepted standards or norms of behaviour but which is not necessarily criminal (although it can be).

In addition to studying crime, criminologists are also interested in actions or behaviour that flout what are regarded as the normal way for persons to conduct themselves. Although deviance includes actions that are defined as illegal, the term has a much broader meaning than 'crime' and embraces other forms of behaviour that mainstream society regards as 'strange', 'odd' or 'weird' and which therefore elicits a negative reaction.

However, this approach provides us with a further way in which we can define crime: it suggests that no act is inherently criminal or deviant – what makes it so is how others react to it. It also helps to explain why some actions that are technically illegal are not viewed as 'bad' by society so that enforcement will lack popular endorsement. This view as to how crime and deviant behaviour is defined is based on interactionism and we shall consider it more fully in connection with labelling theory which is discussed in Chapter 3. However, one aspect of this approach is that it suggests that social control is responsible for creating deviant behaviour (most criminological theories argue it is the other way around) and justifies decriminalization which entails the removal of criminal penalties attached to particular actions.

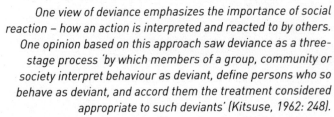

One view of deviance emphasizes the importance of social reaction – how an action is interpreted and reacted to by others. One opinion based on this approach saw deviance as a three-stage process 'by which members of a group, community or society interpret behaviour as deviant, define persons who so behave as deviant, and accord them the treatment considered appropriate to such deviants' (Kitsuse, 1962: 248).

Kitsuse, J. (1962). 'Problems of Theory and Method', *Social Problems* 9 (Winter): 247–56.

An important consideration is the manner in which popular reaction to an act is secured. It may be spontaneous reflecting the fact that large numbers of people disapprove of a particular form of behaviour. However, it can be engineered, in which case this view concerning the definition of an act as deviant shares many common features with the second definition of crime that we considered above, in particular that crime is a socially constructed phenomenon. Moral panics, for example, can be artificially orchestrated against behaviour that powerful interests in society disapprove of and wish to see those who conduct themselves in this manner being condemned as social outcasts.

One consequence of defining deviance in terms of reaction to an act is that this reaction is likely to alter over historical periods of time, making it impossible to statistically compare levels of deviance over historical time periods.

Case study: Crime trends

One difficulty in comparing rates of crime over historic time periods is that the definition of actions regarded as criminal changes. One example of this is prohibition in the United States of America.

In 1920 the Eighteenth Amendment to the Constitution came into force which prohibited the manufacture, sale and transportation of alcohol throughout the country. This action came on the back of earlier measures designed to ban the manufacture and sale of alcohol (most notably the 1919 Volstead Act) whose enforcement had been lax. The impact of the amendment to the Constitution meant that commercial actions that had once been perfectly legal now became illegal and the leisure pursuits of law-abiding citizens became criminalized.

Although the Eighteenth Amendment ensured that the consumption of alcohol diminished, there was much opposition to it. It was seen as a measure promoted by a range of Protestant denominations seeking to impose their religious and moral values over the rest of society, in particular over immigrant communities. The market for alcohol did not disappear and in many cities illegal drinking clubs (termed 'speakeasies') flourished. This continued demand was exploited by organized criminal activity, some of whose leading members (including Al Capone and Bugs Moran in Chicago) became very rich on the proceeds. Nor did this action prevent crime as prohibitionists claimed: in 1929 gang warfare between Capone and Moran led to the murder of seven persons at the St Valentine's Day Massacre in Chicago.

The Prohibition Era ended in 1933 when President Roosevelt signed the Cullen-Harrison Act which legalized weak beers and wines. Later that year, the Eighteenth Amendment to the Constitution was repealed by the Twenty-second Amendment which enabled individual states to ban or place restrictions on the sale of alcohol. These changes meant that actions previously defined as criminal were now perfectly legal.

Similar case studies in England and Wales, whereby changes in the law account for rises and dips in the overall level of crime, include the 1967 Abortion Act (which legalized abortions in certain circumstances) and the 1967 Sexual Offences Act (which decriminalized homosexual acts between consenting adult males aged over 21 years in England and Wales).

The categorization of criminal behaviour

Key idea

Criminal actions are often graded in order of the seriousness with which they are viewed.

Although crime consists of actions that entail a degree of popular disapproval that may be reflected in a county's criminal code, they do not result in identical sanctions being imposed by the state on the offender. Crimes are categorized in terms of the seriousness with which they are viewed and this is reflected in the penalty that is imposed on those who conduct such actions.

In the US a distinction between felonies and misdemeanours is applied at federal (national) level and in many states. Felonies are defined as serious crimes for which the offender can be sentenced to a term of imprisonment of more than one year, whereas misdemeanours are less serious crimes for which the offender can be sentenced to a fine, a period of probation or a sentence of imprisonment of less than one year which is usually served in a county jail. A third category of offences are termed infractions. These constitute the least serious offenses and are usually punishable by a fine. Although the distinction between felonies and misdemeanours originated in England, it no longer applies in that country.

Dig deeper

Hall, S. (2012). *Theorising Crime and Deviance: A New Perspective.* London: Sage.

Newburn, T. (2007). *Criminology.* Cullompton, Devon: Willan Publishing.

Walklate, S. (2011). *Criminology: The Basics.* London: Routledge, 2nd edn.

Fact-check

1 The statement that the law is consensual means:
   A It reflects the views of those who exercise power within society regarding what constitutes right and wrong behaviour
   B It reflects the views held by most members of the general public regarding what constitutes right and wrong behaviour
   C It reflects the corporate views of the judiciary concerning what constitutes right and wrong behaviour
   D It is based on common law rather than on statute law

2 The interactionist view of crime and deviance is that:
   A It consists of an action that conflicts with the law
   B It is an action that undermines a citizen's civil and political liberties
   C The reaction to an act as opposed to the act itself is crucial to defining it as criminal or deviant
   D It consists of actions mainly carried out by members of the working class

3 In the United Kingdom, the 1998 Human Rights Act:
   A Placed the European Convention on Human Rights on a statutory basis and thus enforceable by domestic courts
   B Permitted the use of torture as a response to terrorism
   C Ended the ability of the European Court of Human Rights to intervene in United Kingdom domestic affairs
   D Made it possible for citizens who believed that their human rights had been violated to take their case to the European Court of Justice

4 The term 'deviance' refers to:
   A Perverted behaviour of a sexual nature
   B An action that is commonly disapproved of within society but which is not necessarily criminal
   C Discretion exercised by criminal justice practitioners not to apply the full force of the law against an offender
   D A convicted offender who, on completion of his or her sentence, reoffends

5 In the US the term 'felony' describes:

A A serious criminal offence

B A minor criminal offence

C A conspiracy to commit a criminal act

D Any form of law violation

6 The process that entails the removal of criminal penalties from an act is known as:

A Legalization

B Decriminalization

C Summary justice

D Discretion

2

How do we measure crime?

Information regarding the amount of crime in society at any one time is provided through crime statistics. There are, however, different methods that can be used to compile information of this nature. Crime statistics can be based upon information obtained from police forces that records criminal acts that have been reported to them by members of the general public or may be derived from surveys that seek to identify persons who have been the victims of crime, whether this has been reported to the police or not. This chapter discusses the various means through which information on crime can be gathered and assesses the reliability of the main approaches that are used.

Official crime statistics

Key idea

Official crime statistics provide us with information regarding the amount of crime that exists in society at any one point in time. This is referred to as the *official crime rate*. These statistics are based upon criminal incidents that the police are made aware of.

One source of information regarding the volume of crime is provided through figures that are based upon crime that is reported to law enforcement agencies such as the police. In England and Wales figures provided by the 43 police forces are put together and published on an annual basis. Traditionally, the Home Office published this data but since April 2008 these figures have been published under the supervision of the National Audit Office.

In the US this information is derived from around 17,000 law enforcement agencies and was traditionally published annually by the Federal Bureau of Investigation in a publication prepared under the Uniform Crime Reporting (UCR) Program, entitled *Crime in the United States*. This gave information on the volume and rate of a number of specified criminal offences for the nation, the 50 states and the individual agencies. The UCR system has, however, been replaced in many states by the National Incident-Based Reporting System (NIBRS). This was introduced in the late 1980s and provides a more comprehensive reporting system than the UCR whereby data is compiled on every single crime occurrence as opposed to the more selective approach adopted by the UCR.

There are, however, a number of problems concerning the accuracy of statistics based upon crime incidents being reported to the police. We shall explore this further by discussing the process of crime reporting.

The process of crime reporting

Key idea

The process whereby a crime becomes translated into an official statistic is through a reporting process which comprises a number of stages. Each stage has the potential to reduce the number of crimes that proceed to the next one, so that the final figure represents only a proportion of the total number of crimes that have occurred.

There are a number of stages involved in translating a criminal act that has taken place into an official statistic. Crimes that have occurred may be filtered out at each stage of the crime reporting process, resulting in official crime statistics not providing an accurate portrayal of the actual amount of crime that exists within society. Let us look at this process in more detail.

Key idea

We refer to the gap between the volume of crime that is committed and that which is recorded in official crime statistics as the *dark figure* of crime.

STAGE 1: AWARENESS OF A CRIME

In order for a crime to become entered into official crime statistics, it is first necessary for a witness to have observed a criminal act taking place or for the victim of the crime to be aware that he or she has been on the receiving end of a crime. But this may not always be apparent. For example, a person may attribute the loss of money in the home, the workplace or a public place to personal carelessness as opposed to robbery or theft.

STAGE 2: REPORTING THE CRIME TO THE POLICE

If a person is aware that he or she is the victim of a crime, it does not necessarily follow that this matter will be reported to the police. There may be several reasons why crimes fall out of the reporting system at this stage. The victim may fear that there will be reprisals from the criminal or his or her acquaintances if the police become involved in the incident. Alternatively, the victim may lack confidence in the ability of the police and criminal justice system to deal with the matter fairly. In the UK, this historically meant that victims of hate crime and sexual violence decided not to refer serious incidents to the police.

STAGE 3: RECORDING OF A CRIME BY THE POLICE

Even if a person was aware of being the victim of a crime and then decided to refer the matter to the police, it does not automatically mean that this issue will be reported by the police and become an official crime statistic.

The gap between the amount of crime committed in society and that which enters into official crime statistics is known as the dark figure of crime: 'we can speak of the dark figure of crime, or use the analogy of the official statistics as an iceberg, where what is revealed is a fraction of the actual events capable of being called crime. The actual proportion of crime the dark figure represents is difficult to calculate but it is the majority for many crimes' (Morrison, 1995: 168–9).

Morrison, M. (1995). *Theoretical Criminology: From Modernity to Post-Modernity.* London: Cavendish Publishing.

Key idea

We refer to the gap between crime that is reported to the police and crime that is subsequently recorded by them as the *grey area* of crime.

There are several reasons that might explain why crime that is reported to the police might not enter into official crime statistics.

The police may decide that the issue does not constitute a criminal act or that it was minor and can be responded to unofficially, perhaps by an officer warning an individual not to repeat the behaviour.

Additionally, an officer who receives a report of a crime may decide not to record it because to do so might result in time-consuming paperwork or provide an impression that the locality was a crime-ridden neighbourhood. In England and Wales this process is known as 'cuffing' and was partly caused by the introduction of performance indicators for the police service in the 1990s. Crime statistics were one measure of police performance and high levels of reported crime could imply inefficiency.

The perception that the 43 police forces in England and Wales adopted different standards of crime recording led to the introduction of the National Crime Recording Standard in 2003. This was designed to provide consistency in the way in which all police forces recorded incidents of crime that had been reported to them.

Key idea

In the UK 'cuffing' refers to a decision by a police officer either not to record a crime that has been reported (in which case the crime is said to disappear up a police officer's sleeve) or to downgrade the offence into a crime that is not required to be included in official crime statistics. An attempted burglary, for example, might be downgraded to criminal damage.

Directions from government to law enforcement agencies might dictate that certain types of crime do not appear in official crime statistics. In England and Wales, for example, the police are required to record only what the Home Office refers to as 'notifiable offences'. This means, therefore, that most motoring offences are excluded from crime statistics as they are not required to be included in them.

Instructions of this nature may also determine the manner in which multiple crimes are recorded. This term refers to a series of crimes committed by a person (or group of persons) either in quick succession either in one specific place or directed against one victim. In England and Wales Home Office Counting Rules govern the way in which multiple crimes are recorded.

In the US the *hierarchy rule* was employed by the Uniform Crime Reporting system so that, if in the course of one event a victim was subjected to several crimes (for example, assault, rape and robbery), or in one place several crimes occurred (for example a number of people were robbed and one of the victims was murdered), only the most serious offence would be recorded.

These procedures have the effect of reducing the overall volume of crime that is recorded in crime statistics.

Crime statistics are socially constructed

Although positivist criminology believes that crime statistics constitute useful facts regarding the level of crime in society on which policy can be formulated, criminology based upon interactionist and left idealist approaches is more sceptical of their accuracy. Interactionism has put forward the argument that crime statistics are socially constructed, in the sense that they reflect responses to social behaviour and which are constantly subject to change.

What is termed the 'institutionalist' approach regards official crime statistics not as true portrayals of the volume of crime in society but, rather, as 'outcomes of social and institutional processes' (Coleman and Moynihan, 1996: 16).

One aspect of this view suggests that 'People are not randomly observed, stopped or searched by the police. Instead, their age, social class, skin colour, sex, accent and style of dress all affect their chances of attracting attention from the police in the first place and subsequently affect whether the police will classify, record and prosecute their actions as "criminal"' (Davidson and Layder,1994: 72).

Coleman, C. and Moynihan, J. (1996). *Understanding Crime Data: Haunted by the Dark Figure*. Buckingham: Open University Press.

Davidson, J. and Layder, D. (1994). *Methods, Sex and Madness*. London: Routledge.

The above discussion has suggested that official crime statistics do not provide an accurate statement of the number of crimes that have taken place at a particular point in time. We have argued that these are manufactured by a procedure that tends to filter out crime at each stage of the recording process.

Additionally, factors other than those discussed above influence the production of official crime statistics. These include:

▶ **Attitudes within society as to what constitutes acceptable and unacceptable behaviour:** Traditionally, this has meant that actions discussed in Chapter 7 that relate to white-collar and related criminal activities have been neglected and that crime statistics reflect a bias towards sanctioning working-class crime. However, attitudes regarding right and wrong behaviour change over time. This may result in actions that were previously tolerated becoming criminalized or actions that were once unlawful being regarded as acceptable behaviour. These changes have the effect of increasing or reducing the overall level of crime that is recorded in official statistics whereas, in reality, behaviour may not have changed at all.

▶ **Changes affecting the public's reporting practices:** Technological developments such as mobile phones make reporting crime easier than was once the case. Additionally, new incentives may be placed on the public to report crime. In the UK, for example, insurance companies insist on a police crime number in order to process claims related to burglary. This tends to mean that crimes of this nature are reported to the police, which may not have always been the case in times when relatively few householders possessed personal insurance.

▶ **Police operational practices:** These may derive from aspects of police culture (for example institutional racism that results in minority ethnic groups being targeted in police operations) or from pressures placed on the police service to take robust action against particular crimes. The media may be at the forefront of campaigns which may mean that actions once tolerated by the police are suddenly subjected to a vigorous crackdown: conversely, this change affecting police priorities may mean that other criminal actions previously targeted by the police are downgraded in terms of importance. The reduced recording of such incidents may give the false impression that the problem has been solved whereas in reality it still exists but is being ignored.

▶ **Changes affecting police recording practices:** A criminal activity may be taken from an existing category of offences and recorded as a separate crime. Changes of this nature may derive from police preferences or occur as the result of external pressure from politicians or the general public. This may give an illusion that a particular activity is a serious, new problem, which in reality is not the case.

It might thus be concluded that official crime statistics do not provide us with objective statements relating to the amount of crime in society but are instead the product of a complex process of interplay between the main stakeholders of the criminal justice system – politicians, the media, criminal justice practitioners, victims and the public. They reflect not the volume of crime in society but, rather, attitudes towards social behaviour which change across historical time periods. This is what we mean by stating that crime statistics are socially constructed (or socially produced).

In the following chapter, we will consider a closely related issue and discuss the role played by the media in the social construction of crime.

Victimization surveys

Problems that have been identified in the previous section regarding the accuracy of official crime statistics have led to the use of a number of other approaches to discover the level of crime in society. One of these alternative approaches is victimization/victim surveys.

Key idea

A victimization (or victim) survey seeks to discover the level of crime in society by asking members of the general public if they have been on the receiving end of criminal behaviour.

As it would be impossible to ask every member of the general public to provide researchers with their experiences concerning crime, victimization surveys rely on the use of a randomly selected sample of the general public who are asked if they have suffered from crime over a specific period of time (such as the past year). The experiences of this sample are then translated to provide an estimate of the overall level of crime experienced by the population as a whole.

In other words, if 20 per cent of a sample reported that they had been the victim of a domestic burglary in the previous 12 months, the survey would indicate that 20 per cent of the general population had experienced such a crime during this period.

Victimization surveys are used quite widely. The British Crime Survey (BCS) is used in England and Wales to gain information on crime that has been committed in the previous year. In the United States the US Census Bureau (acting on behalf of the Bureau of Justice Statistics) administers a victimization survey called the National Crime Victimization Survey. This was introduced in

Although different methodologies will produce different estimates concerning the level of crime in society, they may reveal similar trends which indicate falls or rises in crime rates. In connection with England and Wales, 'both the 2009/10 BCS and police recorded crime are consistent in showing falls in overall crime compared with 2008/09. Overall BCS crime decreased by nine per cent (from 10.5 million crimes to 9.6 million crimes), and police recorded crime by eight per cent (from 4.7 million to 4.3 million crimes)' (Flatley et al., 2010: 2).

Flatley, J., Kershaw, C., Smith, K., Chaplin, R. and Moon, D. (2010). *Crime in England and Wales, 2009/10.* London: Home Office, Home Office Statistical Bulletin.

1973 and is used to gather information on the occurrence of specified types of crime by interviewing a random sample of households at six-monthly interviews for a period of three years. Victimization surveys may also be conducted at international level. One example of this is the International Crime Victims Survey which commenced in 1989 and enables comparative data on householders' experiences of crime, policing, crime prevention and feelings of insecurity to be collected.

Case study: The British Crime Survey (BCS)

The British Crime Survey constitutes an important example of a victimization survey.

The BCS began in 1982 and from 1992 was published every two years. Since 2001 it has been published on an annual basis.

Each survey involves interviewing a randomly selected representative sample of the general public (currently around 51,000 people aged 16 and above living in households) to gather information relating to their experiences of victimization in the previous year (although some categories of crime are omitted from the statistics). The sample was initially derived from the electoral register, but since 1992 has been based upon the postcode address file.

Additionally, statistics on the victimization of children aged 12–15 were included in the 1992 BCS. Information on the victimization of children aged 10–15 was presented in the 2010/11 figures for which a sample of around 4,000 was used. The information that was disclosed included bullying at schools.

The BCS possesses important advantages over official crime statistics, one of which is that it is not affected by changes to reporting and recording practices, and ought thus to provide a more accurate measurement of national crime trends over historic periods.

The BSC suggests a higher level of crime in society than does official crime statistics. In 2010/11, for example, the BSC estimated that 9.6 million crimes had been committed whereas the police had recorded only 4.2 million in this period.

Victimization surveys tend to report a higher overall level of crime than that recorded in official crime statistics. One reason for this is that such surveys are able to acquire information on those crimes that are traditionally under-reported by members of the public. This can include a range of serious wrongdoings that includes all forms of hate crime and sexual offences where a victim may be embarrassed to report the crime to the police or feel that the criminal justice system will not deal with the matter fairly.

Victimization surveys may obtain other information related to crime. The American National Crime Victimization Survey also secures information on the impact of crime on victims and on the profiles of offenders, and the British Crime Survey provides findings on the proportion of households suffering from specific types of crime and public perceptions regarding crime and the likelihood of being victimized. Since 2009/10 the BCS has also included questions regarding public awareness and use of online crime maps.

However, such surveys also contain weaknesses. These include respondents including crimes that took place outside of the period being surveyed or failing to remember crimes that should be included. Additionally, some of the supposed benefits of victimization surveys are not always realized in practice: victims of domestic violence and sexual assault may prefer not to disclose their experiences to those conducting victimization surveys.

A final difficulty is that victimization surveys cannot include crimes that were unobserved. This problem may be tackled by a different methodology – self-report studies.

Self-report studies

Self-report studies ask individuals to record their own criminal activities. They typically consist of a series of questions addressed to selected groups asking them about their personal involvement in criminal behaviour.

In America, the first major self-report study was conducted by James Wallerstein and Clement Wyle in 1947. This questioned a sample of men (1,020) and women (678) regarding their participation in a number of crimes. Most (90%) admitted they had participated in at least one of these specified crimes. In England and Wales a more recent example was the Crime and Justice Survey that was introduced in 2003. This was based upon interviews with around 12,000 people aged between 10 and 65.

Self-report studies may provide us with useful information on crime including that associated with youth culture. However, these studies are not targeted at a representative group of society and they rely on the honesty of those participating in such studies who may exaggerate or downplay their personal involvement in criminal activities.

Spotlight

Self-report studies often reveal information about activities not widely regarded as criminal. Although many employees would not regard using company facilities for their personal use as a crime, activities of this nature are costly – employee use of work Internet and email facilities costs businesses in the UK around £10 billion each year. This has given rise to Acceptable Use Policies in which employers provide details of how employees should use communication facilities in their workplace.

Dig deeper

Coleman, C. and Moynihan, J. (1996). *Understanding Crime Data: Haunted by the Dark Figure.* Buckingham: Open University Press.

Croall, H. (2011). *Crime and Society in Britain*, 2nd edn. Harlow: Longman.

Williams, K. (2012). *Textbook on Criminology*, 7th edn. Oxford: Oxford University Press.

Fact-check

1 In the United Kingdom, the term 'cuffing' refers to:
   A An informal punishment administered by a police officer for wasting his or her time
   B A process whereby a police officer fails to record a crime that has been reported by a member of the general public
   C A decision by the Crown Prosecution Service not to prosecute a case referred to them by the police
   D The gap between the amount of crime committed and the number of successful prosecutions

2 The British Crime Survey and the American National Crime Victimization Survey:
   A Seek to provide an estimate of the amount of crime by sampling the public and asking them whether they have been a victim of crime in the past year
   B Are based on reports filled out by victims of crime when they report the incident to the police
   C Are conducted by insurance companies to ascertain whether actions by the victim contributed to the crime
   D Ask members of the public to disclose any criminal activity that they have committed during the past year

3 In England and Wales approximately how many crimes were committed in 2010/11 according to official crime statistics based on crimes recorded by the police?
   A 9.6 million
   B 8.2 million
   C 6.2 million
   D 4.2 million

4 The term 'dark figure of crime' refers to:
   A Crimes such as serial killing that reveal the dark side of the human personality
   B Crimes that have been committed at night
   C The gap between the number of crimes that are committed and the number that lead to a conviction
   D The gap between the number of crimes that are committed and the number that are officially recorded by the police

5 In England and Wales the National Crime Recording Standard sought to:

  A Make it compulsory for citizens to report all crimes of which they had first-hand knowledge, either as a victim or a witness

  B Standardize the way in which police forces recorded incidents of crime that were reported to them by the general public

  C Measure the extent of antisocial behaviour in each neighbourhood

  D Compare the level of crime that had occurred in each of the 43 police force areas

6 A self-report study is:

  A An estimate of the level of crime based on surveys that ask members of the public to disclose any crime they have committed in the past year

  B A facility whereby victims of crime can report the latter online rather than having to attend a police station to do so

  C Another term used for a confession in which a person officially admits to having committed a crime

  D Part of a job application form which requires potential employees to declare if they have ever been in trouble with the law

3

Why do people commit crime?

There is no simple answer to the question 'Why do people commit crime?' There is a wide range of possible (and, indeed, conflicting) explanations for criminal behaviour. An important debate that underpins these diverse explanations seeks to establish whether those who commit crime do so as the result of making a deliberate choice to act unlawfully or whether they are forced into such a course of action by forces over which they have no control. The aim of this chapter is to provide you with an understanding of the key reasons that have been put forward to account for crime. Let us start at the beginning and examine classicist criminology.

Classicist criminology

Classicist criminology arose in the later decades of the eighteenth century: its major figures were Cesare Beccaria (Italy) and Jeremy Bentham (UK). Their key focus was on the operations of the criminal justice system – in short, they believed that people committed crime because it was not clear what would be the consequences of their actions.

Key idea

Classicists assumed that the sure knowledge of the consequences of criminal action would be a deterrent that convinced rational beings not to commit it.

Underpinning classicist thinking was a belief that humans were rational beings who weighed up the consequences of their actions before undertaking them. When applied to criminal behaviour, this meant that a person would evaluate the potential benefits that he or she would derive from committing the crime (perhaps monetary gain) and the potential disadvantages that might arise (in the form of punishment). If the latter outweighed the former, a rational person would decide not to carry out the criminal activity.

However, the accuracy on which this calculation was based relied on a criminal justice system that was completely predictable in its operations. This was not the case anywhere in Europe in the late eighteenth century. The shortcomings of policing made it uncertain that those who committed crime would be apprehended and, if they were, the sentences delivered by the courts were unpredictable. One reason for this in the UK was a reluctance by judges to administer the death penalty which was the theoretical punishment that applied to a very wide range of criminal offences.

A potential criminal, therefore, was uncertain of the consequences of his or her actions and the feeling that 'if I do it, I might get away with it' served as an incentive to carry out criminal acts.

Therefore, classicists wished to eliminate uncertainty from the operations of the criminal justice system to ensure that all citizens were aware of what would happen to them should they commit crime: they would be aware that this action would lead to their arrest and would know in advance exactly what sentence a magistrate or a judge would deliver. This would thus deter rational beings from committing crime.

> An important criticism made by classicist criminologists of the operations of late eighteenth century European criminal justice systems was the inconsistent application of the law and the penalties that it proscribed. They believe that this situation encouraged crime: 'One of the greatest curbs on crime is not the cruelty of punishments, but their infallibility. [...] The certainty of punishment, even if it be moderate, will always make a stronger impression than the fear of another which is more terrible but combined with the hope of impunity; even the least evils, when they are certain, always terrify men's minds' (Beccaria, 1764: 58–9 of the 1963 translation).
>
> Beccaria, C. (1764) *On Crimes and Punishments*, trans. H. Paolucci (1963). Bobbs-Merrill Educational Publishing, Indianapolis.

Accordingly, classicists set about promoting reforms to the criminal justice system that would guarantee a uniform and consistent approach to criminal behaviour. This entailed:

▶ reforming the archaic system of policing that relied on voluntary effort, replacing it with professional police forces in which police officers were paid a wage to carry out their duties;

▶ reforming the penal code to provide for situations in which punishments should be graded to fit the crime: the main consequence of this was to remove the death penalty from a wide range of criminal acts in favour of other punishments that included imprisonment. It was assumed that this would ensure that magistrates and judges would adopt a more consistent approach to sentencing;

▶ reforming the operations of prisons, viewing them as mechanisms whereby those who had acted irrationally by committing crime could be transformed by the prison regime into rational beings who would lead law-abiding lives in the future.

Positivist criminology

A key difficulty with classicist criminology was its insistence that crime was a rational act based upon an individual's calculation of the gains and losses that would arise from committing the crime. This assumption was challenged towards the end of the nineteenth century by positivism which, alternatively, argued that an offender's action was motivated not by rational choice but because of factors over which he or she had no control. This also implies that treatment rather than punishment is the appropriate response to an individual's criminal behaviour.

Key idea

Positivist criminology rejected the classicist belief in *free will* and instead argued that crime arose because individuals were motivated by forces over which they had no control. We refer to this belief as *determinism*.

Unlike classicist criminology whose ideas were based on beliefs and value judgements, positivist criminology sought to demonstrate the truth of its assertions through scientific investigation. The nature of investigations that were underpinned by positivist criminology were varied and were derived from three separate academic disciplines:

1 biology

2 psychology

3 sociology.

In the following sections we will consider how each of these academic disciplines contributed to our thinking about why people commit crime.

CRIME AND BIOLOGY

Theories that link crime and biology argue that crime is caused by faults in an individual's biological make-up. There was also an initial tendency in theories of this nature to suggest that biological imperfections in an individual gave rise to physical blemishes which thus made it easy to identify criminals and distinguish them from law-abiding citizens.

The suggestion that an individual's behaviour was fashioned by their biological make-up was initially put forward by the Italian positivist criminologist Cesare Lombroso who wrote the first edition of his book *The Criminal Man* (*L'uomo delinquente*) in 1876.

Spotlight

The criminologist Cesare Lombroso has sometimes been erroneously named in student essays as Cesare Lambrusco. Remember in your work to avoid confusing a founding father of criminology with an Italian wine!

Lombroso suggested that criminals were individuals who had failed to evolve at the same pace as the remainder of the human race (a view that is referred to as *atavism* which argues that a criminal is a throw-back to an earlier, more primitive version of human beings whose behaviour was characterized by savagery) and that criminals could be identified by their physical characteristics (or blemishes that he referred to as *stigmata*) which indicated their biological inferiority. He based his views on data that included autopsies that he conducted of convicted criminals. Although these views are contentious, Lombroso succeeded in altering the focus of criminology away from the criminal justice system and made the individual criminal the focus of investigation. For this reason he has been described as the 'father of modern criminology'.

Lombroso's suggestion that a criminal was 'born bad' paved the way for later biological theories of crime that emphasized the importance of heredity (that is, that a person inherited their imperfect biological make-up from their parents). This gave rise to quests which included investigations as to whether there might be genetic explanations for crime whereby genetic imperfections were passed from one generation to the next so that crime 'runs in families'.

However, studies derived from other academic disciplines challenged such conclusions by arguing that crime was caused by factors that were external to the individual. This dispute is known as the 'nature versus nurture' debate: the essence of the debate is whether crime is caused by factors related to an individual's biological make-up or whether it arises from factors such as parental upbringing, peer group pressure or social and economic circumstances.

CRIME AND PSYCHOLOGY

Key idea

Psychological explanations of crime argue that the workings of the human mind are the root cause of criminal behaviour.

Whereas approaches that we have considered above argue that a person's biological make-up influences his or her behaviour, psychological explanations of crime turn attention to the workings of the mind and assert that criminal behaviour is based on problems that include neurological disorders or personality disturbances.

The belief that human behaviour is governed by processes that occur in the mind of the individual was based upon the pioneering work of Sigmund Freud in the early decades of the twentieth century. He drew particular attention to the importance of memories or traumatic experiences that occurred during childhood which became stored in the unconscious part of the psyche (or the mind) but which influenced an individual's conscious thoughts and behaviour and resulted in a range of personality disorders which could give rise to criminal acts.

His treatment for problems of this nature was psychoanalysis which sought to unlock and bring to the surface repressed experiences and traumatic memories. This was designed to give the patient an insight into the causes of his or her behaviour and provide the basis for corrective treatment.

Freud's approach reflected positivist views of crime as deterministic – it arose as the consequence of irrational conflicts that occurred within the subconscious mind of the individual over which he or she had no control. During the 1960s further contributions regarding the psychological causes of crime were put forward by Hans Eysenck who disagreed with Freud and argued that personality was fashioned not by childhood experiences but by biological and social factors. He especially drew attention to criminals as individuals with extrovert personalities who were impulsively driven to commit actions that provided them with excitement and pleasure regardless of the consequences that arose through such actions.

CRIME AND SOCIOLOGY

Key idea

Sociological explanations of crime emphasize the importance of social factors in determining human behaviour.

Ideas considered in the previous two sections highlight views that suggest that human actions are influenced by the biological make-up of the body or by the operations of the mind. A third approach based on sociology focuses attention on the manner in which adverse social circumstances (which might include poverty, deprivation or unemployment) can influence an individual's actions.

An important contribution to discussions regarding the impact of social conditions on human behaviour was made by Emile Durkheim at the end of the nineteenth century. He put forward the concept of *anomie* to describe a state of social indiscipline in which established rules of behaviour that included the criminal law were inadequate to prevent individuals from engaging in behaviour that was designed to benefit them, regardless of the impact of their actions on others. Situations of this nature occurred during times of major social upheaval (such as the boom and slump of capitalist economies) which challenged the fundamentals of the existing social order and led to the adoption of an 'every man for himself' attitude towards the attainment of his or her personal goals.

> *Robert Merton put forward social strain theory to explain crime. It arose as a consequence of 'a breakdown in the cultural structure, occurring particularly when there is an acute disjunction between cultural norms and goals and the social structured capacities of members of the group to act in accord with them. [...] It is the conflict between the cultural goals and the availability of using institutional means [...] which produces a strain towards anomie' (Merton, 1968: 216 and 220).*
>
> Merton, R. (1968). *Social Theory and Social Structure*. New York: Free Press.

The concept of anomie was subsequently developed by Robert Merton during the 1930s. He believed that society (not the individual) established success goals which individuals sought to achieve. Merton depicted these as the pursuit of wealth (the 'American dream'). However, not all members in society were in a position to achieve these through legitimate means since social factors that might include poor education or inadequate employment opportunities prevented their attainment. In this situation, some people might decide to achieve society's success goals through unlawful means. Thus, according to Merton, crime might arise as the consequence of a mismatch between the socially induced aspirations to achieve success and the structurally determined opportunities through which to achieve them. This mismatch is referred to as *social strain*.

Anomie, therefore, arose not in times of social disintegration (as Durkheim suggested) but was a constant condition in society that especially affected those at the lower end of the social ladder whose limited opportunities and prospects made it difficult for them to attain society's success goals.

The behaviour of persons suffering from adverse social circumstances was further developed by subcultural theorists, one of whom was Albert Cohen who wrote during the 1950s. Whereas Merton focused on the response of individuals whose social disadvantages made it hard to achieve society's success goals, Cohen examined the behaviour of groups in this setting. He suggested that those whose social circumstances made it difficult for them to attain society's success goals might substitute them for alternative values which came to constitute subculture that was identified by mainstream society as delinquent. This underpinned actions that were designed to secure status and prestige among those with whom the delinquents associated rather than to achieve material benefits such as financial rewards. Thus a person may steal a car to demonstrate his prowess as a 'joy rider' to his friends rather than to sell it and make money from the illegal transaction.

OTHER SOCIOLOGICAL EXPLANATIONS OF CRIME

There are a number of sociological explanations of criminal behaviour in addition to those that have been referred to above.

▶ The Chicago School

The prime concern of this approach was to explain why crime and delinquency appeared to be a constant feature of certain neighbourhoods. Clifford Shaw and Henry McKay who wrote in the 1940s argued that there was a specific geographic area within cities which was characterized by delinquency. This was labelled the *zone of transition* and was the area in which newly arrived immigrants would initially settle and who would move when established, to be replaced by more new arrivals. This made for an area of rapid population change in which existed a range of social problems that included crime, delinquency and immorality and the absence of a sense of social solidarity arising from a multiplicity of values that characterized such areas. These features made it impossible for mechanisms such as the family or the Church to effectively uphold society's conventional values. The ineffectiveness of informal mechanisms to shape communal behaviour gave rise to a neighbourhood that was characterized by *social disorganization*. This approach gave birth to what we now refer to as *ecological theories of crime* and legitimized the objective of community empowerment as a means to remedy this problem.

► Social learning theories

These suggest that crime is a learned response that may be derived from a range of influences that are external to the individual, especially those that are present in childhood. These include personal relationships such as peer groups and impersonal experiences that derive from the media. One of the most important social learning theories is *differential association* that was developed by Edwin Sutherland during the 1930s and 1940s. This suggested that criminal behaviour was likely to arise when a person was situated in an environment in which violation of the law was more widely endorsed than compliance to it – he or she copied the dominant influence to which they were subjected.

► Opportunity theory

This asserted that criminal behaviour arose from a rational assessment that it was impossible to achieve success in society through legitimate means. This calculation induced those who shared this assessment to band together and embrace a delinquent subculture. However, although this situation resulted in gangs primarily composed of lower-class youths, the character of the subculture they embraced was not consistent but was fashioned by the illegitimate opportunities that were present in the local environment. Thus, in areas where strong criminal structures existed, gangs would be incorporated into that environment and perform activities such as theft that were compatible with dominant criminal enterprises. However, in socially disorganized areas that lacked such existing criminal structures the delinquent subculture was less organized and was characterized by gang warfare that sought to secure territorial control of a neighbourhood.

Labelling and conflict theories

This section discusses a number of theories that examine crime from a different perspective to that employed above. Rather than focus on why criminals carry out criminal acts, these theories alternatively consider the nature of crime and deviancy and the manner in which the ability to define acts as criminal or deviant ensures that the existing power relationships in society are maintained. The starting point for this new approach came during the 1960s and was associated with an approach termed 'new deviancy' (or 'interactionism'), whose discussion of labelling theory made an important contribution to criminological study.

Key idea

The terms 'crime' and 'deviance' are sometimes used interchangeably but they embrace different concepts. Whereas crime might be defined as breaking the law, deviancy refers to actions committed by individuals that society disapproves of and responds to in a negative manner. Those who carry out such actions may encounter hostility from their fellow citizens and become regarded as outcasts from society.

New deviancy argued that society was not founded on consensual values but, instead, operated in the interests of those who controlled the operations of the state and who were able to use their power to have actions labelled as deviant of which they did not approve and which they believed could undermine their social status. Labelling indicated that society as a whole disapproved of their actions and as a consequence of this sanctions were deployed against the deviant.

Labelling theory was especially concerned with how an individual whose actions had been declared to be deviant and had been subject to sanctions would subsequently act. Those subjected to it might henceforth be regarded both by themselves and others as social outcasts. This adverse effect on the individual's self-perception might result in the deviant associating with others whose actions had been similarly labelled.

An individual's reaction to the social stigma arising from labelling might also result in actions designed to live up to the label that would otherwise not have taken place – we refer to this as a *self-fulfilling prophecy*.

Marxist criminology developed ideas that had been put forward by new deviancy criminology and argued that the unjust social system that was the product of capitalism was maintained by the use of the law to criminalize those whose actions posed a challenge to the existing power relationships in society. Inequality was viewed as the underpinning of such challenges, which might embrace crime or other forms of challenge by those seeking to improve their economic and social position within society (such as industrial unrest or rioting). What is termed 'critical criminology' subsequently developed the criminological agenda by giving prominent attention to the structure of power within society. Their concern extended beyond class to embrace race and gender inequalities and to consider the processes through which these inequalities were reproduced, the nature of the conflicts that arose to challenge them and how these challenges were resolved.

One difficulty with conflict theories is a tendency to glamorize crime as a mechanism that challenges the structure of power within society and thus to see the process through which actions were criminalized as a mechanism to maintain the existing power relationships in society. In reality, however, crime is an activity that distresses large numbers of 'ordinary' citizens, including poorer people who lived in areas that experience high crime rates. This standpoint was embraced by a criminological school referred to as 'left realism' that emerged during the 1980s. Unlike the stance adopted by more traditional arguments relating to crime that are founded on Marxist perspectives (which henceforth were known as 'left idealism'), left realism argued that it was important to take the problem of crime seriously and to put forward practical remedies to counter it. These remedies were typically based on evidence of people's experiences of crime that were derived from localized crime surveys.

Case study: Moral panics

The concept of moral panics is rooted in the interactionist perception that crime is a socially constructed phenomenon.

Criminological theories that assert challenges to the existing social order are resolved by the process of criminalization imply that a tough 'law and order' response is deployed in response to crime and other forms of social disorder. However, in liberal democratic political systems, punitive responses of this nature would be successful only if they secured a widespread degree of public support. The concept of a 'moral panic' was developed to explain how popular support for policies of this nature could be secured.

A moral panic emerges at the time of public concern about the way in which society is operating. An issue is then selected that epitomizes this concern and a particular set or group of individuals (termed 'folk devils') are depicted as being responsible for this and similar issues. These are frequently young people, often of working-class origin. The negative manner in which this group is depicted underpins a tough law-and-order response to their activities which is delivered with a considerable degree of public support.

The media are given a major role in the production of a moral panic: it is they who select the issue that they depict as a cause of public concern, identify those responsible for the problem and advocate solutions that entail a firm response to it by the law, the actions of the police and the sentencing policies of the courts.

The intention of orchestrating a moral panic is to divert attention from fundamental causes of social problems (which Marxists would define as the operations of capitalism) and to channel public concerns into demanding action against symptoms of these problems. This view, however, ignores the possibility that the cause of concern embraced by a moral panic is a genuine cause of public concern and that the media's intervention is to reflect this concern rather than to artificially create it.

Examples of moral panics that you may wish to research for yourselves include:

► clashes between 'mods' and 'rockers' at holiday resorts on the South Coast of England in the 1960s

► 'mugging' in the 1970s

► the abduction and murder of Jamie Bulger in 1993.

Important literature that you may wish to consult in examining moral panics include: Cohen, S. (2011). *Folk Devils and Moral Panics*, 3rd edn. London: Routledge.

Hall, S. Critcher, C., Jefferson, T., Clarke, J. and Roberts, B. (1978). *Policing the Crisis: Mugging, the State, and Law and Order*. Basingstoke: Macmillan.

Pearson, G. (1983). *Hooligan: A History of Respectable Fears*. Basingstoke: Macmillan.

Conservative criminology

The main concern of conservative criminology is defence of the existing social order – it wishes to maintain society's key institutions and core values and to take actions to defend them when threatened by activities that include crime, disorder or forms of immoral behaviour.

Key idea

The terms 'left' and 'right' are often applied to criminological theories.

These are political descriptions that relate to attitudes towards social, economic and political change. However, when applied to criminology they indicate a distinction between theories that locate the causes of crime in the operations and functioning of the state (perhaps because it fails to treat all social groups equally) and ideas that locate the explanation for crime in the failings of the individual who is seen to make a deliberate choice to commit crime.

Conservative criminology believes that all persons have the potential to act in an unsocial manner but most people are able to exercise self-restraint to overcome any temptation to give in to these instincts. Those who do so are deemed responsible for their actions which are seen as being driven by moral failings. Conservative criminology believes that it is the purpose of the criminal justice system to reinforce other social structures and processes such as the family unit and to take firm action against those who threaten to undermine the fabric of society.

The practical application of these ideas was associated with 'new right' criminology that emerged in the US and the UK in the latter decades of the twentieth century. It arose within the context of the adoption of free market economic policies to tackle problems affecting the global economy, which made it necessary to find ways other than social welfare policies to regulate the criminal and disorderly behaviour of the poorer and underprivileged members of society. Its most notable feature was to inspire a response to crime that has been dubbed 'penal populism' or 'populist punitiveness'. The main component of this approach was a harsh response to crime whereby those who committed it would receive their 'just deserts'. It was assumed that this reaction to crime was what the majority of the general public wanted. Imprisonment was a key aspect of penal populism: rising prison numbers demonstrated to the public that crime was being effectively tackled by the criminal justice system and the politicians who controlled it.

New right criminology echoed the views of classicist criminology that criminals were responsible for their actions and could not blame their behaviour on factors such as social or economic exclusion.

This view was put forward in the UK by the then Home Secretary who stated that he would have 'no truck with trendy theories that try to explain crime away by blaming socio-economic factors. [...] Criminals are responsible for crime and they should be held to account for their actions' (Howard, 1993).

Howard, M. (1993) speech at the Conservative Party Conference, 6 October.

Feminist criminologies

The study of female crime was a traditionally neglected area within criminology, for reasons that included the relatively small number of female offenders and the nature of crimes they committed (which were rarely spectacular crimes involving physical violence). Accordingly, explanations for offending behaviour by females tended to be rooted in late nineteenth-century biological positivism and failed to take into account any of the subsequent explanations that were put forward to explain criminal behaviour that have been discussed earlier in this chapter.

> *Late nineteenth-century biological positivism underpinned explanations of crime committed by women. This behaviour was thus attributed to 'impulsive or irrational behaviour caused by a reaction to factors which included hormonal changes occasioned by biological processes of menstruation, pregnancy and childbirth' (Smart, 1995: 25).*
>
> Smart, C. (1995). *Law, Crime and Sexuality*. London: Sage.

A key development associated with feminist criminology was the publication by Carol Smart of her book *Women, Crime and Criminology* in 1977. This helped to establish a new approach towards an understanding of the causes of female criminality and the experiences of women in the criminal justice system. The agenda that was subsequently developed was diverse and lacking coherence – hence we use the term feminist *criminologies* rather than *criminology*.

The main themes developed within feminist criminologies were:

WHY DO WOMEN COMMIT CRIME?

This aspect of feminist criminologies sought to include more women in evaluations of the causes of criminal behaviour and was responsible for arguments that explained it by factors other than impulsive responses to biological circumstances. These alternative ideas frequently depicted female crime as a rational act motivated by factors that included deprivation.

DOES THE CRIMINAL JUSTICE SYSTEM TREAT WOMEN OFFENDERS FAIRLY?

This approach within feminist criminology sought to analyse whether women who committed crime were treated in a discriminatory manner by the key criminal justice agencies. In particular, arguments that suggested female criminals were treated more leniently (an approach referred to as *male chivalry*, which suggested that the male-dominated criminal justice professions such as the police service or the courts sought to protect rather than harshly punish female criminals) was countered by a new concept, that of *double deviance*.

This suggested that women offenders were treated more harshly than male criminals within the criminal justice system as their punishment reflected both the nature of the crime that had been committed *and* also the extent to which this crime deviated from their conformity to the role that women were expected to play in society. Thus, a female who had displayed violence towards children (contrary to the role expected of her to display love and kindness towards them) would expect a harsher punishment than a man would get who committed the same offence.

The difficulty of finding a sample of male and female offenders who committed a crime in identical circumstances makes it impossible to judge the accuracy of such assertions.

DOES THE CRIMINAL JUSTICE SYSTEM TREAT WOMEN WHO ARE VICTIMS OF CRIME FAIRLY?

This aspect of feminist criminologies argues that the criminal justice system fails to provide justice to women who are victims of crime, especially crimes of violence that include sexual abuse, domestic violence, and rape. The failure to make adequate responses to such actions is reflected in criminal justice practices that might be used to excuse or mitigate inappropriate behaviour by men towards women as an aspect of the socially acceptable 'attribute' of masculinity (by arguing, for example, that a female wearing a short skirt who accepted a lift from a male stranger who then raped her was partly responsible for the crime as her actions and style of dress encouraged this response from a man). This perspective views crime towards women as an aspect of oppression derived from a patriarchal society – in other words, as a way of keeping women 'in their place' as socially inferior to men. It is also reflected in the way in which the criminal justice system has traditionally discriminated against women who seek employment or who work within the criminal justice system.

TO WHAT EXTENT DO GENDER ROLES INFLUENCE BOTH MALE AND FEMALE CRIMINALITY?

This aspect of feminist criminology views crime as the product of socially constructed gender roles – that is, the wide difference in male and female offending rates is explained not by inborn biological factors but from attitudes and opportunities that derive from the differential way in which boys and girls are brought up. Girls are taught to be passive and conform to their social role of housewife and mother while toughness and aggression (which might lead to crime) are seen as acceptable values for boys to exhibit. This view is put forward as an explanation both of the relatively high levels of male criminality and the relatively low levels of female offending.

Postmodern criminology

Social, economic and cultural changes that occurred in the late decades of the twentieth century have given rise to a society that is sometimes depicted as different in nature to the one that preceded it and is described as 'late' or 'post' modern. What has been termed 'postmodern criminology' rejects universal explanations for criminal behaviour and instead argues that there is a wide range of explanations that may be derived from individuals attaching different meanings to similar actions. The methods used to study criminal behaviour are typically multidisciplinary, reflecting the view that criminal behaviour cannot be understood from the viewpoint of one single academic discipline or one single theoretical perspective.

Dig deeper

Bernard, T. and Snipes, J. (2009). *Gerould A. Vold's Theoretical Criminology*. Oxford: Oxford University Press, 6th edn.

Burke, R. (2009). *An Introduction to Criminological Theory*. Cullompton, Devon: Willan Publishing, 3rd edn.

Newburn, T. (2009). *Key Readings in Criminology*. Cullompton, Devon: Willan Publishing.

White, R. and Haines, F. (2004). *Crime and Criminology: An Introduction*, 3rd edn. Oxford: Oxford University Press.

Fact-check

1 Atavism is:

A A theory of crime that argues criminals are a throw-back to a bygone generation

B A theory of crime that argues criminal behaviour is the product of social circumstances

C A theory that links crime to behaviour learned from violent television programmes

D A term applied to a theory of crime that is outdated

2 Anomie is:

A A theory of crime that is supported by only a few people

B A theory of crime that links criminal behaviour to adverse social circumstances

C A theory of crime that argues criminal behaviour is the product of bad childhood experiences

D A theory of crime that is comprehensible only to Emile Durkheim

3 A key belief of classicist criminology was:

A The death penalty was the appropriate solution to crime

B Criminals in the United Kingdom should be transported to Australia

C Criminals were rational beings who possessed free will as to whether they committed crime or not

D Poor people committed most crime

4 Labelling theory argued:

A Criminals should be forced to carry placards to warn the public that a bad person was in the neighbourhood

B It was easy to identify criminals by the clothes that they wore

C Crime was a label applied by the powerful in society to outlaw actions that were against their interests

D There was no one theory to explain criminal behaviour

5 Positivist criminology believed:

A Those who committed crime had made a deliberate choice to do so

B Criminals committed crime because they thought they would get away with it .

    C It was impossible to totally eliminate crime from society

    D Those who committed crime were forced to do so by
       circumstances over which they had no control

6 Sigmund Freud believed:

    A Crime was committed by persons of low intelligence

    B Criminals were 'born bad' and had no control over their actions

    C Crime arose from repressed childhood experiences that
       could be revealed by psychoanalysis

    D Social disadvantage was the main cause of crime

How can we prevent crime?

In the previous chapter we examined a number of theories that seek to explain why people commit crime. In this chapter we will consider the practical measures that are designed to prevent it. These two chapters are linked since, if we know why people commit crime, it becomes possible to put forward initiatives that seek to stop it happening. However, the wide range of theories that have been put forward to explain the causes of crime makes it impossible to agree on one single remedy to prevent it. Accordingly, there exists a wide range of approaches to crime prevention and we will consider these in this chapter.

What should be the focus of crime prevention?

Key idea

An important issue that underpins crime prevention is where to direct initiatives – what should be the *focus* of these activities?

Crime prevention may be directed at a variety of targets. What is termed 'primary crime prevention' focuses on the physical environment within which crime occurs and entails initiatives designed to make it harder for any member of the general public to commit crime in that location.

Other methods of crime prevention focus on potential offenders. These may be those who are deemed to be at risk of offending (perhaps because of their family background or the area in which they live) or those who have already offended where the aim is to prevent repeat behaviour of this nature. These approaches are referred to as *secondary* and *tertiary* crime prevention, respectively.

Situational methods of crime prevention

Key idea

Situational methods of crime prevention focus on the environment within which crime may occur and aim to make it less attractive to conduct criminal activities.

Crime prevention initiatives that are based upon a situational approach are based upon the concept of *opportunity reduction*: they are concerned with interventions that are designed to make it harder to commit crime or which seek to deter people from committing it by the use of initiatives that increase the likelihood of offenders being subsequently detected.

> *The situational approach is American in origin and typically entails '(1) measures directed at highly specific forms of crime; (2) that involve the measurement, design or manipulation of the immediate environment in as systematic and permanent way as possible; (3) so as to increase the effort and risks of crime and reduce the rewards as perceived by a wide range of offenders'*
> (Clarke, 1992: 4).
>
> Clarke, R. (1992). *Situational Crime Prevention: Successful Case Studies.* New York: Harrow and Heston.

Typically situational methods of crime prevention are based upon an analysis and evaluation of crime that has occurred in order to work out whether there are any factors that seem relevant to explain what has happened which can then form the basis of preventive measures. This approach frequently relies on what has been described above as physical measures of crime prevention and is associated with a very wide range of actions which we will now consider.

ACTION DIRECTED AT THE TARGET(S) OF CRIME

Key idea

Situational crime prevention may entail actions that focus on the potential target of criminal activity and seek to make it less susceptible to such activities.

Some initiatives based upon situation methods of crime prevention entail measures designed to influence the behaviour of those who may be tempted to commit crime by making the target(s) of crime less attractive. This approach may entail:

▸ *Target removal* – when a potential target of crime is taken away: an example is when a firm pays its employee wages into their bank accounts rather than paying them in cash on a weekly or monthly basis. In this example, the target that has been removed is cash in transit in the form of a payroll that would be delivered to a firm;

▶ *Target hardening* (or *target insulation*) – when measures are taken to make it more difficult for a potential target to be the subject of crime: examples include the installation of burglar alarms and car steering locks or measures to deny access to residential property by those not authorized to be there;

▶ *Target devaluation* – when actions are initiated that seek to ensure that goods are of use only to their authorized owners and are useless if stolen. An example is the use of dye to stain banknotes stolen from a cash machine.

ACTIONS DESIGNED TO ENHANCE SURVEILLANCE

Key idea

Situational crime prevention may involve actions that seek to increase the likelihood of criminal action being observed, thus increasing the possibility of detection. These approaches seek to prevent crime through enhanced methods of surveillance.

It might be argued that crime is less likely to occur if the person who commits the crime is aware that he or she may be observed while doing it. This will increase the risk of detection. Some situational methods of crime prevention seek to enhance the likelihood that a criminal's actions will be observed by others – an approach that we term 'surveillance'.

The belief that the possibility of a criminal act being observed in England and Wales was historically performed by police patrols and public officials that included park keepers and bus conductors and also by ordinary members of the general public who were willing to get involved in tackling crime. Various factors resulted in the reduction of these traditional forms of 'capable guardians' and have prompted technological innovations to carry out the functions that they once performed.

The use of closed-circuit television (CCTV) is one example of a technological development that has been used as a mechanism that seeks to prevent crime: it may be employed to protect residential property or business premises from burglars or be used by public authorities, for example, to deter crime in a busy city centre.

> *Closed-circuit television plays an important part in contemporary crime prevention policy in England and Wales, although its effectiveness is debated: 'CCTV does have a preventative value in deterring crime. The deterrent, however, does not necessarily come from the television itself but from the potential of being discovered. [...] It may contribute towards prevention when applied properly in the appropriate setting and when monitored'* (Arrington, 2007: 151).

Arrington, R. (2007). *Crime Prevention: The Law Enforcement Officer's Practical Guide.* Sudbury, MA: Jones and Bartlett.

Spotlight

CCTV has been widely used in England and Wales as a method of situational crime prevention. By the late twentieth century it was estimated that a person in a major city could be filmed up to 300 times each day by these devices when visiting shops, banks and places of work or merely walking around the streets. Although this has given rise to accusations of the surveillance society in which personal freedoms are undermined, it has also helped to promote television programmes such as *Big Brother* in which in the name of entertainment participants agree to their actions being subjected to intensive scrutiny by CCTV.

> *Surveillance seeks to persuade individuals not to engage in criminal behaviour – 'the threat of potential surveillance [...] acts to produce a self-discipline in which individuals police their own behaviour'* (Armitage, 2002: 2).

Armitage, R. (2002). *To CCTV or not to CCTV? A Review of Current Research into the Effectiveness of CCTV Systems in Reducing Crime.* London: NACRO, Community Safety Practice Briefing.

An alternative approach that seeks to enhance the possibility of criminal behaviour being observed requires the physical reconstruction of residential areas. This approach is based upon the belief that certain types of environmental design aid crime to be committed. The remedy, therefore, is to redesign localities to enhance the potential that criminal behaviour will be observed – an approach that we refer to as *designing out* crime.

Case study: Designing out crime

The relationship between the physical environment and crime was highlighted by Jane Jacobs (1961) and Oscar Newman (1972). These works put forward the concept of *defensible space*.

This argued that urban crime arose from the breakdown of social mechanisms that once kept crime in check and the solution was to reconstruct residential environments to foster a sense of territoriality or ownership among those who lived there and to facilitate natural surveillance whereby residents could look out both for themselves and each other. In the UK, for example, this approach often led to the tearing down of high-rise blocks of flats or apartments and replacing them with constructions that were similar to the old low-rise terraced property that they had replaced.

The redesigning of residential areas sought to eliminate those design factors that were alleged to lead to crime, thereby empowering residents to regain control of their immediate environment. These included anonymity, lack of surveillance and ease of escape for the criminal. Other remedies that were designed to create defensible space included improved street lighting and reducing the amount of open space for the use of the general public.

One difficulty with this approach is that the emphasis on the environmental factors that contribute to crime ignores other issues that may be of equal or even greater importance. These include social conditions and economic factors that are frequently argued to underpin criminal behaviour.

A final situational method of crime prevention that is based upon improved levels of surveillance entails a community taking measures to defend itself against crime. This approach is based not upon the physical redesign of neighbourhoods but, rather, on the introduction of structures through which community spirit can be developed and 'good neighbourliness' promoted. One important development in the US and the UK that was based upon this approach was Neighbourhood Watch.

Neighbourhood Watch was introduced in America by the City of Seattle's Police Department in 1974. It was subsequently adopted in many areas of England and Wales. We refer to the process by which initiatives pioneered in one country are copied in others as *policy transfer*.

Neighbourhood Watch seeks to involve members of local communities in crime prevention. It entails groups of neighbours becoming organized and keeping an eye on each other's property. They take note of anything suspicious and pass on relevant information to the police. There is no organizational blueprint for these schemes whose operations are thus subject to considerable variation.

Neighbourhood Watch has many benefits that include transforming neighbourhoods from a group of anonymous individuals leading individualized lives into a community of active citizens who work together and co-operate with each other in order to combat crime.

However, such schemes have weaknesses. They are based on a belief that the crime that takes place within neighbourhoods is perpetrated by outsiders who can be readily identified by those who live there and whose speedy reporting of incidents makes it possible for the police to apprehend them. However, this is not always the case – crime is often committed by persons who live in the locality, thus reducing the effectiveness of schemes of this nature.

An assessment of situational methods of crime prevention

In the previous section of this chapter we have considered some of the activities that are associated with situational methods of crime prevention. Although schemes of this nature possess considerable benefits, there are also weaknesses to this approach. One of the most important of those is *displacement*.

The term 'displacement' is capable of several definitions. At its simplest it suggests that situational methods of crime prevention may not actually stop crime from being committed but simply alter the patterns of criminal behaviour: thus, a burglar who is deterred from entering a property that is protected by a burglar alarm or CCTV may rob from another property that is not protected by situational methods of this nature. We refer to this as *spatial displacement* – the burglar simply conducts crime elsewhere from where had originally been intended.

Other definitions of displacement suggest that situational methods of crime prevention may result in a crime being committed at a time different to that initially intended by the criminal (termed *temporal displacement*), or lead to the criminal using different methods to commit a crime, taking into account situational initiatives such as target hardening (*tactical displacement*) or lead to the criminal undertaking a different form of criminal activity from the one he or she initially conducted – situational methods to protect houses, for example, might persuade a burglar to instead engage in street crime (or 'mugging') as a form of criminal enterprise. We refer to this as *target* or *functional displacement*.

Problems of this nature lend support to an alternative approach through which to tackle crime. This is known as the *social approach* to crime prevention whose aim is to tackle the social problems that are deemed responsible for causing criminal behaviour.

The social approach to crime prevention

Key idea

Whereas situational methods of crime prevention seek to alter the environment in order to make it harder to commit crime in that vicinity, social approaches to crime prevention seek to eliminate criminal behaviour by tackling its underlying social and economic causes.

The social approach to crime prevention has a broader agenda than that of situational crime prevention. Its approach seeks to address the underlying causes of criminal behaviour with the aim of totally eliminating behaviour of this nature.

Unlike situational methods of crime prevention that seek to combat crime by making the environment less attractive to the criminal, social methods of crime prevention seek to tackle the underlying causes of criminal behaviour. 'Situational and opportunity factors might help to determine when and where crime occurs, but they do not play a role in whether crime occurs. [...] The only way to prevent crime is to deal with its root causes through psychological, social or political interventions' (Clarke, 2005: 57).

Clarke, R. (2005). 'Seven Misconceptions of Situational Crime Prevention', in N. Tilley (ed.), *Handbook of Community Safety and Crime Prevention*. Cullompton, Devon: Willan Publishing.

The social approach to crime prevention may embrace a wide range of initiatives. It underpins approaches that view deprivation as an underlying cause of crime and seeks to remedy this problem by policies that aim to improve social and economic conditions experienced by the poorer sections of society. Social approaches to crime prevention may be concerned with activities that seek to divert groups from criminal behaviour, for example by providing youth clubs whose facilities and supervision enable youngsters to remove themselves from the streets where they may carry out antisocial or criminal actions. Additionally, social approaches to crime prevention may entail identifying factors that increase the risk of criminal behaviour and introducing measures designed to prevent these actions from occurring. Programmes that seek to provide resources to deprived neighbourhoods to be used in ways that include family support services is an example of this.

Social approaches to crime prevention typically involve the expenditure of considerable sums of public money. In contrast, situational methods of crime prevention often entail individuals assuming responsibility for the protection of themselves and their property. A further difficulty with the social approach to crime prevention is that of evaluation – unlike many situational methods of crime prevention, social approaches to crime prevention may not easily lend themselves to analysis on which their effectiveness can be judged.

Community safety

The term 'community safety' involves a variety of measures that are designed to address specific forms of criminal behaviour that occur in particular neighbourhoods. The measures that are put forward to achieve this are usually delivered by a wide range of agencies working in partnership and may employ both situational and social approaches to combating crime.

Key idea

Community safety has a broader agenda than crime prevention and seeks to formally involve a wide range of agencies to initiate actions designed to tackle both the symptoms and causes of crime in specific neighbourhoods. Additionally, it entails the involvement of local people, giving them some sense of ownership of the processes that are initiated.

Community safety has assumed considerable prominence in England and Wales since the end of the twentieth century and has entailed local government assuming an important role in crime prevention. A key mechanism through which community safety is delivered is a Crime and Disorder Reduction Partnership (now commonly known as a Community Safety Partnership). This is organized at the level of local government and places a statutory requirement on a range of agencies that include the police service, local government, the Probation Service, and health authorities to co-operate in developing and implementing a strategy to reduce crime and disorder in their locality.

Dig deeper

Hughes, G. and Edwards, A. (eds) (2002). *Crime Control and Community: The New Politics of Public Safety.* Cullompton, Devon: Willan Publishing.

Hughes, G., McLaughlin, E. and Muncie, J. (eds). *Crime Prevention and Community Safety.* London: Sage.

Tilley, N. (ed.). *Handbook of Community Safety and Crime Prevention.* Cullompton, Devon: Willan Publishing.

Welsh, B. and Farrington, D. (1999). 'A Review of the Costs and Benefits of Situational Crime Prevention'. *British Journal of Criminology*, 39: 345–68.

Fact-check

1 Situational methods of crime prevention:
   A Focus on tackling the social factors that cause crime
   B Involve the use of closed-circuit television as a crime prevention measure
   C Is concerned with evaluating situations that might contribute to causing crime
   D Promotes changes to the environment to make it harder for crime to be committed

2 One meaning of the term 'crime displacement' in relation to crime prevention initiatives is:
   A The effectiveness of these initiatives leads to criminals transferring their activities to less well-protected neighbourhoods
   B Crime is totally eliminated from the neighbourhood
   C Suspected criminals are rounded up and forced to live in another location
   D Convicted criminals are expelled from the neighbourhood in which they live

3 The term 'designing out crime' refers to:
   A Penalties inflicted on convicted criminals that require them to wear unfashionable clothes
   B Education programmes to convince young people not to commit crime
   C Measures pursued jointly by a number of criminal justice agencies that are designed to prevent crime
   D Initiatives affecting housing developments that seek to create an environment in which it is difficult to commit crime

4 Social methods of crime prevention:
   A Urge communities to join together and undertake activities to prevent crime
   B Want crime prevention measures to include an element of fun in order to encourage people to participate in them
   C Seek to address the underlying causes of criminal behaviour
   D Require the police to encourage communities to undertake initiatives to combat crime

5 The term 'community safety' refers to:
   A Police methods that provide a highly visible presence in communities in order to deter crime
   B A community that pursues effective measures to protect itself from crime
   C An approach that acknowledges that the task of preventing crime is not solely the responsibility of the police
   D A community that is crime free

6 Neighbourhood Watch is sometimes unsuccessful because:
   A It cannot operate in remote rural areas
   B It acts on the assumption that crime within a neighbourhood is committed by outsiders
   C Neighbours sometimes do not get on well with each other and do not wish to work together
   D Crime is committed during the hours when most people are at work

5

How is crime detected?

Once a crime has been committed it is necessary to discover who has carried out the offence so that he or she can be punished for their actions. We refer to the task of discovering those responsible for criminal behaviour as 'detective work'. There is a wide variety of ways that are available to detectives to aid them in their work. These range from the skilled questioning of a suspected offender to scientific innovations. In this chapter we will consider the various methods that have been and are employed to detect those who have committed criminal offences.

Detection as a function of the police

Key idea

The detection of crime is a specialist task within policing that involves discovering those responsible for committing crime.

Although a key role of the police is to prevent crime, they will never be totally successful in eliminating all forms of criminal activity. When crime occurs, police work entails discovering who committed it with the objective of charging them and bringing them before the courts. The detection of crime is a specialist function within policing that is performed by detectives.

In some countries, there was an historical reluctance to combat crime with the use of detectives. Unlike police officers engaged in preventative police work, detectives wore no uniforms and were not immediately recognizable as police officers. In England and Wales, concerns that detective work would be used as a mechanism to spy on the population and, in particular, to monitor their political opinions, explained the relatively slow growth of this specialism within policing.

Detective work was slow to develop in England and Wales during the nineteenth century as an aspect of professional policing. 'When the "new police" came into being in 1829, resistance resulting in part from prejudice and partly from fear and suspicion [...] inhibited the formation of a detective unit or plain-clothes branch. The principal aims of the police at the time were the prevention of crime and the maintenance of order, as opposed to investigation and detection' (Matassa and Newburn, 2007: 43).

Matassa, M. and Newburn, T. (2007). 'Social Context of Criminal Investigation', in T. Newburn, T. Williamson and A. Wright. *Handbook of Criminal Investigation*. Cullompton, Devon: Willan Publishing.

How can crime be detected?

Key idea

A wide range of methods can be used in an attempt to discover who has committed a crime that has taken place.

OBSERVATION

The actions of a person who commits a criminal act may be observed by others. These may include police officers, victims and witnesses of crime.

QUESTIONING A SUSPECT

A person suspected of having committed a crime may be taken to a police station where detectives will question him or her. The aim of this questioning is to discover whether the answers to questions justify the police charging the suspect, a process which is simplified if, as the result of the questioning, the suspect admits to the offence. The extent to which a person in these circumstances is required to answer questions varies from one country to another.

A more robust form of questioning is termed 'interrogation', the aim of which was often to obtain a confession from the person suspected of having committed a crime. This involved a more aggressive stance being taken by a police officer which in extreme circumstances could result in physical maltreatment. In England and Wales, concerns that such behaviour sometimes occurred resulted in the 1984 Police and Criminal Evidence Act which introduced the tape-recording of interviews taking place in police stations.

Case study: Detectives and the treatment of suspected criminals after 1945

A major issue that surfaced in England and Wales after 1945 was the way in which detectives treated those whom they suspected of having committed a crime.

In this period the courts expected that a person brought before them would have signed a confession. The absence of this would cast doubt in a judge's mind of the suspect's guilt.

In order to obtain a confession, some detectives resorted to rule bending whereby questioning gave way to physical forms of abuse. This situation was abetted by the absence of legislation governing how the police should treat those detained in custody. Their treatment was regulated by Judges' Rules which had initially been formulated in 1912. These established norms of behaviour which, if breached, might technically cause a trial judge to exclude evidence such as a confession that had been obtained under duress. This course of action was, however, rare.

Well-publicized episodes of police mistreatment of suspects caused public concern. These included a suspect being beaten with a rhino whip by Sheffield detectives in 1963 and the planting of evidence designed to convict protesters by Detective Sergeant Harold 'Tanky' Challenor in 1963. The mistreatment of suspects resulted in the conviction of three boys of the murder of Maxwell Confait in 1972. The eldest was 18 but had a mental age of eight. They were freed by the Court of Appeal in 1975 and the police handling of the matter was criticized by one of the judges, Lord Scarman.

This resulted in an enquiry conducted by Sir Henry Fisher with a remit to examine the application of Judges' Rules to those suspected of crime. Although his report in 1977 stated that 'on the balance of probabilities' two of the boys charged were guilty of the murder, it prompted the creation of a Royal Commission on Criminal Procedure in 1979. This resulted in the 1984 Police and Criminal Evidence Act and the 1985 Prosecution of Offences Act.

The 1984 legislation provided safeguards for the treatment of suspects while in police custody. This included the length of time they could be detained and also required the tape-recording of interviews. The latter made it impossible to verbally or physically mistreat suspects.

The perception that close police involvement with a case sometimes made them bend the rules in order to obtain a conviction lay behind the creation of the Crown Prosecution Service (CPS) by the 1985 legislation. Henceforth, the role of the police was to gather the evidence which would be reviewed by a solicitor working for the CPS who would determine whether the case would proceed to court.

INFORMANTS

An informant is a person who associates with a criminal gang and passes on information to the police that enables them to arrest persons who have committed a crime. The informant may be a criminal who has agreed to co-operate with the police (perhaps because of the promise of financial rewards) or may be a police officer working undercover who has managed to infiltrate a criminal organization. The term 'supergrass' is used to describe the activities of informants who name a large number of their criminal associates in return for which they may be given reduced sentences (or, in some cases, immunity from prosecution). In England and Wales an important example of a supergrass was Bertie Smalls whose actions secured the conviction of a large number of criminals in the early 1970s.

> *Informants have played an important part in investigating crime but some aspects of their activities are problematic. 'Informants, appropriately employed, are essential to criminal investigations and, within limits, ought to be protected. The police must not embark on a course which will constrain them to withhold information from or mislead a court in order to protect an informant' (Morton, 2002: xii).*
>
> Morton, J. (2002). *Supergrasses and Informants and Bent Coppers.* London: Time Warner Books.

One difficulty with the use of informants is that they may act as agents provocateurs – that is, they may incite people to commit a criminal act that they otherwise would not have carried out. We use the term 'entrapment' to describe actions of this nature and legal safeguards exist in many countries as a defence against the criminal liability of a person in this situation. A further problem is the reliability of informants who have a criminal background and who may give false information regarding the activities of their former accomplices with whom they have fallen out.

Forensic science and the detection of crime

Key idea

Forensic science refers to the application of scientific techniques to the detection of crime.

Forensic science (which is sometimes referred to as 'legal medicine' or 'medical jurisprudence') makes an important contribution to the detection of crime. It builds upon an approach that entailed meticulous observation of the scene of a crime (perhaps using a magnifying glass) in order to obtain evidence that might lead to the apprehension of an offender. Forensic science gathers material at the scene of a crime which is then scientifically analysed in an attempt to detect the offender. The evidence that is collected may constitute a wide range of material ranging from fingerprints, footprints, bullets and trace evidence (such as fabric, hair, skin, blood, saliva and semen), while in cases of murder a dead body may also be an important source of evidence. The items that are collected will then be subjected to analysis by professionals who include pathologists, toxicologists and DNA analysts whose methods of investigation include autopsies, microscopes and DNA scanners. Although we may view forensic science as a relatively recent phenomenon, many of the techniques that are now used to solve crime by scientific analysis have historic origins.

Microscopes were initially developed in the late sixteenth century and considerable improvements were made by the Dutch amateur scientist Anton van Leeuwenhoek in 1670. The microscopic analysis of samples taken from a crime scene remains an important aspect of detective work. A further important development relates to adipocere. This is a wax-like substance that forms on decaying corpses, first discovered by the Englishman Sir Thomas Browne in 1658. This enables contemporary forensic scientists to estimate the time of death of a victim of crime. The use of fingerprints to identify criminals was a nineteenth-century development, the use of which became widely adopted following the publication of the book *Finger Prints* by the British anthropologist Francis Galton in 1892. This work proved that each individual's fingerprints were unique.

Forensic science considerably developed during the twentieth century and a number of national facilities were set up to make use of this approach to the detection of crime. In 1932 the American FBI established the Technical Laboratory (now called the FBI Laboratory) and in the United Kingdom the Forensic Science Service was formed in 1991 by the amalgamation of existing regional forensic laboratories. Its role (until its abolition in 2012) was to provide forensic services to all 43 police forces in England and Wales. This work has also been popularized by television programmes that include *CSI: Crime Scene Investigation*, which was first screened in 2000.

In the following section we discuss some contemporary techniques to detect crime that are associated with forensic science.

FINGERPRINTS

A person who has committed a crime may leave some form of personal trace at the scene of the crime which enables him or her to be subsequently identified. An early development that concerned the application of scientific procedures to detective work was that of fingerprints which could be examined by magnifying glasses or microscopes.

As has been stated above, fingerprints are unique to an individual and, if the police have previously fingerprinted a suspect and stored the record, it is possible to identify an offender if he or she commits a further criminal offence.

DNA PROFILING

A further application of scientific techniques to detective work has been provided by DNA profiling. As with fingerprints, a person's DNA profile is unique to him or her and can be provided through a range of samples that might be left at the scene of a crime, including, hair, blood, saliva or semen.

DNA has become an important tool in detective work and has been of especial use in revisiting crimes committed many years before to see whether specimens that could not be analysed at the time can now be examined because of developments in DNA profiling. The term we give to this procedure is 'cold case review'. It is widely used in a number of countries including the US. In England, improvements in DNA profiling enabled two persons to be convicted in 2012 of the murder of Stephen Lawrence, a notorious crime that had been committed in 1993 (see Chapter 19).

However, DNA profiling is not without its drawbacks and is not totally infallible. One difficulty is that a match between a profile stored on a database such as the United Kingdom National DNA Database (a national facility for the storage of DNA samples) and that found at the scene of a crime has to be made by a human being and the findings may thus be subject to human error. There are also civil liberty issues arising from the storage of profiles, especially when these relate to a person not subsequently charged with a criminal offence.

POLYGRAPHS

Polygraphs are usually referred to as 'lie detectors' and are used to measure a person's stress level. This is revealed by a number of physiological indicators that include pulse rate, blood pressure, skin conductivity and respiration. Polygraphs operate on the basis that an untruthful answer will produce physiological responses that differ from reactions to truthful answers.

The polygraph was invented in the US: in 1917 William Moulton Marston pioneered a polygraph that relied solely on the measurement of blood pressure and in 1921 John A. Larson invented a more comprehensive device that additionally measured heart rate, skin conductivity and respiration.

However, despite the popularity of lie detector tests in television programmes that include the *Jeremy Kyle Show* (where this method is used in connection with personal relationship issues), the use of the polygraph in crime detection is limited. Polygraph tests do not consistently detect untruthful answers, which reduces their worth as evidence presented before a court of law and also undermines their claim to be a scientific tool of investigation. For this reason, many countries do not regard polygraph testimony as admissible evidence, although it may be undertaken voluntarily by a defendant to bolster his or her defence. In America, it is permitted as testimony in a number of states although it is more widely used as a tool in criminal investigations by American (and also Canadian) law enforcement officers.

Other related methods that are used in crime detection and which may be considerably developed in usage in the twenty-first century include the electroencephalograph (EEG) (also known as 'brain fingerprinting') which measures electrical activity in the brain and judges a person's brain reaction when shown items such as images or words that relate to a crime scene. If these fail to produce a reaction from the subject, it is assumed that he or she has no knowledge of them and is thus not a party to the crime. Although this method is regarded as accurate, the analysis of results obtained may be subject to human error.

Technology and crime detection

Key idea

Technological advances made during the twentieth century have provided additional ways to detect criminal behaviour.

In addition to forensic science, contemporary methods used to detect crime make use of other forms of technology. Below we will consider some of these applications.

SURVEILLANCE

We have examined forms of surveillance such as closed-circuit television (CCTV) in Chapter 4 in connection with the prevention of crime, but these methods may also be used in connection with the detection of offenders. CCTV was widely used to apprehend those who had committed criminal acts such as looting in the August 2011 riots in England and was used alongside other technical devices such as images taken from mobile phones.

Surveillance of vehicles may be conducted through Automatic Number Plate Recognition (ANPR) whereby vehicle registration plates are photographed by devices that include closed-circuit television or speed enforcement cameras and the images obtained are read by a process that is termed 'optical character recognition'. There are problems with the accuracy of this form of surveillance and civil liberty objections have also been raised concerned the monitoring of citizens' movements.

Other forms of surveillance may also be used in connection with preventing and detecting crime and apprehending criminals. Various forms of eavesdropping that include telephone tapping, email interception and planting bugs may be employed, especially in connection with serious crime. In the United Kingdom, the procedure under which such methods made be employed are laid down by the 2000 Regulation of Investigatory Powers Act. However, although what is termed 'intercept evidence' may provide a useful form of intelligence that enables criminals to be apprehended, the evidence obtained by many of such methods is not admissible in a court.

A further problem is that technological devices that may detect crime can also be used to commit it: the interception of telephone conversations was at the heart of the phone hacking allegations in the United Kingdom when it was alleged that the telephones of a number of persons were intercepted by journalists in order to provide newsworthy stories for the newspaper for whom they worked (see Chapter 7).

Key idea

Methods not reliant on technology have also been developed to detect criminals in the twentieth century.

CRIMINAL PROFILING

Criminal profiling (which is sometimes referred to as offender profiling) is derived from the academic discipline of psychology and entails a forensic psychologist constructing a profile of a criminal that is derived from the nature of the offence that has been committed and the manner in which it has been carried out. This profile consists of personality traits that enable a description of the offender to be constructed that will lead to his or her arrest. The work of criminal profilers has been glamorized in television programmes that include *Cracker* in the United Kingdom and *Criminal Minds* in America.

Criminal profilers are sometimes used in contemporary crime investigations. 'The usual pattern is that they are thoroughly briefed by senior officers. [...] They are then allowed access to most of the important documents, photographs and videos of the case, and they usually visit the crime scene. The written profiles they eventually produce might suggest the age of the offender, his family background, the formative experiences of his life, his work, his personality, his internal conflicts, his family life and the quality of his relationships with other people. The police might then find the profile useful in narrowing down their list of suspects or prompting a new line of inquiry, and they might take advice from the profiler on the timing and manner of arresting someone. Profilers offer advice on the best way of interviewing suspects, but they do not conduct interviews with suspects, or even sit in on interviews' (Cook, 2002: 12).

Cook, S. (2002). *The Real Cracker*. Basingstoke: Channel 4 Books.

There are, however, a number of problems related to criminal profiling. Those who use it are not always psychologists and the method is not totally reliable – there are occasions in which the profile bore little or no relationship to the offender when he or she was eventually caught and which thus may lead law enforcement agencies on wild goose chases. One example of this was the profile constructed in relation to the Beltway sniper attacks. These occurred in 2002 in Washington, DC, Maryland and Virginia in which ten people were killed and three others seriously injured. Criminal profiling suggested that these crimes were carried out by a middle-class white male whereas the offenders were two black males, one of whom (Lee Boyd Malvo) was aged 17 years.

We will return to criminal profiling in our discussion of serial killers in Chapter 6.

Psychics

In relation to the detection of crime, a psychic is a person who claims to possess paranormal psychic abilities that enable him or her to visualize information that is relevant to a criminal case such as the location of a body or the whereabouts of a kidnapped person. Police forces throughout the world are generally loath to involve psychics in criminal investigations (or, at least, are loath to admit that they have involved them) unless the absence of other leads results in this course of action more or less as an act of desperation.

Detection work – how successful is it?

Key idea

Although technological developments have aided the detection of crime, in most countries its success is limited.

In addition to the statistics that are employed to measure how much crime exists within society (which we considered in Chapter 2), statistics are also used to evaluate how much crime is detected. The term 'clear-up rate' is sometimes used in connection with these statistics.

Spotlight

The mythical late nineteenth-/early twentieth-century detective Sherlock Holmes enhanced the prestige of detective work – the use of logical reasoning coupled with forensic science enabled even the most complex cases to be solved. The reality is, however, different. In 2010/11 in England and Wales, only 1.15 million of the 4.15 million crimes recorded by the police (28%) were subject to a sanction detection. For offences against vehicles and burglary the figure was much lower – 11.1% and 13.3%, respectively.

In most countries, the detection rate overall is low, although it is subject to widespread variations between categories of crime.

In England and Wales, for example, the detection rate for murder is high whereas the detection rate for household burglary is low – not much over 10 per cent.

There is also variability as to what constitutes a detection. In England and Wales a distinction is made between *sanction detections* (in which the offender receives some form of penalty) and *non-sanction detections* (in which no penalty is given to the person who committed a criminal act).

In England and Wales one controversial form of non-sanction detection is that of Taken into Consideration (TIC). This occurs when a person who has been apprehended for a criminal offence is invited by the police to admit to other crimes on the understanding that no proceedings will be brought against the person willing to give this information. Its main advantage is that it enables the police to 'close their books' on crime that is subject to this kind of confession. However, it is a process that is subject to abuse which may arise if there is no corroborating evidence that links the crime to the person who is willing to admit to it: he or she may do so, for example, in order to curry favour with the police and obtain benefits from them.

Dig deeper

Bell, S. (2012). *A Dictionary of Forensic Science*. Oxford: Oxford University Press.

Morton, J. (2002). *Supergrasses and Informants and Bent Coppers*. London: Time Warner Books.

Newburn, T., Williamson, T. and Wright, A. (2007). *Handbook of Criminal Investigation*. Cullompton, Devon: Willan Publishing.

1 In England and Wales, the term 'non-sanction detection' refers to:
   A An offence that has been detected by the police but for which no penalty is inflicted on the offender
   B An incident that is reported to the police but which does not constitute a criminal offence
   C A decision by the Crown Prosecution Service to discontinue a case that the police have referred to them
   D A decision by the police to stop investigating a crime as they believe they will never be able to find the offender

2 Forensic science entails:
   A Evaluating the methods that most effectively combat crime
   B The application of scientific techniques to the detection of crime
   C Calculating the costs of crime to the economy
   D Assessing the risk that offenders pose to the community in order to determine whether they should receive a custodial sentence or a community penalty

3 In England and Wales the proportion of reported crime that was detected in 2010/11 and for which a penalty was applied to the offender was approximately:
   A 18%
   B 28%
   C 38%
   D 58%

4 In England and Wales DNA profiles are stored on:
   A The Police National Computer
   B The National Register of Convicted Offenders
   C The National DNA Database
   D The Home Office Large Major Enquiry System

5 The term 'cold case review' refers to:
   A A process whereby a convicted offender can seek to have his or her conviction overturned in the light of new evidence that was not available at the original trial
   B The superintendence of murder investigations by senior detectives

    C The reopening of unsolved serious crimes that occurred many years previously in the hope that new scientific tools will result in the detection of the offender

    D A procedure whereby a person convicted of an offence admits to having committed other similar crimes but receives no penalty for them

6 The term 'supergrass' refers to:

    A A prolific drug trader

    B A detective who is good at his or her job

    C An informant who provides information that leads to the arrest of a number of his or her accomplices

    D A person who confesses to having committed a serious crime

6

Serial killers

Persons who commit several murders over an extended period of time have always fascinated the general public and their actions receive considerable attention in the media. This interest often derives from the nature of the crimes that have been committed, especially when these exhibit gory characteristics. This chapter examines the phenomenon of serial killers and illustrates this topic with case studies. It discusses what is meant by this term and puts forward explanations that have been offered to explain criminal behaviour of this nature.

What is a serial killer?

Key idea

A serial killer is defined as a person who commits a string of murders over an extended period of time.

Serial killers are the subject of much popular fascination. Criminal acts that entail the use of violence receive considerable media attention and this is heightened when a number of related crimes are committed over a period of time and appear to be the work of one person. So let us first define what a serial killer is and how this offender can be differentiated from other persons who commit more than one murder.

A serial killer commits a string of murders that take place intermittently over a period of time and frequently uses a similar method of killing (which we refer to as a *modus operandi*). There may also be a similarity in the targets that are selected to become a serial killer's victims. There is no minimum or maximum number attached to the number of murders that have to be carried out in order for the offender to be labelled a 'serial killer', although three or more murders is sometimes used as a criterion and those who carry out a large number of killings are sometimes described as 'prolific' serial killers. Nor is there any limit set to the period of time over which the offences take place – it may be months, years or even decades. It is important, however, to the definition of a serial killer that there is a gap (sometimes referred to as a 'cooling off period') between each episode of murder.

Spotlight

Remember to spell this term correctly – *serial* killers should not be confused with *cereal* killers. However, the latter term could be used to describe environmental activists who destroy genetically modified (GM) crops.

The term 'serial killer' needs to be differentiated from other forms of killing that involve multiple murders.

A large number of people may be killed in a single, one-off event. We refer to this as a *mass killing* and it is typically carried out by means such as planting a bomb in a place frequented by large numbers of people. The scale of deaths associated with an episode of mass killing is much greater than that associated with a serial killer and mass killing usually entails violence that is directed at its victims in an indiscriminate way in the sense that the specific victims are not singled out by the killer – anyone who happens to be in the wrong place at the wrong time is a potential victim of this form of murder. Terrorists may be regarded as mass killers, and even if they subsequently repeat their actions they will not totally replicate all aspects of their previous crime.

> *Serial murder has always excited the public imagination: 'People have always been fascinated by it. They want every last grisly detail, preferable with accompanying pictures. Nowadays we have twenty-four-hour news channels to satisfy that need. A hundred years ago when cheap, mass-produced printing was state-of-the-art, there were illustrated tabloids. Only the technology has changed. The public's appetite for sensational, true-crime stories has remained exactly the same' (Schechter, 2003: 3).*
> Schechter, H. (2003). *The Serial Killer Files: The Who, How, When, What and Why of the World's Most Terrifying Murderers.* New York: Ballantine Books.

A killer may murder several people over a relatively short period of time, perhaps in one single episode of violence or in several episodes that take place in close proximity to each other that enable all the acts of violence to be regarded as related and constituting one event. We refer to this phenomenon as a *spree killing*. Its main difference from serial killing is that the episode is not repeated – very often because the murderer commits suicide or is killed by the law enforcement authorities. In the UK examples of spree killers include Thomas Hamilton who killed 16 children and one adult at Dunblane, Scotland, in 1996 and Derrick Bird whose killing spree in West Cumbria in June 2010 left 12 people dead and 11 injured.

There is nothing new about serial killers and the exploits of one known as 'Jack the Ripper' in London in the 1880s has been the subject of intense interest that has spanned many decades. However, the term 'serial killer' was applied to a number of cases that took place in the US during the 1970s, particularly to Ted Bundy who was estimated to have murdered between ten and 20 women in that period. He was convicted of some of his crimes in 1979 and executed in 1989.

Case study: The Whitechapel Murders

Eleven murders took place between 1888 and 1891 in the impoverished, run-down and violent Whitechapel area of East London. The victims were all women, most of whom (and possibly all) were prostitutes.

At least five of these murders carried out in 1888 were attributed to a serial killer known to history as 'Jack the Ripper'. This name appeared in a letter that was claimed to have been written by the murderer, although doubt was subsequently cast on the authenticity of the letter. Two of these deaths occurred on one night in September 1888. These were set apart from the other murders that occurred in Whitechapel by the extremely violent, brutal and grotesque nature of the killings. The victims had their throats cut and in most cases the lower abdomen of their bodies had been savagely mutilated. In some cases organs had also been removed.

There is no certain explanation as to why the murders ceased in 1891. The Metropolitan Police, the City of London Police and a private organization, the Whitechapel Vigilance Committee, were involved in the search for the killer but the murderer was never caught. The nature of the wounds inflicted on the women gave rise to suggestions that the murderer had anatomical knowledge and may have been medically trained. Responsibility has been directed at a large number of people, some of whom were extremely well-connected. These included the Queen's grandson Prince Albert Victor and her personal doctor, Sir William Gull. Blame was also directed at an Irish American, Francis Tumblety, who fled to France and later to America while on bail. He died in 1903 and his possessions included two rings that were identical to those of one of the victims.

What makes a serial killer?

There are a number of reasons that might explain the phenomenon of serial killing. The theories of crime that we considered in Chapter 3 have relevance to this discussion and it may be argued that factors that cause individuals to become serial killers include biological, psychological and social and cultural conditioning factors. Anomie theory (which suggests that criminals are those who feel no bonds of attachment to society) is often put forward as an explanation of serial killers – the absence of attachment perhaps being derived from factors that relate to childhood such as parental neglect or physical or sexual abuse.

> *The actions of serial killers are explained by a variety of factors: 'The cause of serial murder eludes criminologists. Such disparate factors as mental illness, sexual frustration, neurological damage, childhood abuse and neglect, smothering relationships with mothers [...], and childhood anxiety are suspected. Many experts view serial killers as sociopaths who from early childhood demonstrate bizarre behaviour such as torturing animals. Some are sadists who enjoy the sexual thrill of murdering and who are both pathological and destructive narcissists' (Siegel, 2012: 353).*
>
> Siegel, L. (2012). *Criminology.* Wadsworth, Cengage Learning: Belmont, California, 11 ed.

In the following sections we shall consider some of the main explanations that have been put forward to explain the motives of serial killers.

SERIAL KILLERS AND FINANCIAL MOTIVES

Key idea

Some serial killers murder in order to financially profit from their activities.

Some serial killers may do it for money – to them it is a job of work. There are various descriptions that are applied to this form of serial killer that include 'hit man' or 'contract killer'. Their activities are often performed at the request of organized criminal gangs. One example of this was Richard Kuklinski who worked as a contract killer for American criminal families in Newark and New York City. It is alleged that he may have killed as many as 250 men between 1948 and 1986.

Serial killers who do not regard killing as a job or work may, nonetheless, be driven in whole or in part by the desire to secure financial gain from their actions. This was a major motive in the crimes carried out by Dr John Bodkin Adams, a general practitioner in Eastbourne, England. Although he was never convicted of murder, he was convicted of misusing dangerous drugs.

Although serial killers tend to be mainly male, some are female and financial motives underpin their crimes in the majority of cases. These include murdering husbands or partners in order to financially benefit from life insurance policies – the description 'black widow' is applied to this type of female serial killer.

SERIAL KILLERS AND PLEASURE SEEKING

Key idea

Serial killers may commit multiple murders because it provides them with a sense of thrill and excitement.

Serial killers may act as they do because they experience thrill and enjoyment from their actions. We refer to this as *hedonism*. This may derive from the sense of fear that their actions instil in the victim or may be associated with the sexual gratification that they achieve either from murder or from activities associated with it such as kidnap and rape.

Examples of hedonistic serial killers include Jeffrey Dahmer in the US who killed a number of young males between 1978 and 1991. He was convicted and received 15 consecutive life sentences in 1992, totalling over 950 years. He died in prison in 1994 at the hands of another inmate.

SERIAL KILLERS AND POWER CONTROL

> **Key idea**
>
> Serial killers may murder because they wish to exercise domination over other human beings.

Some serial killers derive gratification because murderous acts provide them with an opportunity to exercise power and control over fellow human beings and ultimately to be in a position where they are able to determine whether they will allow that person to live or die. For this type of serial killers, sexual abuse of the victims may be an aspect of behaviour that seeks to dominate.

SERIAL KILLERS AND MENTAL DISORDERS

> **Key idea**
>
> Serial killers may suffer from personality disorders that force them to murder.

Serial killers may act in the way they do because a force over which they have no control drives them to regularly commit the crime of murder. This may take the form of the killer hearing voices and feeling compelled to do as they say. Hearing voices is a common symptom of schizophrenia. These voices may be assumed to come from God or the devil: the American serial killer David Berkowitz known as 'Son of Sam' (who killed six people in New York City in 1976 and 1977 and injured several more) believed that a demon transmitted orders that he should kill through his neighbour's Labrador dog.

Alternatively, serial killers may suffer from psychopathic or sociopathic personality disorders. These are characterized by factors that include a disregard for society's standards of behaviour, impulsive or antisocial behaviour, and the absence of feelings of fear or guilt. They have low autonomic arousal, which means that they do not display obvious signs of emotion or affection.

Serial killers and a sense of mission

Key idea

Some serial killers are driven to kill by a sense of purpose or mission: these are referred to as 'missionary serial killers'.

Serial killers may view themselves as instruments to rid society of individuals, groups or organizations that they regard as an evil, exerting a detrimental impact on its wellbeing. Various manifestations of hate crime may be driven by impulses of this nature, characterized by random attacks on individuals who are members of marginalized or socially excluded groups such as prostitutes. Missionary serial killers may also direct their activities at more carefully selected targets, performing acts of violence that share many characteristics with terrorism.

In the US Ted Kaczynski (otherwise known as the Unabomber) provides us with an example of a serial killer motivated by a sense of purpose. His mail bombing campaigns especially targeted universities and airlines which he regarded as being responsible for promoting the modern industrial-technological system. He especially objected to the loss of personal freedom which this system entailed. His campaign commenced in 1978 and was conducted over a period of around 20 years; three people were killed (the first of which was a computer store owner in 1985) and 20 injured.

Case study: Ted Bundy

Ted Bundy was an American serial killer whose victims were young white females, many of whom were university students aged between 15 and 25 years of age and from middle-class backgrounds. His crimes also included kidnap and rape. Shortly before his execution he confessed to having committed 30 killings across seven states between 1974 and 1978, although the number is likely to have been higher than this, perhaps as many as one hundred.

Bundy's modus operandi varied but often entailed impersonating an authority figure or feigning disability as a pretext for stopping a victim who was then taken to a secluded location and attacked. Death occurred from strangulation. Alternatively, he broke into the victims' residences and savagely assaulted them with a blunt instrument. Some of his victims were decapitated and in other cases he practised necrophilia on the corpses. He also frequently took pictures of his victims' dead bodies.

In 1976 Bundy was convicted of aggravated criminal assault and kidnapping in Utah, but managed to escape in 1977 when he had been extradited to Colorado in connection with a charge of murder. Although quickly recaptured, he again escaped. While 'on the run' he committed further murders before being recaptured in Florida in 1978. One of these episodes in January 1978 involved an attack on four female students in a Florida State University sorority house: all were sexually attacked and two were murdered. The following month he sexually assaulted and murdered a 12-year-old girl. He was subsequently apprehended for driving a car with stolen licence plates. Forensic evidence and eyewitness accounts linked him to the Florida attacks and he was tried in two separate trials for the three murders. After multiple appeals and numerous stays of execution, he was executed in 1989.

Bundy's motives for murder appear to be the satisfaction he derived from the control he was able to exert over his victims and the pain he was able to inflict on them, which included torture. His crimes bore the hallmarks of someone suffering from antisocial personality disorder, termed a 'sociopath', who was unable to experience feelings of guilt or remorse.

Although serial killing is not unique to America, it is a serious problem in that country: 'in the early 1990s, an FBI Behavioural Sciences Unit survey of news clippings estimated 82 serial murderers were active between 1900 and 1970, and 365 between 1970 and 1992 [...] the potential scale of the problem seemed alarming; at one point it was claimed that around a quarter of US murders were committed by a few serial killers' (D'Cruze et al., 2006: 141).

D'Cruze, S., Walklate, S. and Pegg, S. (2006). *Murder.* Cullompton, Devon: Willan Publishing.

Do serial killers possess any obvious characteristics?

There is no general set of characteristics that are possessed by serial killers. Although as a generalization they may be of lower average intelligence than the general population, many do not match this profile. Ted Kaczynski, for example, was extremely intelligent and well educated. The English serial killer Dr Harold Shipman (who was convicted in 2000 for murdering 15 of his patients but may have killed considerably more than this by administering lethal doses of a strong opiate) enjoyed a successful career as a general practitioner.

Nor are serial killers set apart by leading a solitary life – many have families, hold down a steady job and engage in a range of social activities. Ted Bundy, for example, took an active interest in politics in the 1970s while another American serial killer, Dennis Rader (who killed at least ten people in Kansas between 1974 and 1991), was a Boy Scout Leader and an elected Church Council President.

There may, however, be factors that many serial killers share, one of which is suffering abuse (sexual, physical or emotional) by a family member as a child. Alternatively, they may have been abandoned by their parents as a baby or in early childhood and brought up by other relatives or in a foster home or have been brought up in the environment of a family breakdown. This profile fits David Berkowitz ('Son of Sam') who believed that his natural mother had died during childbirth (which was not the case) and who was brought up by an adopted family.

In 1963 J.M. Macdonald put forward the Macdonald triad which associated three practices in childhood – animal cruelty, obsession with fire, and bedwetting beyond the age of five years – with violent behaviour, especially murder. Although dispute was later cast on the importance of bedwetting to serial killing, the triad has some relevance – Dennis Rader, for example, was associated with the sadistic killing of animals.

Key idea

Criminal profiling is one method that has been developed to track down serial killers.

The absence of any general set of characteristics possessed by serial killers makes the task of detection hard. One method that was developed in America was that of criminal profiling. This approach was not entirely new. In the 1880s a police surgeon, Thomas Bond, sought to profile the personality of Jack the Ripper. However, the technique was developed by the FBI's Behavioral Science Unit in the 1970s.

The aim of profiling is to construct a picture of the criminal's personality derived from a detailed examination of patterns of behaviour revealed in connection with a murder. There are four key areas that contribute to this analysis:

1 antecedent

2 the method or manner by which the murder was committed

3 the way in which the body was disposed of

4 the offender's behaviour following the murder.

From this information, a picture is compiled of the offender's personality that seeks to identify key characteristics such as age, intelligence, physical characteristics, personality features and style of living. This picture is then compared to the list of suspects that has been compiled by the police.

The crime scene is especially important to the profile, enabling organized or disorganized crime scenes to be identified. An *organized crime scene* exhibits features that include evidence of advance planning and the removal of the body and the murder weapon from the vicinity of the crime. A *disorganized crime scene* suggests that the murder was spontaneous and the body and murder weapon are likely to be left there.

The features of the crime scene are then related to particular offender profiles. A disorganized crime scene suggests an offender whose characteristics include average or above-average intelligence, who is in work and mixes normally with other people. A disorganized crime scene suggests an offender whose characteristics include below-average intelligence, who is unskilled and likely to be unemployed or with an erratic employment record and who is likely to live alone, finding it hard to mix with other people.

Dig deeper

Berry-Dee, C. (2003). *Talking with Serial Killers: The Most Evil People in the World Tell Their Own Stories*. London: Blake Publishing.

D'Cruze, S., Walklate, S. and Pegg, S. (2006). *Murder*. Cullompton, Devon: Willan Publishing.

Schechter, H. (2003). *The Serial Killer Files. The Who, How, When, What and Why of the World's Most Terrifying Murderers*. New York: Ballantine Books.

Wilson, D. (2011). *A History of British Serial Killing: The Shocking Account of Jack the Ripper, Harold Shipman and Beyond*. London: Sphere Books.

Fact-check

1 A serial killer is a murderer who:

  A Commits a number of offences in a relatively short space of time using similar methods

  B Is constantly in the news headlines because of the nature of his or her crimes

  C Carries out a number of murders at the same time

  D Has been convicted but, on release, carries out a similar crime

2 Murders that occurred in Whitechapel, London, between 1881 and 1891 (some of which were attributed to the serial killer Jack the Ripper) stopped because:

  A He was apprehended by the police

  B He got fed up with his life of crime

  C He died

  D Nobody knows for sure

3 An important motive that drives serial killers to murder is:

  A They were born bad and cannot avoid this form of behaviour

  B They derive pleasure from the exercise of power over their victims

  C They crave the publicity that the media gives to their crimes

  D They regard murder as a ritual that cleanses the soul

4 A contract killer carries out murders:

  A For fun

  B For religious reasons

  C For money

  D Out of a sense of duty

5 A person who draws up a picture of an offender based upon the nature of the crimes they have committed is known as:

  A A detective

  B A scene of crime investigator

  C A criminologist

  D A criminal profiler

6 In the United Kingdom the name of the general practitioner who was convicted in 2000 of having killed 15 people but was suspected of having killed many more was:

A Dr Hawley Harvey Crippen

B Dr Harold Shipman

C Dr John Bodkin Adams

D Dr Michael Swango

7

The crimes of the powerful

Many of the theories of crime that we considered in Chapter 3 are concerned with explaining crime that is committed by those at the lower end of the social ladder. This does not mean, however, that persons of higher social status always lead completely law-abiding lives. This chapter considers crime that is carried out by those deemed 'respectable' members of society. It differentiates between behaviour undertaken by individuals to further their own interests and that undertaken by business corporations to benefit their commercial prospects. In particular, it poses the question as to whether activities of this nature are treated by society with the seriousness that they deserve.

White-collar crime

Key idea

White-collar crime refers to criminal activities carried out by persons who are not drawn from the lower end of the social scale and which do not pose a threat of physical violence by the criminal towards the victim.

The term 'white-collar crime' was associated with an American criminologist, Edwin Sutherland, who challenged the perception that crime was an activity associated with working-class people. He believed that this behaviour could also be exhibited by those who were of higher social standing.

The original definition of white-collar crime was 'a crime committed by a person of respectability and high social status in the course of his occupation' (Sutherland, 1949: 9).

Subsequent discussion of this concept differentiated white-collar crime into corporate (or organizational) crime and occupational crime: corporate crime is defined as 'offences committed by corporate officials for the corporation and the offences of the corporation itself' (Clinard and Quinney, 1973: 188).

Occupational crime 'is committed largely by individuals or small groups of individuals in connection with their occupation. [...] It includes violations of law by businessmen, politicians [...] lawyers, doctors [...] and employees who embezzle money from their employers or steal merchandise or tools' (Clinard and Yeager, 2006: 18).

Clinard, M. and Quinney, R. (1973). *Criminal Behaviour System: A Typology.* New York: Holt, Rinehart and Winston.

Clinard, M. and Yeager, P. (2006). *Corporate Crime.* New Brunswick: Transaction Publishers.

Sutherland, E. (1949). *White Collar Crime.* New York: Dryden.

Sutherland's original definition of white-collar crime has been subsequently developed to embrace three different forms of criminal enterprise:

1 *Occupational crime:* This refers to crime carried out by employees within the workplace who seek to advantage themselves at the expense of the company for whom they work. They may be of any social status;

2 *Middle-class crime:* This embraces activities carried out by persons of relatively high social status but not necessarily within the setting of a workplace: it entails activities that are designed to benefit them personally, such as insurance fraud and tax evasion;

3 *Corporate crime:* This involves activities carried out by the employees of a company whose prime aim is to benefit the company rather than the individuals who carry out the criminal act. Examples of this may include bribery and corruption that is designed to secure lucrative contracts for the corporation or compromising safety standards for the company's consumers or workers in order to maximize its profits. Those who own companies may also carry out illegal actions that include a range of fraudulent activities such as embezzlement, misappropriation of funds and false accounting.

Case study: The LIBOR scandal of 2012

Although corporate crime may benefit a commercial organization, those who conduct it may also benefit from it. They may be rewarded by the company whose interests they have furthered in the form of promotion or other financial benefits, or they may themselves profit financially from their illicit actions.

The dual nature of corporate crime was evidenced in the LIBOR scandal that initially affected Barclays Bank in the UK in 2012. LIBOR stands for the London Interbank Offered Rate. This is the interest rate that banks in London charge to lend money to each other for short-term borrowing periods.

In 2012 Barclays Bank was fined £290 million following an investigation by the UK's Financial Services Authority and the USA's Department of Justice Commodity Futures Commission which revealed several banks had conspired to manipulate this rate.

Although this action on the part of Barclays traders was designed to make the bank seem more financially stable than it actually was during a period of economic crisis, some traders also made personal profits arising from these activities. The bank's chairman and chief operating officer resigned in the wake of these allegations.

Although there remains a tendency to use the term 'white-collar crime' to refer to all of these activities, we sometimes place the three forms of crime outlined above under the one heading of 'economic crime'. This includes actions such as bribery and corruption; various forms of fraud committed against individuals or the state; crime that is committed with the aid of computers and actions associated with organized crime such as money laundering. In contrast to the theories of crime that are discussed in Chapter 7, none of these actions entail the use of (or the threat to use) physical violence against persons who are the victims of them.

The scale of the problem

Key idea

The activities that have been discussed above are a significant aspect of contemporary crime and measured in financial terms are much larger than the losses caused by 'ordinary' crimes.

Spotlight

Workplace crime can sometimes reach enormous proportions and have catastrophic consequences. Unauthorized speculative trading by a derivatives broker, Nick Leeson, employed by Baring's Bank, resulted in losses that totalled £827 million in 1995. This sum was double the bank's trading capital and led to it being declared insolvent in 1995. His actions caused the demise of Britain's oldest investment bank, whose origins dated to 1762.

The types of crime that have been referred to in the previous section of this chapter have become increasingly important aspects of contemporary crime. By the end of the twentieth century it was estimated that the annual cost of white-collar crime in the US amounted to more than $400 billion and in the early years of the twenty-first century activities that included embezzlement, fraud, money laundering and corruption cost British businesses around £32 billion. Negligent actions undertaken by companies and businesses have also caused loss of life.

> The financial cost of white-collar crime is large: 'white collar crimes exact a heavy aggregate toll, one that dwarfs comparable losses to street criminals' (Shover, 1998: 140).
>
> However, although white-collar crime entails high economic costs, it is a relatively neglected phenomenon in criminology: 'Homicide and other "street crimes" probably receive so much attention because they threaten us personally and violate our sense of security. Yet this fact leads us to neglect the gravity of "white collar crime" which in many ways is more harmful than street crime. [...] Estimates of the costs of white collar crime dwarf those of street crime. For example, although the Federal Bureau of Investigation (FBI) estimates that property crime costs the public about $17 billion in direct costs, the monetary costs of white collar crime may exceed $700 billion. Similarly, whereas almost 16,300 people died from homicide in 2008, the annual number of deaths from white collar crime [...] may exceed 100,000' (Barkan and Bryjak, 2011: 6).
>
> Barkan, S. and Bryjak, G. (2011). *Fundamentals of Criminal Justice: A Sociological View*, 2nd edn. Sudbury, MA: Jones and Bartlett Learning.
>
> Shover, N. (1998). 'White Collar Crime', in M. Tonry (ed.), *The Handbook of Crime and Punishment*. Oxford: Oxford University Press.

The various forms of criminal activity that have been discussed above have increased in extent in recent years. There are various reasons that might explain this. The growth of information and communications technology has created a range of new criminal opportunities that can be exploited by workers within a company (including low-level misdemeanours that include 'surfing the Net' in company time) or persons outside of the workplace. The latter includes cybercrime, which broadly refers to crime that involves the use of computers. This may embrace *computer-assisted crime* (in which computers are used to carry out crimes such as fraud and theft which existed before computers were invented) or *computer-focused crime* (where computer technology has resulted in the emergence of new crimes such as hacking and deliberately planting viruses to sabotage computers owned by individuals or business enterprises).

Crime committed by business corporations has especially grown in recent decades. In criminology we tend to use the term 'corporation' broadly to encompass all forms of commercial enterprise whether carried out by large multinational organizations or smaller businesses organizations.

In addition to 'traditional' forms of corporate crime whereby injuries and deaths are caused to workers, consumers and the general public arising from commercial practices that seek to maximize profits, the process of deregulation in both the UK and the US since the 1970s (whereby governments remove regulations affecting the conduct of business in order to encourage enterprise) may help to further stimulate commercial wrongdoings. The inadequacy of regulation covering all aspects of commercial enterprise has also been exploited by organized crime through activities that include money laundering.

However, corporations may be on the receiving end of contemporary aspects of occupational crime. A key feature of modern business enterprises is the divorce of ownership and control which means that the employees may possess too much autonomy in the conduct of their activities. They may exploit this absence of adequate supervision for their own benefit (perhaps embezzling money from the company) or, alternatively, undertake unauthorized actions which can have disastrous commercial consequences.

Case study: *News of the World* phone hacking scandal

The media possesses considerable power in liberal democratic societies and is a key source of information for the general public on a wide range of issues. The need to stay ahead of a rival media outlet may result in the use of practices which are immoral or even illegal. This case study considers events that led to the closure of a major newspaper in Great Britain, the *News of the World*.

The *News of the World* newspaper was published by News International, a subsidiary of News Corporation which is owned by the media tycoon Rupert Murdoch. Allegations were made that journalists working for this newspaper (and other tabloids published by News International) had engaged in a number of malpractices that included hacking voicemail messages and bribing public officials in order to obtain information that would form the basis of exclusive newsworthy stories.

Initially, it was assumed that the victims of such activities were celebrities, politicians and members of the Royal Family. In January 2007 a *News of the World* editor and a private detective were jailed in connection with intercepting voicemail messages on the phones of royal aides. However, it subsequently emerged in 2011 that ordinary members of the public had also been targeted in this way. These included relatives of British soldiers killed in action, victims of the July 2005 London bombings and the phone of the murdered schoolgirl Milly Dowler. Public distaste towards these activities resulted in advertisers withdrawing from the *News of the World* and culminated in a decision by Rupert Murdoch to close the newspaper in July 2011.

News International initially tried to blame the affair on the actions of one rogue reporter, but subsequently admitted that the practice was more widespread. Rupert Murdoch took out a series of adverts in UK newspapers to apologize for the actions of the *News of the World* and subsequently out-of-court damages were paid to a number of victims.

One key issue in this scandal concerned the extent to which senior executives within News International were aware of the malpractices of their journalists. It seemed that a powerful media outlet with high-powered connections could break the law with impunity. This belief seemed justified in connection with police investigations into the hacking allegations. In 2006 the Metropolitan Police launched an investigation. Police officers subsequently alleged that News International had attempted to thwart the original police inquiry in 2006. They refused to relaunch this in 2009 but did reopen the case in 2011.

The perception that the newspaper was untouchable was aided by the appointment of a former editor of the *News of the World*, Charles Coulson, as Director of Communications by incoming Prime Minister David Cameron in 2010. He resigned from his post in 2011 and it was subsequently alleged that he was aware of the extent of phone hacking and also that he authorized payments to police officers in return for providing information to journalists. He was later arrested in connection with the bribery allegation.

Heads started to roll in 2011. A number of resignations occurred within the News International empire (including its chief executive, Rebekah Brooks) and outside of the organization. These included the Chief Commissioner of the Metropolitan Police, Sir Paul Stephenson. He had hired as a public relations advisor a former *News of the World* executive, Neil Wallis, who had been questioned by the police in connection with the hacking scandal. The Assistant Commissioner of the Metropolitan Police who had checked the credentials of Mr Wallis also resigned.

The scandal raised a number of important issues that related to the regulation of the press, media ownership and the extent to which those who owned major corporations were fully aware of the practices undertaken by their employees. A number of inquiries were held into this affair which included the Leveson Inquiry into phone hacking and police bribery conducted by the *News of the World* and an investigation mounted by the Home Affairs Committee. In the US (which houses the headquarters of News Corporation), an investigation was mounted by the Federal Bureau of Investigation in July 2011 to determine whether News Corporation accessed voicemails of victims of the 9/11 attacks.

The scandal affecting the *News of the World* did not end in 2011. In January 2012 four current or former employees of Rupert Murdoch's *Sun* newspaper and a police officer were arrested on suspicion of corruption. The following month a further five journalists employed by Rupert Murdoch's *Sun* newspaper were arrested in connection with allegations related to the bribery of public officials to obtain information.

The regulation of white-collar and corporate crime

Key idea

Activities that have been described above as white-collar, middle-class and corporate crime have traditionally not been viewed as priorities for interventions by the state.

It is widely assumed that there is an official reluctance to initiate criminal actions against white-collar, middle-class and corporate wrongdoers. Although there are examples where this does occur, criminal law is not consistently deployed in connection with the activities that we have considered in this chapter. This may give rise to a perception that the state is tolerant towards certain types of wrongdoings, perhaps to justify or legitimize a wider range of criminal actions undertaken throughout society.

In the UK this issue was raised in 2011 in connection with the manner in which Her Majesty's Revenue and Customs department dealt with the resolution of tax issues (including disputes over outstanding tax) from large companies which totalled £25 billion. The House of Commons Public Accounts Committee was worried that large companies were treated more favourably than other taxpayers and that they appeared to receive preferential treatment compared to small businesses and individuals. The Committee argued that all taxpayers should be seen to be treated equally before the law.

The failure to take adequate actions against white-collar, middle class and corporate wrongdoers sends out wrong messages to society as a whole regarding the need to combat crime: 'as long as legislators and administrators of criminal justice fail to take appropriate measures against white collar crime, it is nonsensical to expect the penal system to be successful in its fight against the ordinary thief and burglar and small fry' (Mannheim, 1946: 119).
Mannheim, H. (1946). *Criminal Justice and Social Reconstruction*. London: Routledge and Kegan Paul.

There are several reasons that might account for the apparent official reluctance to take robust action to counter the activities that are the focus of this chapter. Perhaps the most important of these is that crime of this nature is 'victimless' in the sense that it did not specifically target an individual and deliberately set out to cause him or her harm. The crime does not target specific individuals and is thus victimless – the state, for example, is the sufferer of tax evasion. Additionally (as we have argued above), this type of crime is often characterized by the absence of physical violence towards the victim, which is frequently the rationale for punitive responses by the state.

It is alleged that a particular deficiency to tackle activities discussed in this chapter is the absence of a robust response to corporate crime by the use of the criminal law. One explanation for this is that whereas 'ordinary' crimes such as theft and burglary challenge the underlying capitalist value of property ownership, corporate wrongdoings offer no such challenge – indeed, the motivation of many of these actions is to maximize profits and accumulate capital and thus they are in accordance with the cardinal aims of a capitalist society.

Other reasons which may explain the state's reluctance to intervene in corporate wrongdoings are:

▶ Corporate wrongdoings often consist of actions that are perhaps immoral but not illegal and thus do not constitute a crime. Exploiting workers in developing nations by taking advantage of low wages in order to buy products cheaply which are then sold as expensive items is an example of this;

▶ It is sometimes difficult to ascertain whether an action attributable to a corporation that causes injury or death was the result of incompetence or hard luck rather than being the product of a criminal wrongdoing.

For reasons such as these, intervention regarding corporate wrongdoings often takes the form of regulation rather than the use of the criminal law.

Regulatory supervision of corporate wrongdoings

Key idea

Corporate activities are frequently controlled by the criminal law.

There have been some initiatives to extend the scope of the criminal law to regulate corporate wrongdoings.

Much corporate crime takes place on a global scale and frequently involves politicians or public officials being bribed in order to further corporate business interests. Accusations of this nature have been especially directed at the operations of multinational companies operating in developing nations. Attempts at regulation include the Convention on Combating Bribery in International Business Transactions, which was initiated by the Organization for Economic Co-operation and Development (the OECD) in 1999. This sought to impose and enforce common rules against companies and individuals seeking to bribe foreign public officials for business purposes and resulted in some countries introducing legislation to further its objectives.

In the UK this took the form of the 2010 Bribery Act. This covered issues such as the bribery of foreign officials and the failure of a commercial organization to prevent bribery conducted on its behalf by its employees. One concern with this legislation is that it will place UK businesses at a disadvantage by criminalizing behaviour that is deemed acceptable commercial practice outside of the UK.

Other legislative endeavours in the UK have been directed against activities by business concerns that result in a major loss of life. Episodes of this nature included the sinking of the ferry the *Herald of Free Enterprise* (in which 192 died) and the King's Cross underground fire (which killed 31 people) in 1987; the fire on the *Piper Alpha* oil rig in the North Sea (which killed 167 workers) and the Clapham rail crash (in which 37 persons died) in 1988; the *Marchioness* riverboat sinking in 1989 (in which

51 people perished when the ship collided with the dredger the *Bowbelle*), the 1999 Paddington rail disaster (in which 32 people died) and the 2000 Hatfield rail disaster (where an unrepaired broken rail caused the deaths of four people).

In response to public concerns regarding such events, the 2007 Corporate Manslaughter and Corporate Homicide Act made it possible for companies and organizations (but not senior executives of these organizations) to be found guilty of a criminal offence if it can be proved that injuries or deaths were caused by a management failure that constituted a gross breach of the duty of care. The penalties on conviction can entail an unlimited fine, publicity orders or remedial orders requiring a firm to put right any management failure that results in death.

Key idea

Corporate activities are often subject to regulatory supervision rather than the criminal law.

However, the favoured form of intervention regarding corporate wrongdoings is that of regulatory supervision rather than the criminal law.

Regulatory supervision may take two forms. The activities of corporations are sometimes controlled by *self-regulation* whereby companies that operate within specific commercial sectors effectively police themselves. The justification for this process is that 'insiders' may possess a better grasp of corporate practices than outsiders and are thus better placed to spot wrongdoings and immediately initiate procedures to stop them. However, self-regulation may result in abuses being covered up in order to prevent the whole industry being associated with wrongful actions.

External regulation is an alternative way of supervising the activities of corporations. In the UK regulatory supervision is conducted by agencies that are external to the business sector over which they exert control. Examples include the Health and Safety Executive, the Environment Agency, the Office of Fair Trading and the trading standards departments that are operated by local authorities. The remit of these agencies often covers commercial practices in general rather than activities associated with specific commercial enterprises. Regulatory agencies have the power to prosecute commercial concerns that have undertaken actions leading to the death or injury of workers employed in an industry, the consumers of its products or the general public, but they frequently seek to secure compliance with laws and regulations through ways other than prosecution, which is used only as a last resort. Additionally, the penalties arising from prosecutions are often an inadequate response to the scale of harm that has been caused. This is especially the case with commercial activities that pollute the environment.

Dig deeper

Croall, H. (2001). *Understanding White Collar Crime*. Buckingham: Open University Press.

Furnell, S. (2002). *Cybercrime: Vandalizing the Information Society*. Edinburgh: Pearson Education.

Payne, B. (2012). *White Collar Crime: The Essentials*. London: Sage.

Tombs, S. and Whyte, D. (2011). *The Corporate Criminal*. London: Routledge.

Fact-check

1 Cybercrime is:
   A A term applied to a wide range of crimes that are carried out with computers
   B Crime committed by Cybermen whose actions were challenged by Dr Who
   C Another term for hacking
   D A term applied to the theft of computers and related software

2 The view that crime is sometimes carried out by persons of respectability and high social status in the course of their occupation is associated with the work of:
   A Edwin Sutherland
   B Donald Sutherland
   C Kiefer Sutherland
   D Graham Sutherland

3 The term 'corporate crime' refers to:
   A A business concern that has gone bankrupt
   B A business concern that is the victim of criminal activity such as fraud
   C A series of related crimes carried out by an organized criminal gang
   D Crime that is designed to aid the commercial interests of a business concern at the expense of its customers and/or workers

4 The term 'occupational crime' is applied to:
   A Professional criminals who have graduated at the University of Crime and for whom crime is a full-time job
   B Crime committed by an army that invades another country which it then occupies
   C Crime committed by employees within the environment of the workplace
   D Crime committed by people who have jobs as distinct from crime committed by those who are unemployed

5 The term 'victimless crime' refers to:
   A A crime of which the victim is not aware
   B A crime that does nobody any harm

   C A crime that lacks a specific victim in the form of a person or persons who directly suffer from the criminal act

   D A situation when insurance companies make good any loss suffered by a victim of crime

6 The term 'economic crime' means:

   A Crime that is conducted by business and commercial organizations

   B Crime that is cost effective for a criminal to carry out and from which he or she can expect to make a profit

   C Crime that benefits a country's economy

   D A wide range of crime that is conducted within, against and by commercial organizations

8

Political crime

What is termed 'political crime' refers to illicit actions that are undertaken by persons who hold political office. These usually seek to bring some form of personal benefit to the politician who performs the act. The term also applies to unlawful actions that are designed to further a political cause or interest and which often entail the use of violence. This chapter examines the concept of political crime which embraces three activities – activities that are committed by politicians who abuse the trust placed in them and the power they possess, crime committed against the state and its citizens in the form of terrorism and crimes committed by a state against other states and nations.

Politicians and the abuse of trust and power

In liberal democratic countries such as the UK and the US, politicians are elected into office in order to serve the nation and defend the more localized interests of their constituents, those who elected them. However, although most politicians do perform these roles, there have been examples of politicians using their office in order to further their own interests (or those of the political party that they represent) in order to secure financial benefits or other forms of advantage. These actions may include criminal behaviour or may embrace activities that are immoral rather than being illegal.

Key idea

The term 'sleaze' has been coined to describe actions undertaken by politicians that entail the abuse of the trust and confidence placed on them by those who elected them to office and which are designed, instead, to further their own interests.

There is nothing new in the situation whereby the actions of politicians go beyond serving the interests of the nation and raising the concerns of those who elected them into office. British and American history contains numerous examples of scandals that are based upon the inappropriate action of elected officials. Attempts by politicians to cover up activities of this nature also form an aspect of abuse of power, perhaps the most infamous of which was the episode relating to Watergate in 1972.

Case study: Watergate

The Watergate scandal provides a good illustration of crime committed by powerful people.

On 17 June 1972 five men were arrested for their part in a break-in that occurred at the Watergate complex, Washington, DC, which housed the headquarters of the Democrat National Committee during the 1972 Presidential election. The aim of this burglary was to plant phone-tapping devices. It had occurred in May 1972 but problems with the quality of information that they provided prompted a further break-in on 17 June 1972 which was observed by a security guard. He called the police and five men were arrested. The key issue was who had organized these break-ins.

Information found on the burglars linked them to a fund-raising group that was campaigning for the re-election of President Nixon. This suggested that senior members of the Nixon administration may have organized the burglaries. Although this was vehemently denied by the President, investigations by the FBI concluded that the break-ins were part of a wider campaign of spying and sabotage conducted against the Democrats.

In November 1972 President Nixon was comfortably re-elected, but the scandal refused to die down. Two reporters on the *Washington Post* (Bob Woodward and Carl Bernstein) published material that suggested knowledge of the break-in and attempts subsequently to cover it up reached the higher echelons of the Nixon administration including the President himself.

The trials of the burglars produced further allegations of a cover-up and resulted in the resignation (and subsequent conviction) of two of the President's most influential aides. A new Attorney General was also appointed with a remit to appoint a special counsel to conduct an investigation into the Watergate episode.

These responses did not, however, satisfy the Senate which established a committee to investigate the affair in February 1973. The committee's hearings established that the President tape-recorded conversations in his office. These tape recordings might shed light on the Watergate affair, in particular regarding who had knowledge of what was taking place. The special counsel asked for these tapes, but the President refused on the grounds of executive privilege. On 24 July the Supreme Court ruled that he had to hand over these recordings.

The tapes, when released, revealed that the President was aware of the break-ins and was implicated in attempts to cover it up, including an attempt to get the CIA to block the FBI's investigation on the grounds of national security. This suggested that the President was involved with a criminal conspiracy to obstruct justice. In March 1974 a grand jury indicted seven people (including some senior Presidential aides) for conspiracy to hinder the Watergate investigation.

On 6 February 1974 the House of Representatives overwhelmingly voted to give its Judicial Committee the authority to investigate impeachment proceedings against the President. In July 1974 the House of Representatives passed three articles of impeachment against the President and in the face of likely impeachment by the House of Representatives and the strong possibility of a conviction in the Senate, President Nixon resigned from office on 9 August 1974. His successor, Gerald Ford, issued him with a pardon.

Historically, the term 'corruption' was applied to actions of this nature. However, during the 1990s an alternative description, that of sleaze, tended to be used. This term especially related to actions that entailed inappropriate sexual behaviour, sometimes coupled with attempts to deny that such actions had occurred.

In Britain one aspect of sleaze that emerged during the 1990s was accusations that one or two members of a Conservative government that emphasized the importance of society returning to traditional values based on self-discipline and the family were engaged in extramarital affairs. Such actions, although not illegal, were widely viewed as hypocritical. In the US, an important example of sleaze affected President Clinton who was accused of having a sexual affair with an intern, Monica Lewinsky.

Initially, both Lewinsky and the President swore on oath that they had not had an affair. However, doubt was subsequently cast on the truthfulness of these denials which led the President to admit having had an 'inappropriate' physical relationship with Ms Lewinsky. A subsequent report of a special counsel, Kenneth Starr, to the House of Representatives Judiciary Committee accused the President of perjury, abuse of power, obstruction of justice and witness tampering. In December 1998 this committee approved four articles of impeachment, two of which were then endorsed by the House of Representatives. This led to a trial before the Senate, at which President Clinton was acquitted in February 1999.

The use of the term 'sleaze' during the 1990s also embraced more traditional forms of behaviour based upon the abuse of political power for a politician's personal gain.

Key idea

Lobbying seeks to influence decisions taken by government and is an activity which may enable politicians to use contacts derived from the office they occupy (or have occupied) to their financial advantage.

In the UK a 'cash for questions' allegation arose in 1994 which accused a small number of Conservative Members of Parliament of accepting money from lobbying firms in return for tabling parliamentary questions in the House of Commons. This resulted in the appointment of a Committee on Standards in Public Life, whose recommendations included establishing an independent Parliamentary Commissioner for Standards. The importance of this reform was that it ended the ability of the House of Commons to totally regulate its own internal affairs.

However, allegations relating to the inappropriate conduct of Members of Parliament were not completely resolved by this reform. Towards the end of the 1990s, it was alleged that aides to ministers were prepared to use their position inside government to offer lobbying firms access to ministers or to secure confidential information and, additionally, some former aides to ministers utilized their contacts to gain access to ministers. This 'cash for access' scandal resulted in the government bringing forward a new code in 1998 to regulate lobbying, whose provisions included prohibiting a minister's former aides from leaking confidential information to lobbyists. However, this failed to provide a total remedy regarding the activities of lobbying forms and in 2010 three former Labour Cabinet ministers were accused of involvement in an 'influence for cash' scandal which alleged that they were willing to use their past contacts in government to secure changes in legislation desired by lobbyists.

Allegations concerning the behaviour of politicians in connection with the activities of lobbying firms were also a concern in the US. Here, the lobbying activities directed at the federal (national) government are regulated by the 1995 Lobby Disclosure Act (in part amended by the 2007 Honest Leadership and Open Government Act). This legislation requires firms to register with the clerk of the House of Representatives and the Secretary of the Senate within 45 days of having been hired. Lobbyists are required to file quarterly reports and list the issues on which they have lobbied and the institutions which they have contacted. An early reform of President Obama was to prohibit officials from taking jobs in lobbying firms while the administration that had appointed them remained in office.

Key idea

In the UK the issue of MPs' expenses accounts constituted a further example of suggestions that politicians sought to further their own interests rather than those of the general public.

The relationship between lobbying firms and politicians constitutes one mechanism through which inappropriate behaviour may arise. However, there are other ways through which actions of this nature may arise. In 2009 a national UK newspaper published details of the expense accounts submitted by Members of both houses of Parliament, the overall bill for which was footed by the taxpayer. In addition to mortgages on MPs' second homes, claims included the cleaning of a moat, the upkeep of a swimming pool, the maintenance of a 'helipad', the tuning of a piano, the purchase of horse manure as a garden fertilizer and a contribution towards wages paid to a housekeeper. Although in the vast majority of cases the politicians had broken no law (and in many cases voluntarily paid money back to which they were legally entitled), public opinion was concerned about the wide range of matters for which MPs could legitimately claim expenses.

This issue resulted in the resignation of the Speaker of the House of Commons, Michael Martin, in 2009 and ensured that the desire to 'clean up politics' received a high profile in the 2010 UK general election. Subsequently, three former members of the House of Commons and two members of the House of Lords received prison sentences in connection with false expense claims.

Politically motivated violence

A totally different form of political crime to that discussed in the previous section arises from activities that entail some form of violence to further a political objective.

Although in liberal democracies such as the UK and US political change is secured through the ballot box, there are alternative ways whereby political objectives can be accomplished. Some of these entail the use of violence, the most extreme form of which is terrorism.

Key idea

Terrorism may be defined as the use, or threat to use, violence to secure political change. It seeks to obtain its objectives through intimidation and instilling fear in the population.

Although terrorism is not a new form of activity, it has assumed considerable importance in recent years. It formed an integral feature of the campaign by the Provisional IRA to achieve their objective of removing the British presence from Northern Ireland in which bombing campaigns were conducted both in Northern Ireland and, commencing in 1973, on mainland Britain. In more recent years, terrorism has been associated with Islamic fundamentalism and al-Qaeda whose activities included the 9/11 attacks on the World Trade Center in New York and the Pentagon building in Washington in 2001, which resulted in the deaths of around three thousand people. Attacks associated with the same cause occurred in Madrid in 2004 and London in 2005, one feature of which has been the use of suicide attacks.

Spotlight

Terrorism is a notoriously difficult term to define – a problem that mainly stems from people having different views concerning the legitimacy of acts of violence, in particular the cause that these actions intend to promote. It is in this sense that it has been argued one person's 'terrorist' is another person's 'freedom fighter'.

Politically motivated violence may be directed at specific targets (such as politicians, judges, magistrates, police officers or soldiers) or it may be indiscriminate in nature whereby violence is directed at the general public with the aim of causing a sense of fear or panic, the intention of which is to exert pressure on the government to give in to the terrorists' demands.

In 2001 the former President of America, Bill Clinton, defined the purpose of terrorism as being 'not military victory, it is to terrorize, to change your behaviour if you're the victim by making you afraid of today, afraid of tomorrow and in diverse societies [...] afraid of each other.'

Clinton, B. (2001). 'The Struggle for the Soul of the Twenty-first Century'. The Dimbleby Lecture, BBC 1 television, 16 December.

The legislative response to terrorism

Key idea

States that are subject to terrorist campaigns will respond by enacting antiterrorist legislation which provides new powers with which to combat the threat.

The use of violence to secure a policy change is not confined to public policy and can also be directed against commercial practices which opponents wish to alter. In the former case, the dividing line between direct action and terrorism can be hard to draw when it entails the use of coercive means. However, in recent years, terrorism has been especially associated with attempts to change the direction of state policy.

States in which violence of this nature occurs may respond with a range of measures. Typically, these create a specific offence of terrorism. For while it has always been illegal to kill members of the public, murder or manslaughter might be hard to prove whereas accusations of involvement in terrorist activities constitute a more general charge for which it is easier to obtain convictions.

The measures that are provided to combat terrorism typically include:

- New powers for the police to stop and search persons who may be involved in activities of this nature;

- Provisions to enable personnel working at border controls to detain and question those suspected of terrorism;

- Changes to judicial proceedings.

In Northern Ireland during the 1970s the latter took the form of removing juries from trials connected with terrorist offences so that the case was tried before one judge. The name 'Diplock Court' was applied to this procedure, named after the judge who proposed its adoption. Antiterrorist measures may also contain speedier deportation procedures that can be applied against suspected terrorists and provisions to make it illegal to be a member or active supporter of an organization that embraces terrorism as its political activity.

Legislation to combat terrorism is frequently embodied in special legislation that makes terrorism a specific criminal offence. Examples of this include the United States' 2001 USA Patriot Act and the UK's 2012 Terrorism, Prevention and Investigation Measures Act.

Measures of the sort referred to above may constitute limitations on a citizen's civil and political liberties and there is thus the need to ensure that these correctly balance the twin requirements of *security* and *liberty*. On the one hand, a state has to take adequate measures to ensure that its citizens are free to go about leading their lives without the fear of being subject to terrorist-inspired violence. On the other hand, it is equally important that the measures that are adopted are proportionate to the threat that a nation faces and do not unnecessarily restrict fundamental freedoms that we associate with liberal democratic nations.

> Although states that are subject to terrorist campaigns need to take action to safeguard their citizens, this is often at the expense of civil and political liberties. 'The power of states to proscribe organizations as terrorist, financially cripple them, and criminalize and financially penalize those that associate with them, expands dramatically executive power, undermines due process protections and provides states with powerful weapons with which to deal with political opposition' (McCulloch and Pickering, 2005: 482).
>
> There is a danger that interventions of this nature may erode the very fabric of the liberal democratic state 'by declaring to be illegitimate political and industrial activities which had previously been thought to have distinguished a liberal democracy from an authoritarian or fascist society' (State Research, 1979: 4).
>
> McCulloch, J. and Pickering, S. (2005). 'Suppressing the Financing of Terrorism, Proliferating State Crime, Eroding Censure and Extending Neo-colonialism'. *British Journal of Criminology* 45: 470–86.
>
> State Research (1979). 'Introduction', in E.P. Thompson, *The Secret State*, State Research Pamphlet No. 1. London: Independent Research Publications.

In the UK this issue was especially raised in connection with internment. This involves arresting and placing in custody persons suspected of terrorist offences without there being any intention to bring that person to trial. It thus constitutes a direct violation of the concept of the citizens' civil liberties which in the US are embodied in the Fifth and Sixth Amendments to the Constitution.

Internment had been briefly used in Northern Ireland in the early 1970s as a measure to combat violence associated with the Provisional IRA and was introduced in mainland Britain under the 2001 Anti-terrorism, Crime and Security Act, especially in a desire to thwart activities associated with al-Qaeda. However, in December 2004, the Law Lords ruled that it contravened Articles 5 and 14 of the European Convention on Human Rights, in response to which the government enacted the 2005 Prevention of Terrorism Act which replaced internment with a form of house arrest that was termed 'control orders'. Current restrictions imposed on suspected terrorists to prevent or disrupt their engagement with terrorist activities are contained in the Coalition government's 2012 Terrorism Prevention and Investigation Measures Act.

The police response to terrorism

> ### Key idea
> The police will formulate responses to combat terrorism. An especially contentious tactic is that of 'shoot to kill'.

The police will make use of powers specifically provided to them to combat terrorism but in addition to these they will devise tactics to counter the terrorist threat. These may embrace a range of measures related to the gathering of intelligence that is designed to prevent terrorist attacks from occurring. It may also involve the use of lethal force against those who are suspected of mounting terrorist attacks.

It was alleged that the Royal Ulster Constabulary utilized this tactic in Northern Ireland during the early 1980s and particular concern was directed at six deaths in County Armagh in 1982. It was subsequently used in London in the early years of the twenty-first century to counter the threat posed by Islamic fundamentalists associated with al-Qaeda. Their use of the tactic of suicide bombing required lethal force to consist of shooting a suspect in the head before a suicide bomb could be detonated. There are a number of problems associated with a policy of shoot to kill, in particular that the role of police officers to arrest suspects becomes altered to that of becoming a judge and jury, with the power to sentence a person whom they suspect of this crime.

However, the most serious problem that is raised concerns whether a police officer's suspicion that a person is a terrorist, and thus should be shot dead, is accurate. This situation occurred in 2005, when a young Brazilian man, Jean Charles de Menezes, who was on his way to work, was mistaken for a terrorist suspect and shot dead by police officers in the carriage of an underground train in Stockwell, South London. Although he was completely innocent of any crime, he had been shot in the head seven times.

State-sponsored violence

Terrorism often entails the state and its citizens being subjected to extreme forms of violence that are designed to advance a political objective. However, governments may themselves be willing to sanction or sponsor violence or other forms of illicit activity to further their own political agendas.

Key idea

Although nations may be on the receiving end of terrorist violence, their governments may also conduct similar activities themselves to achieve their political ends.

There are many methods that governments may use that entail the use of violence against other nations or individuals within them. Conventional warfare is one option, examples of which include the US-led invasion of Iraq in 2003.

Conventional warfare is waged according to the rules of war but may be costly in both financial and political terms. There are other ways whereby a nation may conduct violent actions against another nation of whose government it disapproves, perhaps by supporting groups that are engaged in conflict with that government. This may be conducted in a secret manner. In the US, one example of this was the Iran–Contra affair in the 1980s which concerned alleged involvement of the administration of President Reagan in the illicit transfer of profits made from the sale of arms to Iran to guerrilla groups fighting the socialist Sandinista government in Nicaragua which America wished to see removed.

Governments that are faced with terrorist campaigns may also decide to meet fire with fire and combat these groups with violent responses which may be legally dubious under international law. One example of this was the mission by

American Special Forces into Pakistan in 2011 that resulted in the killing of the leader of al-Qaeda, Osama bin Laden. A further example concerns the use of what is termed 'proxy torture'. This entails nations that have banned the use of torture secretly sending suspected terrorists whom they have captured or abducted to countries where the practice is used in order to obtain information and intelligence that may thwart terrorist attacks. This process is sometimes referred to as 'rendition'. Documents that came from the Libyan foreign ministry following the 2011 civil war suggested that the US Central Intelligence Agency and the UK's Secret Intelligence Service (MI6) rendered suspects to Libya knowing that they would be tortured.

Although crimes such as terrorism are often directed against the state, the state can also be responsible for similar activities itself. We refer to these as state crime, which is defined as 'illegal or deviant acts perpetrated by, or with the complicity of, state agencies' (Green and Ward, 2005: 431). It embraces 'a broad spectrum of forms of criminality, including genocide, human rights abuses, war crimes, corporate misdeeds, environmental abuses and others' (Jamieson and McEvoy, 2005: 505).

Green, P. and Ward, T. (2005). 'Introduction', *British Journal of Criminology* 45: 431–3.

Jamieson, R. and McEvoy, K. (2005). 'State Crime by Proxy and Juridical Othering', *British Journal of Criminology* 45: 505–27.

Nations that are involved in violent actions that entail activities such as seeking to destabilize regimes they regard as enemies or conducting or condoning assassinations of political figures are most unlikely to view their actions as constituting terrorism. They may instead regard actions of this nature as essential in protecting national interests. This highlights the intensely subjective nature of terrorism – that is, an action defined as terrorism by one group of people may be seen in a totally different light by others. This is summarized in the argument that 'one man's terrorist is another man's freedom fighter'.

Dig deeper

Beckman, J. (2007). *Comparative Legal Approaches to Homeland Security and Anti-terrorism.* Aldershot: Ashgate.

Harris, R. (2003). *Political Corruption: In and Beyond the State.* London: Routledge.

Hoffman, B. (2006) *Inside Terrorism*, rev. edn. New York: Columbia University Press.

Fact-check

1 In England and Wales, a scandal affecting Members of Parliament in 2009/10 focused on:

A Their salaries

B Their moral conduct

C Their expense claims

D Their hours of work

2 What group was associated with events that took place in New York and Washington, DC in 2001, Madrid in 2004 and London in 2005:

A The Real IRA

B Al-Qaeda

C The Angry Brigade

D The anti-capitalist movement

3 The term 'rendition flights' is associated with:

A Aerial surveillance carried out by small, unmanned aircraft

B Flights that entail released hostages being brought home to their country of origin

C Flights conveying suspected terrorists to countries where information will be obtained from them through the use of torture

D Flights that contain terrorists who are travelling to countries where they intend to carry out acts of violence

4 What event led to the resignation of Richard Nixon as President of the United States of America in 1974?

A The Iran–Contra affair

B An inappropriate sexual relationship with an intern

C The Teapot Dome scandal

D The Watergate break-in

5 A terrorist organization that uses indiscriminate tactics targets:

A Senior politicians

B The general public

C Police officers

D Members of the judiciary

6 What tactic to combat terrorism was declared to be incompatible with the European Convention on Human Rights by the United Kingdom's Law Lords in 2004?

A Control orders

B Internment

C The random use of stop and search powers

D Deportation

9

Organized crime

Many contemporary forms of criminal activity are similar to big business in terms of the revenue that they generate and the way in which they operate. The term 'organized crime' is used to describe criminal enterprises of this nature. This chapter is concerned with explaining the nature of organized crime and discussing the various forms of criminal enterprise that are embraced by this term. It also examines the way in which contemporary manifestations of organized crime have contributed towards the international co-ordination of criminal justice policies in order to combat crime of this nature.

What is organized crime?

Key idea

The term 'organized crime' is a complex one to define. However, it is commonly associated with a number of key characteristics which include a formal or semi-formal network whose role is to supply goods for which there is a demand. Violence may also be a feature of organized crime.

To an extent all crime requires some form of organization – even the petty thief acting in isolation is likely to require contacts with other criminals in order to be able to sell the proceeds of his or her crime.

However, when we use the term 'organized crime', we tend to regard it as crime that is conducted by a group of people who operate in some kind of formal network. This network may operate in a manner that is similar to a secret society which is bound together by ties of loyalty which are frequently based upon family networks or ethnic social groups and within which a hierarchy exists as it would in a legitimate business enterprise.

One definition of organized crime by an American criminologist emphasized the importance of the word 'organization': 'the organized criminal [...] occupies a position in a social system, an "organization", which has been rationally designed to maximize profits by performing illegal services and providing legally forbidden products demanded by the broader society within which he lives' (Cressey, 1969: 72).

Cressey, D. (1969). *Theft of the Nation: The Structure and Operations of Organized Crime in America.* New York: Harper & Row.

In common with legitimate commercial activity, organized crime operates in accordance with the laws of supply and demand by providing products or services for which there is a demand but which are not available legally. These may include drugs or pornography. The activities that are associated with organized crime are typically conducted on a large scale (which is increasingly international in scope and also tends to involve a range of criminal actions rather than one specific type of crime) and involve large sums of money, while those involved may be willing to use illicit means including corruption and violence to achieve their ends.

There are, however, difficulties with the picture that this depicts and in the following section we shall explore various forms of criminal activity that may be described as 'organized' but which do not exhibit all of the features that have been described above.

Key idea

The mechanisms through which organized crime may be carried out are varied. They include traditional forms of organized crime, organization that is centred on specific crime targets, and criminal gangs. Organization may also be provided by business corporations or white-collar criminals.

Traditional forms of organized crime

Traditional forms of organized crime embrace groups that include the Sicilian Mafia, Chinese Triad and Tong Groups and the Japanese Yakuza.

Any reference to the term 'mafia' might make our minds focus on films such as *The Godfather* trilogy and the operations of the Sicilian Mafia that they depict. Although the term 'mafia' is often used in connection with any form of organized criminal gang, the Mafia and other traditional criminal groups constitute a specific form of organization that have long historical heritages and initially were not necessarily associated with criminal enterprise. An important early function of the Sicilian Mafia, for example, was to provide a sense of order and stability in an area that lacked effective government by providing protection services and adjudicating disputes between peasants and landowners. Centralized power and family ties (albeit involving an extended network of related families) were integral aspects of its organization and structure that were bound together by honour.

Chinese organized crime embraces two major groups:

1 *The Triads* derived from secret societies in China and subsequently spread to other countries through emigration.

2 *The Tongs* emerged within Chinese communities where these had been established in other countries.

Japanese organized crime is centred on the Yakuza which claims an historical heritage that dates back to the samurai warriors.

Traditional organizations involved in organized crime developed in a number of ways during the twentieth century. In Italy, for example, the Sicilian Mafia engaged in new forms of criminal activity that had previously been avoided (such as drugs and prostitution) and expanded its political and economic power until, by the 1970s, it virtually occupied the position of 'a state within a state'. Chinese Tong groups were initially similar to street gangs but over time developed more structure. In Japan, the Yakuza extended its more traditional operations (which included drug trafficking and the management of prostitution and gambling) into areas that included political corruption. Traditional organizations also became more international in focus and by the late 1950s in the US, all forms of organized crime in that country were attributed to the Mafia (sometimes referred to as the Cosa Nostra). This led to organized crime being viewed as an alien conspiracy conducted by Americans of Italian heritage.

Organized crime is often associated with groups such as the Mafia and are termed 'traditional' organized crime groups: 'These groups are [...] traditional in the sense that they have their own mores, customs and rites of passage the origins of which are in the historical conditions surrounding their inception. Their traditions are also subject to a degree of continuity, although they are now at the service of criminal objectives' (Wright, 2006: 100).

Wright, A. (2006). *Organized Crime*. Cullompton, Devon: Willan Publishing

Project-based crime

In England and Wales much of the crime that took place before the Second World War was of localized nature and was carried out by individual criminals. For many of these, crime was a full-time occupation often involving skilful actions that included 'safe cracking'. The Second World War expanded the opportunities for criminal activity (involving actions that included looting bomb-damaged homes and businesses and supplying goods that were subject to rationing and other forms of control by the government). These tended to require criminals involved in these activities to co-operate but did not entail the creation of highly developed organizational structures.

However, significant changes occurred to the pattern of crime after 1945. Traditional forms of criminal activity were joined by a new and less localized form of enterprise that was termed 'project-based' crime. This was planned by criminal masterminds who recruited teams of criminals to carry out a specific criminal enterprise (a 'project') which was designed to secure significant financial rewards. The 'Great Mailbag Robbery' in 1952 was an early example of this form of organized criminal activity (in which £287,000 was stolen), though the most infamous example was the 'Great Train Robbery' in 1963.

Spotlight

It was estimated that the proceeds of the 'Great Train Robbery' that occurred in the UK in 1963 amounted to £2.5 million, which at that time was the biggest theft that the world had known. In today's currency the amount stolen would be equivalent to around £40 million.

Although project-based crime was a form of organized criminal activity, the organization with which it was associated was loosely structured and of an ephemeral nature (that is, the membership of the teams that were recruited to carry out the crime were not constant and individuals were chosen in relation to their skills being appropriate to the target that was to be attacked).

Criminal gangs

Key idea

Criminal gangs exhibit wide variations in connection with factors that include structure and organization, motivation for membership, and links with other forms of criminal enterprises.

Project-based crime was conducted by criminal gangs which lacked a formal structure. Other forms of criminal gangs possess a more permanent structure and organization even if the membership of these is subject to variation. Gangs of this nature give organization to criminal activity which is typically diverse in nature and carried out in a relatively localized setting – for example a neighbourhood, a housing estate or, on a grander scale, a city. It may entail the use of, or the threat to use, violence.

As we have discussed in Chapter 1, in the US the Prohibition Era (1920–33) imposed a ban on the manufacture, sale and transportation of alcohol. However, as demand for alcohol remained high, organized crime was able to step in and supply the product illegally. Organized crime in this era often entailed existing gangs (whose crime was centred on enterprises such as controlling gambling outlets) moving into this new area of work, which was frequently conducted alongside other criminal activities. Crime bosses who engaged in a number of illegal operations wielded considerable power in the area within which it was conducted. An infamous example was Al Capone in Chicago.

In England and Wales there are numerous examples of criminal gangs that sought to exert territorial control over an area within which they could construct a criminal empire. The Sabinis in South London controlled protection rackets in the interwar years that were centred on racecourses. Similar protection activities related to gambling and drinking clubs were carried out by the Richardsons in South London and the Krays in East London in the 1950s and 1960s. In these examples gang leadership was derived from family ties and, although crime was primarily conducted as a source of income, the territorial control with which it was associated also gave leaders considerable prestige and status within the neighbourhood.

In recent years criminal gangs have been especially associated with youth/juvenile or street gangs. The extent to which these are organized in a formal sense varies, and in some cases they consist of loose attachments of peer groups. These also operate in relatively small geographic areas, and exerting territorial control over that location (their 'turf') is an important aspect of gang activity. Gangs of this nature may form a relationship with more established criminal organizations in areas where links to these are readily available, especially in connection with drug trading, and may also provide individual members with the stepping stones to a career in crime.

> One problem related to the study of juvenile gangs is that of definition: 'many contemporary gang researchers note the absence of definitional consensus. They subsequently identify two widely used benchmarks for assessing whether a given social group is a gang: (1) youth status, defined as an age classification ranging between 10 and the early 20s or even older, and (2) the engagement by group members in law-violating behaviour or, at a minimum, "imprudent" behavior' (Esbensen et al., 2001: 106).
>
> Esbensen, F., Winfree, L., He, N. and Taylor, T. (2001). 'Youth Gangs and Definitional Issues: When is a Gang a Gang, and Why Does it Matter?', *Crime and Delinquency* 47:105–30.

There have been many examples of gangs of this nature in post-1945 England and Wales. Their formation is often associated with social and economic deprivation and social exclusion in which crime is embraced as a form of livelihood or as a means of excitement. Gangs may also be formed for primarily social reasons, in which case members may derive from more affluent backgrounds.

In the US ethnicity underpinned the formation of street gangs in areas containing significant Black and Hispanic populations. These date from the 1920s in California and in the 1970s were supplemented by Asian street gangs (initially derived from Vietnam). The membership of youth and street gangs considerably expanded in the latter decades of the twentieth century and organization became more structured. Drug trading was a key criminal activity and violence involving the use of firearms became a trademark of gangs of this nature. In England and Wales the Yardie gangs (which derive from Jamaica) provide an example of minority ethnic involvement in gang-oriented organized crime especially in relation to gun crime and drug trading. However, these gangs are relatively loosely structured in comparison to other forms of organized criminal activity.

Case study: Criminal gangs and the state's response in the UK

An important contemporary concern in the UK has been the emergence of local criminal gangs whose activities frequently involve the use of weapons that include guns and knives. This has prompted a number of initiatives to tackle crime of this nature, including the 1997 Knives Act that prohibits the sale of combat knives and restricted the marketing of knives.

In September 2007 the Tackling Gangs Action Programme was launched. The aim of this programme was to reduce serious violence, especially the use of firearms, carried out by young people as an aspect of gang-related activities. It was followed by the Tackling Knives Action Programme in 2008, one aspect of which sought to alert young people aged 13–19 of the dangers of carrying knives. Both of these programmes were carried out in selected areas.

The murder of 27 young people in London in 2007 by other young people (and a further 20 by mid 2008) in which a knife or a gun was the murder weapon prompted the government into further action. This took the form of a 2008 Home Office policy document which established a link between gangs and the problems of urban violence and rising weapon use in the UK.

This gave rise to the government's proposals for tackling serious crime, Saving Lives. Reducing Harm. Protecting the Public. An Action Plan for Tackling Violence 2008–11.

The specific measures to tackle violence that were put forward included: the introduction of new controls to remove deactivated firearms from Britain's streets; ensuring that witnesses to gang violence received the best possible protection from the earliest stage of the criminal justice process; delivering education to young people on the dangers of carrying weapons; and providing portable knife arches and search 'wands' to the police and other agencies to increase the detection of knife crime.

Corporate and white-collar crime as organized crime

Key idea

Activities conducted by commercial corporations and by white-collar criminals may also constitute a form of organized crime.

Although the forms of organized crime that have been discussed above are characterized by the willingness to use violence to exert control over the organization as well as to achieve its illicit ends, the use of physical violence is not an essential component of contemporary forms of organized crime.

Business corporations that conduct perfectly legitimate business operations may themselves be guilty of criminal actions. Typically, these are designed to further the company's commercial interests and may include actions such as bribing officials or politicians in a country where the company wishes to secure a lucrative contract. It may also entail acts of industrial espionage or spying that seek to prevent a competitor from securing an advantage derived from factors such as superior technology. Large companies may seek to avoid paying taxation. Corporations such as banks may perform actions – sometimes without their knowledge or consent – that aid organized crime. Money laundering is an example of this. This describes a process that enables the proceeds of organized crime to be converted into finance that can be used as income and also to transact legitimate commercial activity in order to make further financial gains. In England and Wales, in an attempt to combat money laundering, the introduction of Suspicious Activity Reports by the 2000 Terrorism Act and the 2002 Proceeds of Crime Act required organizations such as banks to undertake actions that include reporting to the Serious Organized Crime Agency the deposit of large sums of money into an account.

Forms of activity associated with white-collar crime may also be conducted by criminal organizations. Although fraud is a crime that may be carried out by an individual acting in his or her own interests, it may also be carried out on a much larger scale in an organized manner. Technological developments have aided organized white-collar crime. This includes various forms of cybercrime where a criminal organization might seek to extract money from a legitimate business enterprise by planting (or threatening to plan) viruses onto its computer network.

The international dimension of organized crime

Key idea

Organized crime is international in scope and requires a co-ordinated response from a number of countries to combat it.

Organized crime has increasingly assumed an international dimension in recent years. Technology has made it possible for organized criminals operating in one country to perform activities that are conducted in another. The proceeds of criminal activity can be transferred electronically from one country to another, making it extremely difficult for law enforcement agencies to mount effective operations to counter activities of this nature.

The twin forces of globalization and technology have fuelled the growth of organized crime: 'globalization [...] has made it increasingly easy for foreign organized criminals to set up base in major European cities such as London. [...] New technologies

provide new and more effective means to commit crime [...] as well as more secure ways of communicating with criminal groups' (Home Office, 2004: 11).

Home Office (2004). *One Step Ahead: A Twenty-first Century Strategy to Defeat Organized Crime.* London: TSO, Cm 6167.

Tackling the power of organized crime

Contemporary forms of organized crime may exercise considerable power within a state, arising from the links its leaders are able to construct with public officials and politicians and also from the economic resources at their disposal derived from activities that include money laundering, arms trading, trafficking in people, and the production and supply of drugs. They may abuse their power and regard themselves as untouchable by the law enforcement agencies.

Case study: People trafficking

Crime that is conducted across national borders justifies the enhanced co-operation of the criminal justice systems of individual nations. Some aspects of this crime are relatively new, an example of which is people (or human) trafficking.

People trafficking entails the illegal trade in human beings for a range of purposes that include forced labour, bonded labour (or debt bondage) and commercial sexual exploitation. Victims may be involved in such trade through force, fraud or deception. The movement of persons from one country to another is performed without the victims' voluntary consent and the victims are then held against their will in the country to which they have been transported. In many ways, this constitutes a modern-day version of the slave trade.

People trafficking is an aspect of organized crime and is big business conducted on an international scale. In 2006 a report by the United Nations Office on Drugs and Crime identified 127 countries of origin, 98 transit countries and 137 destination countries for human trafficking. Around 800,000 people each year are victims of these activities, of whom the majority are women between 18 and 24 years of age. In 2005 it was the estimated that the annual global profits of human trafficking exceeded $30 billion.

The international scope of this problem requires international action to combat it especially in connection with sharing intelligence and enforcement. This includes the United Nations Convention against Transnational Organized Crime (or the Palermo Convention), which came into force in 2003, one protocol of which seeks to suppress and punish trafficking in persons, especially women and children. This aims to secure international co-operation for investigating and prosecuting human trafficking. Additionally, the Council of Europe Convention on Action against Trafficking in Human Beings came into force in 2008. However, in 2006 there were only around 3,000 convictions worldwide for offences related to people trafficking.

An additional problem is that organized crime is often associated with terrorism, one reason being that terrorist groups may be involved in the trafficking (but not production) side of organized criminal activity in order to make money.

These factors have encouraged countries to take the problem of organized crime seriously and to pursue policies that are designed to combat it. In the US, for example, President Johnson's Commission on Law Enforcement and Administration of Justice (1967) and President Reagan's Commission on Organized Crime (1983) examined the nature of the problem. (Both subsequently attributed much of the problem to the Mafia.) In Italy, vigorous measures to combat the Sicilian Mafia and the Neapolitan Camorra (which included the use of the military) were undertaken towards the end of the twentieth century. In the UK concerns regarding organized crime resulted in the creation in 2005 of a national police organization (the Serious Organized Crime Agency). This is to be replaced in 2013 by the National Crime Agency.

As many contemporary forms of organized crime are international in nature, initiatives to tackle it have entailed co-operation between countries. The importance of these initiatives is emphasized by a trend affecting organized crime whereby organized criminal groups may co-operate with each other, raising the potential of more serious forms of criminal activity being committed. Links between traditional organized crime groups in Italy and Latin America and newer bodies such as the Russian 'Mafia' are an example of this.

In this section we will consider one aspect of such international co-operation that has been pursued within the organizational structure that is provided by the European Union.

The co-ordination of criminal justice policy in the EU

Key idea

The European Union has undertaken a number of initiatives to secure a co-ordinated response to organized crime and terrorism.

The twin pressures of organized crime and terrorism (issues that are often viewed as interrelated) have prompted a number of developments to occur within the European Union (EU) to harmonize the approach adopted by member countries to combat problems of this nature.

These have included the creation of the European Police Office (more commonly known as Europol) which became operational in 1999. Its role is to co-ordinate the sharing of intelligence related to serious forms of organized crime, although future developments (under the auspices of the 2009 Treaty of Lisbon) may also see it assume operational responsibilities.

Judicial co-operation within the EU has been promoted through Eurojust which was set up in 2002. Specific reforms associated with this objective have included the introduction of the European Arrest Warrant in 2004 (which was designed to simplify extradition procedures between EU countries) and the European Evidence Warrant which seeks to create a common warrant for obtaining evidence in one EU country that is needed for a criminal case being conducted in another EU country. This was adopted in the UK in the 2009 Policing and Crime Act.

Co-ordination in EU criminal justice matters has also been promoted by the 1985 Schengen Agreement and 1990 Schengen Convention. A key purpose of the Schengen Agreement was to abolish internal frontier controls between EU member states. The UK and Irish Republic remain outside of these arrangements, although it is intended that the UK will participate in the Schengen Information System (SIS) (an EU-wide database for the collection and exchange of information relating to immigration, policing and criminal law) when the new version (SIS II) becomes available, a development scheduled for 2013.

Dig deeper

Laverick, W. (2012). *Global Injustice*. London: Routledge.

Morton, J. (2003). *Gangland.* London: Time Warner.

Occhipinti, J. (2003). *The Politics of EU Police Cooperation: Towards a European FBI?* London: Lynne Reinner.

Wright, A. (2006). *Organised Crime.* Cullompton, Devon: Willan Publishing.

Fact-check

1 In the US organized crime developed significantly during the Prohibition Era. What merchandise was supplied illegally during this period?

A Drugs

B Alcohol

C Tobacco

D Video games

2 Which family dominated criminal activity in East London during the 1960s?

A The Krays

B The Richardsons

C The Sabinis

D The Smiths

3 What name has been adopted to describe the criminal organization that originated in Sicily in the nineteenth century?

A The Triads

B The Yardies

C The Mafia

D The Yakuza

4 The term 'project-based crime' describes:

A Crime that is organized around attaining a specific objective

B A police operation that is designed to combat a particular type of criminal activity

C Crime that is carried out by a large criminal gang

D A criminal act whose main objective is to secure publicity rather than financial gain

5 The process whereby the economic proceeds of crime are turned into legitimate forms of finance is known as:

A Offshore banking

B Money laundering

C Online banking

D Financial manipulation

6 The European police agency that is responsible for combating European Union-wide crime is known as:

A Interpol

B The Schengen Information System

C Europol

D The Justice and Home Affairs Council

10

Why do we punish criminals?

Those who break the law will be penalized to express society's disapproval of their behaviour. We refer to this as 'punishment'. However, a key concern is what society wishes to achieve by punishing an offender. There are a wide range of possibilities, an important consideration being whether society carries out punishment in order to deter or prevent future acts of criminality or to exact revenge on those who have broken the law. The aim of this chapter is to provide you with an understanding of the wide range of outcomes with which punishment might be associated and to explain why the aims and methods of punishment alter over historical time periods.

Punishment

'Punishment' is capable of several definitions although its meaning is often restricted to measures which are unpleasant and intended to inflict pain on an offender in response to an offence that he or she has committed.

The scientific study of punishment is known as penology, which seeks to provide an understanding of the concerns that underlie the wide range of penal strategies that are available to society. We will consider these later in this chapter.

Punishment is imposed by the state and has been defined as 'the deliberate use of public power to inflict pain on offenders' (Andrews, 2003: 128).

However, inflicting pain is not universally accepted as a goal of punishment. Others prefer the use of the term 'sanction' 'as the general term for any measure which is imposed as a response to crime, with adjectives distinguishing the various kinds of sanction according to their primary purpose – punitive sanctions, rehabilitative sanctions, punitive/rehabilitative sanctions (which are ambivalent about their aims), reparative sanctions and sanctions designed to protect the public through containment' (Wright, 2003: 6–7).

Andrews, M. (2003). 'Punishment, Markets and the American Model: An Essay on a New American Dilemma', in S. McConville (ed.), *The Use of Punishment*. Cullompton: Willan Publishing.

Wright, M. (2003). 'Is It Time to Question the Concept of Punishment?', in L. Walgrave (ed.), *Repositioning Restorative Justice*. Cullompton, Devon: Willan Publishing.

Vigilante justice

Vigilante justice consists of punishments administered by an individual or a group of citizens without the involvement or authority of the state to legitimize their actions. Citizens may justify their intervention by arguing that the punishments available to the state are inadequate to deal with the problem they face.

Vigilante justice embraces a wide range of penalties which include 'necktie parties' (when a mob hangs or lynches a person whose actions they disapprove of), tarring and feathering criminals, or physically driving them away from the community.

The main problem with punishment inflicted by vigilante justice is that it may be directed against groups of people who are disliked (for reasons that include their looks, lifestyle or colour of skin) even if they have not committed a criminal wrongdoing. The victims of vigilante justice are unlikely to be given the opportunity to defend themselves against whatever charges are brought against them and the punishment may be overly severe.

The aims of punishment: reductivism

Those who believe that the main aim of punishment is to ensure that those who have committed crime do not do so again are termed 'reductivists'.

Key idea

The concern of reductivists is with criminal actions that may be undertaken in the future rather than those that have already occurred.

There are a number of methods through which reductivist methods of punishment can be delivered.

DETERRENCE

Key idea

Deterrence operates on the belief that the certainty of punishment will persuade people not to commit crime.

One reason why we may punish offenders is the belief that the unpleasant nature of the punishment will ensure that they never commit crime again. We refer to this as 'deterrence'. There are two forms of deterrence – *individual* or *general*. Individual deterrence seeks to influence the future behaviour of a single convicted offender whereas general deterrence seeks to influence the future actions of the public at large. Both are underpinned by a widespread belief that those who commit crime will be detected by the police and sentenced by the courts.

Individual deterrence may be delivered in a variety of ways and includes the imposition of a custodial sentence on an offender. The loss of freedom, perhaps coupled with other unpleasant aspects of a prison regime, is designed to encourage him or her to refrain from future offending behaviour to avoid a further, and perhaps more severe and/or lengthier, repetition of these unpleasant circumstances.

General deterrence has a broader remit – that of influencing the behaviour of any member of society who might be tempted to commit crime. The approach associated with general deterrence may entail severe penalties (which in the United Kingdom historically included the death penalty and which is still used in a number of US states) based on the assumption that it would be illogical for a person to commit an action attached to dire consequences.

The belief that punishment can deter the future commission of crime is underpinned by a belief that offenders are rational beings who calculate the costs and benefits of their behaviour and will not carry out a criminal act if the nature of the punishment outweighs any benefit that they may derive from the crime. Deterrence therefore ignores the possibility that crime may be a spontaneous act, propelled by factors that override logical considerations, and perhaps over which the individual has no control.

INCAPACITATION
An alternative way through which a reductivist strategy of punishment can be delivered is that of incapacitation.

Key idea
The main concern of incapacitation is to protect society from the actions of criminals.

Incapacitation places potential victims of crime at the forefront of its concern and can be performed through a number of ways that physically remove criminals from society. This was historically accomplished through the system of transportation whereby criminals in the UK were removed to the American colonies and Australia. However, transportation was ended in 1857 when it was substituted for penal servitude. Imprisonment is now the method that is used to isolate criminals from the remainder of society. The idea behind incapacitation is a simple one: criminals cannot terrorize neighbourhoods if they are locked up in prison.

REFORM AND REHABILITATION

A further way to deliver a reductivist strategy is to include provisions within the punishment which is administered that seek to transform the offender into a law-abiding member of society. This aspect of punishment, therefore, seeks to bring about the reform and rehabilitation of the lawbreaker.

Key idea

Methods that seek the reform and rehabilitation of criminals aim that they become law-abiding citizens when the punishment has been completed.

There are various ways whereby a punishment seeks to change the personal values and habits of offenders so that their future behaviour conforms to mainstream social standards. Penal reformers in the late eighteenth and early nineteenth centuries viewed prisons as an arena in which bad people could be transformed into good and useful members of society. Contemporary prisons remain charged with bringing about the reform and rehabilitation of inmates but, as Chapter 12 argues, there are several factors affecting the prison environment that serve to undermine this ideal.

Reform and rehabilitation may also be attempted through programmes directed at tackling offending behaviour, which may be delivered in prison or in the community or in both of these arenas. These programmes may be addressed at the factors that cause criminal behaviour to occur, addressing issues such as anger control and drug and alcohol abuse. More coercive approaches entail interventions that are designed to make it impossible for convicted criminals to repeat their offending behaviour, such as the castration of sex offenders.

RESTORATIVE JUSTICE

Restorative justice is reductivist in intention. However, it is not universally viewed as a form of punishment but is sometimes viewed as a mechanism to enable a dialogue to be entered into whereby those involved in, or affected by, a criminal act can jointly devise a course of action whose aim goes beyond the reform of offenders and which seeks to secure their reintegration into society.

The requirement placed on the offender to accept responsibility for his or her actions, apologize and make recompense to the victim is designed to help both parties put past events behind them, thereby facilitating the offender's reintegration into the community. We will consider restorative justice more fully in Chapter 17.

A particular problem with reductivist strategies is whether behaviour can be altered through punishment (whatever form it takes) since, while punishment may temporarily suppress antisocial behaviour, the previous behaviour may return once the punishment is removed.

Accordingly, it is also necessary to identify and remove the factors which underpin that behaviour in order to prevent future offending: 'people must "internalise" mechanisms that regulate behaviour so that in the absence of the threat of punishment, they will choose not to act aggressively – not because of the threat of punishment, but because they agree with the behaviour which has been taught' (Huesmann and Podolski, 2003: 77–8).

Huesmann, L. and Podolski, C. (2003). 'Punishment: A Psychological Perspective', in S. McConville (ed.), *The Use of Punishment*. Cullompton, Devon: Willan Publishing.

Retributivism

We have argued above that the various strategies associated with reductivism focus their concern on future behaviour – punishment (whatever form it takes) is justified because it may persuade a person or persons not to engage in criminal actions in the future.

An alternative approach is that of retributivism. This is backward-looking, in the sense that punishment focuses on offending behaviour which has already taken place. Although this might also change an offender's behaviour in the future, this is not the prime purpose of punishment which is justified solely by the view that the offender should be held responsible for the wrongdoing that they have committed. Retributivism holds that criminals are punished because they deserve to be.

Key idea

A retributivist view of punishment is similar to vengeance – pain is inflicted on offenders in order that society can 'get its own back' on criminals' acts.

Retributivist responses to crime are historic. The principle of *lex talionis* was referred to in the Old Testament whereby the response to crime was of an equivalent nature to the crime itself ('an eye for an eye and a tooth for a tooth'). The use of the death penalty for murder reflects this historic principle, which further ensures that murder carries a harsher punishment than, for example, burglary.

A difficulty with capital punishment is that the deliberate infliction by the state of violence may legitimize the use of violence by criminals. For this reason, many countries no longer use this form of punishment.

Case study: Capital punishment in the United Kingdom

The execution of offenders who commit serious crimes may be viewed as a deterrent to others not to act in the same manner, but is primarily a form of punishment that is founded on retributivism, whereby society 'gets its own back' on those who commit crime. However, the criminal justice systems of many countries do not possess this sentence.

Until the early years of the nineteenth century, most criminal offences carried the death penalty in England and Wales. There were in excess of 220 crimes that carried this punishment, some for strange actions that included damaging Westminster Bridge or impersonating a Chelsea pensioner. Home Secretary Robert Peel was influential in reducing the number of capital offences in the early decades of the nineteenth century.

However, the death penalty was not regularly enforced and in order to ensure certainty of sentence, classicist criminologists inspired reforms to the penal code designed to ensure that the punishment fitted the crime. Gradually, the death penalty was removed from most offences so that by the twentieth century it applied only to cases of murder where it was a mandatory sentence.

A key difficulty with the death penalty is that nothing can be done to redress harm once execution had taken place, should it subsequently emerge that the person found guilty was innocent of the crime of which they were convicted. In post-war England and Wales a number of executions occurred that questioned the justice of this penalty. These included the executions of Timothy John Evans in 1950, Derek Bentley in 1953 and Ruth Ellis in 1955.

The 1965 Murder (Abolition of Death Penalty) Act suspended the use of executions in the United Kingdom and this suspension was made permanent in 1969. In 1998 the death penalty was removed for offences committed contrary to the Armed Forces Acts. In 1999 the government ratified the Second Optional Protocol on Civil and Political Rights which totally eliminated execution as a penalty in the UK.

Other countries, however, retain the death penalty as a sentencing option. In the US, the states determine whether this penalty shall apply and in recent years increased use has been made of it. Between 1966 and 1982 only nine persons were executed and none between 1968 and 1976. However, in 2010, 46 prisoners were executed and this figure rose to 52 in 2009.

DENUNCIATION

Denunciation is a way through which a retributivist response to crime can be delivered. It focuses on past criminal actions and seeks to enable society to express its outrage at the actions that an offender has committed. This implies that punishment is justified, not because it influences the behaviour of others not to commit similar acts, but simply because it expresses society's abhorrence of crime.

> *The role played by punishment in articulating the disapproval of the public towards criminal actions helps to set the boundaries of society – 'we collectively define what sort of people we are by denouncing the type of people we are not' (Davies, 1993: 15). It is in this sense that punishment may confirm core values which hold society together.*
>
> Davies, M. (1993). *Punishing Criminals: Developing Community-based Intermediate Sanctions*. Westport, CT: Greenwood Press.

Spotlight

An ancient punishment that was used in both the UK and US in the sixteenth and seventeenth centuries to detect witches was that of dunking.

The alleged witch was bound and immersed in a pond or vat of water. If she floated, she was judged to be guilty of witchcraft and executed, by being burnt or hanged. If she sank, she was judged innocent of the charge – but, sadly, would probably have died from drowning.

The rationale of punishment – sociological perspectives

The approaches to punishment that have been discussed above focus on the practical aspects of punishment and seek to provide an understanding regarding the desired outcomes arising from various forms of state intervention. There is, however, another approach to the study of punishment – sociological perspectives that seek to explain alterations in the methods used by society to punish criminals. In the UK, for example, methods of punishment that included execution, transportation, various forms of corporal punishment and placing people in the stocks have passed out of favour and are no longer used. Sociological perspectives seek to explain why these changes occur.

Sociological perspectives concentrate on the concept of punishment itself and seek to 'explore the relations between punishment and society, its purpose being to understand punishment as a social phenomenon and thus trace its role in social life' (Garland, 1990: 10). The focus of sociological perspectives is theoretical rather than practical, aiming to provide an understanding of the factors that underpin society's responses to crime as opposed to explaining what purpose punishment is designed to achieve.

Garland, D. (1990). *Punishment and Modern Society*. Oxford: Clarendon.

Key idea

Sociological perspectives seek to provide an understanding of why methods of punishment change over historical time periods.

KEY IDEAS ASSOCIATED WITH THE SOCIOLOGY OF PUNISHMENT

▶ Emile Durkheim

Durkheim suggested that punishment reflected the nature of society's collective conscience at any one point in time. Changes to society's commonly held beliefs and values would thus be reflected in alterations to the methods used to punish lawbreakers.

Durkheim believed that the main reason why this consensus altered was related to the division of labour that differentiated a feudal society from a modern, industrialized one. He held that punishment became less repressive in modern societies because the consensual values that underpinned punishment were tempered by factors such as moral diversity that made for a more moderate reaction to criminal behaviour.

▶ Max Weber

Weber linked the changing nature of methods of punishment to the sources of authority within society. He believed that in modern capitalist societies authority was based on legal-bureaucratic foundations which meant that localized, inconsistent and irrational responses to crime that were associated with more primitive forms of society became replaced with a rational system of punishment that was universally applied and administered in a dispassionate, impartial and consistent manner by the professional authorities of the central state such as magistrates and judges.

▶ Marxist approaches

Marxist explanations of punishment emphasize the manner in which methods of punishment are underpinned by economic considerations, in particular those relating to the labour market. Thus fluctuations in the way society responded to crime are argued to derive from changes affecting the labour market. A shortage of labour would result in lenient punishments in order to get criminals back into work whereas an abundance of labour would lead to a more severe response to crime which might include the death penalty as additional members of the workforce were not required.

▶ Michel Foucault

Foucault's key concern was the way in which social discipline was maintained throughout society. He argued that the harsh, barbaric but intermittently used methods of punishment associated with pre-industrial societies were ineffective in maintaining social order in more advanced societies where it was necessary to devise a more sophisticated system of social control that would exist permanently and whose hallmark was 'uninterrupted, constant coercion', implemented not by a central form of authority but through a wide range of mechanisms that were spread throughout society. The aim of what was referred to as the 'disciplinary society' was to secure an individual whose obedience and conformity was based on self-control derived from constant surveillance (or the perception that this was taking place) rather than constraints imposed by an external authority.

Dig deeper

Brooks, T. (2011). *Punishment.* London: Routledge.

Foucault, M. (1977). *Discipline and Punish: The Birth of the Prison.* London: Allen Lane.

Hudson, B. (2003). *Understanding Justice: An Introduction to Ideas*, Perspectives and Controversies in Modern Penal Theory, 2nd edn. Buckingham: Open University Press.

Zaibert, L. (2006). *Punishment and Retribution.* Aldershot: Ashgate.

Fact-check

1 Reductivists:

  A Want the state to spend less on the criminal justice system

  B Are concerned to stop a criminal from reoffending in the future

  C Wish to see less crime in society

  D Support the death penalty as a way of preventing criminals from reoffending

2 *Lex talionis* is:

  A A criminal who is often in conflict with Batman

  B An historic document which outlines how criminals were punished in Old Testament times

  C A principle that asserts that the punishment received by a criminal should be in proportion to the nature of the offence that has been committed

  D A form of punishment that is designed to deter criminal behaviour

3 The sociology of punishment is concerned with explaining:

  A How particular forms of punishment are designed to reduce the level of crime in society

  B Why the methods of punishment used by society alter over a historical time period

  C Why many modern societies have abandoned the death penalty

  D Why punishment often fails to bring about the reform of criminals

4 Restorative justice:

  A Is a punishment used in the case of burglary and requires the criminal to restore to the victim the goods that have been stolen

  B Seeks to shame the criminal into admitting that he or she has broken the law

  C Enables the victim of a crime to carry out the punishment imposed on the offender by a court

  D Aims to enable the criminal to make amends for his or her crime and thus be reintegrated back into society

5 A retributivist approach to punishment:

A Believes that criminals should be dealt with leniently

B Is concerned that society should get its own back on those who have broken its laws

C Wishes to ensure that those who have broken the law do not do so again in the future

D Supports capital punishment as a response to crime

6 Penology is:

A The study of why criminals commit crime

B A branch of reproductive medicine

C The scientific study of punishment

D Concerned with prison reform

11

What is the criminal justice system?

When we refer to the criminal justice system, we are considering a range of agencies whose responsibilities include apprehending those who have broken the law, prosecuting persons suspected of having committed a criminal offence, determining the innocence or guilt of those charged with a crime, and punishing those found guilty of a criminal act. This chapter seeks to provide a broad overview of the criminal justice system by discussing the role of the diverse range of agencies that operate within it and considering some of the key principles that underpin their work.

The criminal justice system

Key idea

The aim of the criminal justice system is to uphold the law and to deliver an appropriate response to lawbreaking. It consists of a number of agencies, each of which performs specific functions related to this aim.

The criminal justice system comprises a number of agencies whose main purpose is to bring offenders to justice. Their work entails considerable public expenditure: in England and Wales the annual expenditure on the criminal justice system when the Coalition government entered office in 2010 was around £20 billion. Below we consider some of the key agencies in the criminal justice system and issues that underpin their operations.

THE POLICE SERVICE

The main responsibilities of the police service include preventing crime, investigating criminal acts and preparing the groundwork for the prosecution of those charged with committing crime. We consider their work more fully in Chapter 12.

THE PROSECUTION SERVICE

The manner in which countries organize prosecution services is subject to considerable variation and we consider this issue more thoroughly in Chapter 14. Their responsibilities include charging decisions – that is, whether to bring before the courts a person whom is accused of having committed a criminal offence. In England and Wales this role is carried out by the Crown Prosecution Service (CPS). This was created by the 1985 Prosecution of Offences Act and is headed by the Director of Public Prosecutions.

THE COURTS

The main role of the courts is to determine the guilt or innocence of a person who has been formally charged by a prosecuting authority with a criminal offence. The structure and organization of the courts varies considerably from one country to another and we consider their role more fully in Chapter 13. Trial procedure is separately discussed in Chapter 14.

THE PRISONS

Those convicted of a criminal offence may receive a custodial sentence, in which case they are deprived of their liberty and sent to prison. The main purpose of prisons is to ensure that criminals remain in custody for the duration of their sentence (thus security considerations to avoid escapes are a prominent feature of prison regimes), although prisons in most countries also aim to provide opportunities (such as education and training) that are designed to transform criminals into law-abiding members of society upon their release. In England and Wales prisons in the public sector are the ultimate responsibility of the Ministry of Justice. We consider their role more fully in Chapter 15.

A range of other services also exists within criminal justice systems. In England and Wales the National Probation Service aims to ensure that criminals who receive non-custodial sentences that are to be carried out within the community and those who have been released from sentences served in custodial regimes do not continue a career of lawbreaking. We consider the role of this and similar services operating in different countries in Chapters 15 and 17.

In England and Wales a further body operates within the criminal justice system – the National Parole Board. The main purpose of this body is in connection with persons who have received a mandatory sentence of life imprisonment for murder. In such cases the trial judge will set a minimum period that has to be served in prison. When this term has been served, the prisoner is eligible for apply for release. The application is judged by the Parole Board which judges whether the offender poses a continued risk to society. The Parole Board may thus refuse the application (in which case the prisoner can reapply subsequently) or agree to it in which case the prisoner is freed under license. This means that should the released prisoner reoffend, he or she will be recalled to prison.

A system or a process?

Key idea

An important issue affecting criminal justice is the extent to which the various agencies operate according to the same aims and objectives. This is at the heart of a debate as to whether we should refer to there being a *criminal justice process* or a *criminal justice system*.

Although in the early stages of studying criminology we tend to use the term 'criminal justice system' as a collective term to describe the various agencies that we have listed above (and for convenience this chapter will use this term), a distinction exists between the terms criminal justice *process* and criminal justice *system*.

A criminal justice process consists of a range of agencies, each with their own aims and objectives, which operate more or less in disregard of the operations of the other bodies. In England and Wales, for example, the National Probation Service and the Prison Service historically operated as distinct services, the rationale of the former being to keep offenders out of the hands of the Prison Service.

A criminal justice system also consists of a range of agencies. However, the term system implies a unity of purpose whereby these agencies all pull in the same direction, typically seeking to attain common aims and objectives.

The perception that England and Wales possessed a process as opposed to a system resulted in post-1997 Labour governments inaugurating a series of reforms under the heading of 'joined-up government'. This sought, through various mechanisms, to co-ordinate the work performed by the various criminal justice agencies – in other words, to *systematize* what had previously been a *process*.

In England and Wales post-1997 Labour governments sought to promote a joined-up approach to the operations of the criminal justice system. This meant: 'Making the whole system work

together [...] It means linking up the target's delivery objectives, strategic plans, IT systems and the daily work of every individual working in each criminal justice agency' (Home Office et al., 2002: 145).

Home Office, Lord Chancellor and the Attorney General (2002). *Justice for All.* London: TSO, C, 5563).

Case study: Joined-up criminal justice in England and Wales

The principle of joined-up criminal justice entails a number of different agencies being required to co-operate in order to accomplish common objectives. This co-operation may be formulated by creating machinery to act as an umbrella under which various agencies work together or it can be achieved using other methods, such as targets whose attainment requires the co-operation of a number of bodies.

One important example of joined-up criminal justice in England and Wales was provided through the mechanism of crime and disorder reduction partnerships (CDRPs) (which are now commonly known as community safety partnerships). These were created by the 1998 Crime and Disorder Act and were designed to advance the objective of community safety.

CDRPs operate across the geographic boundaries of local government (usually district councils). They entailed the co-operation of local representatives of traditional criminal justice agencies (such as the police and probation services) and representatives of other local agencies (such as the health service and local authority education and social service departments) that did not traditionally have a role in criminal justice matters but which could exert an important input in securing community safety (which might be threatened by issues that include drug-related crime and truanting by schoolchildren).

CDRPs required participating agencies to see beyond their own organizational priorities and gel behind common objectives. Leadership in a joined-up approach is an important aspect of its success in doing this.

Discretion in the criminal justice system

Although the professionals who work within the criminal justice system operate according to formalized rules and procedures, they also possess some degree of flexibility in connection with the decisions they are required to make. We refer to this as 'discretion'. For example, a police officer who encounters a lawbreaker may decide, if the offence is not a serious one, to informally warn the person not to repeat their behaviour as opposed to taking more formal action (such as an arrest). Prosecutors are often able to determine whether a case should be brought to court and, if so, what precise charge should be levelled against the offender. Plea bargaining between prosecution and defence is a further aspect of discretion at this stage of the prosecution process. Magistrates and judges also possess some degree of flexibility in their sentencing decisions.

As we have argued in Chapter 3, classicist criminologists were firmly opposed to the use of discretion within the criminal justice system as this meant that those who were contemplating breaking the law did not know what the outcome of their actions would be and this situation undermined their ability to make a rational choice concerning the commission of crime.

Attempts to limit the use of discretion within the criminal justice system later became associated with the *justice model* which originated in America in the 1970s and which became associated with retributivist objectives of punishment (a term we have discussed in Chapter 10). In England and Wales the restriction of discretion by criminal justice professionals was implemented by legislation that included the 1994 Police and Magistrates' Courts Act (which enabled the Home Secretary rather than individual chief constables to set priorities for their forces) and the 1997 Crime (Sentences) Act which imposed a raft of mandatory sentences for crimes such as domestic burglary based on the belief that sentencers were often too lenient towards offenders. This legislation was modelled on the American 'three strikes and you're out' approach (the application of policies pioneered in one country to another is a process that we refer to as *policy transfer*).

> *The professionals who work within the criminal justice system are able to temper their decisions with the use of discretion. This term refers to 'the freedom, power, authority, decision or leeway of an official, organization or individual to decide, discern or determine to make a judgement, choice or decision, about alternative courses of action or inaction' (Gelsthorpe and Padfield, 2003: 1).*
>
> Gelsthorpe, L. and Padfield, N. (2003). 'Introduction', in L. Gelsthorpe and N. Padfield (eds), *Exercising Discretion: Decision-making in the Criminal Justice System and Beyond.* Cullompton, Devon: Willan Publishing.

Victims in the criminal justice system

Key idea

The criminal justice system needs to strike a balance so that it fairly treats those who are suspected of breaking the law while at the same time delivering justice to those who have been victims of crime.

A key purpose of the criminal justice system is to punish those who have broken the law. However, it is necessary to treat all parties involved in a criminal act fairly.

The rights of those who are accused of committing a crime need to be safeguarded. In many countries the starting point for such protections are the presumption of innocence – that is, a person accused of a crime is considered to be innocent and it is up to the prosecution to prove that this is not the case. The intention of this procedure is to ensure that no person should be punished for a crime that he or she did not commit: should this happen, we refer to it as a *miscarriage of justice*.

However, it is also important that the operations of the criminal justice system secure the confidence of victims of crime (and more broadly the general public) so that they feel that justice has been delivered thus providing them some relief from the pain that they have experienced from the criminal's actions. If a criminal justice system fails to do this, the public will lose confidence in the 'official' way of tackling crime. This may result in the use of vigilante justice in which the public deal with offenders themselves by taking the law into their own hands.

Criminal justice systems can be underpinned by one of two perspectives. One is the *crime control model* which regards securing the conviction of offenders to be the main purpose of the criminal justice system. The other is the *due process model* which regards the need to protect the rights of those accused of crime as the prime operating principle of the criminal justice system.

Two key values that underpin the operations of the criminal justice system are crime control and due process. These models were initially defined by Herbert Packer (1964) and in a subsequent work he differentiated between them as follows: 'The value system that underlies the Crime Control Model is based on the proposition that the repression of criminal conduct is by far the most important function to be performed by the criminal process. The failure of law enforcement to bring criminal conduct under tight control is viewed as leading to the breakdown of public order and thence to the disappearance of an important condition of human freedom. If the Crime Control Model resembles an assembly line, the Due Process Model looks very much like an obstacle course. Each of its successive stages is designed to present formidable impediments to carrying the accused any further along in the process' (Packer, 1968: 158 and 163).

Packer, H. (1964). 'Two Models of the Criminal Process', *University of Pennsylvania Law Review* 113: 1–68.

Packer, H. (1968). 'Two Models of the Criminal Process', in H. Packer, *The Limits of the Criminal Sanction*. Stanford, CA: Stanford University Press.

It is important, therefore, that the correct balance is struck between these two perspectives. A heavy leaning towards the crime control model will make convictions easier to obtain but at the cost of an increased number of wrongful convictions. On the other hand, a criminal justice system which places prime emphasis on the due process model runs the risk of being regarded as too lenient towards offenders, especially when these are let off for procedural reasons.

Attempts to readjust this balance are frequently depicted as what is termed a zero-sum game: that is, it is argued that any attempts to increase the protection that is afforded to victims by the criminal justice system must be at the expense of a loss of right of suspects and offenders; while, alternatively, attempts to increase the protection offered to suspects and offenders are viewed as necessarily resulting in a loss of protection that the criminal justice system affords to those who are victims of crime.

In the following section we will consider how this dilemma was played out in England and Wales.

Rebalancing the criminal justice system in England and Wales

Key idea

A number of initiatives have been pursued in England and Wales to give victims of crime a fairer deal from the operations of the criminal justice system.

Rebalancing the criminal justice system indicates a desire to make the system provide an improved level of service to victims of crime and offer an enhanced level of protection to the general public by tackling the perceived bias that had traditionally been displayed towards offenders.

The objective of rebalancing the criminal justice system was a major concern of post-1997 Labour governments and became an important aspect of criminal justice policy between 2005 and 2010 which sought to close the gap between what the public expected of a criminal justice system and what they saw it delivering. In particular, it sought to ensure that victims and witnesses of crime received just treatment from the operations of the criminal justice process.

There were a number of ways through which this objective was pursued after 2005. They included:

▶ The 2003 Criminal Justice Act

This act's provisions included:

▶ The abolition of common law rules that governed the admissibility of evidence relating to a defendant's previous bad character in criminal proceedings;

▶ The ability to retry a person for the same crime for which he or she had been previously acquitted in the event of 'new and compelling' evidence emerging;

▶ Giving judges the ability to dispense with a jury where there was a danger of jury tampering.

▶ The 2004 Domestic Violence, Crime and Victims Act

This proposed the appointment of an independent commissioner for victims and witnesses. In 2005 a Code of Practice for the Victims of Crime was put forward. This set out what protection, practical support and information victims had a right to expect from criminal justice agencies.

▶ The 2008 Criminal Justice and Immigration Act

The provisions of this act included the removal of the use of procedural irregularities to overturn the sentences of those who were plainly guilty of the offence for which they had been convicted.

Additionally, use was made of targets to rebalance the criminal justice system by requiring all criminal justice agencies to meet the needs of victims and witnesses.

The private (or commercial) sector and the criminal justice system

Key idea

Criminal justice services were traditionally performed by agencies that operate in the public sector. However, the private sector also performs activities that are related to criminal justice activities.

Private policing

England and Wales and the US have a long tradition of police services being performed by private bodies. This is sometimes referred to as 'commercial policing' as the bodies concerned operate in the private sector according to commercial lines (that is, they seek to make a profit from the services that they provide). There are two main areas of work performed by private policing organizations – *security work* and *detective work*.

Security work encompasses a wide range of activities that range from patrol work and the installation of crime prevention devices such as burglar alarms to transferring money ('cash in transit') or other valuable items from one location to another. In England and Wales the growth of what has been termed mass private property (that is, private property used by members of the general public including shopping centres and nightclubs) has helped to increase the numbers employed in this aspect of private policing.

Private detectives are a well-known institution in both Britain and America. The British fictional detective, Sherlock Holmes is perhaps the best known of all private detectives, and the exploits of fictional American private detectives such as Thomas Magnum and Mike Hammer were regularly aired in television programmes shown on both sides of the Atlantic.

In reality, however, the work of private detectives is less glamorous than literature or the media would suggest. Personal relationships (husbands or wives seeking proof of their partner's infidelity) form the bread-and-butter work of many private detectives, although they do perform other functions that include debt collection, tracing missing persons and the investigation of insurance fraud.

Some bodies provide both security and detective work. An important example of this was the American Pinkerton National Detective Agency (whose employees were usually referred to as 'Pinkertons'). This organization (which still exists) was established in 1850 and was especially renowned for its role in anti-trade union activity in the latter decades of the nineteenth century and early years of the twentieth.

The main problem of private policing is that of standards – the pay that is offered and the training that is provided mean that the job does not attract high-calibre applicants. Some countries such as the US attempted to maintain standards through a licensing system but this was traditionally resisted in England and Wales where an alternative approach was adopted that sought to provide piecemeal regulation of the activities used in the private policing sector.

However, in 2001 the Private Security Industry Act established a licensing system whereby a newly created body, the British Security Industry Association (BSIA), became responsible for licensing those who sought employment in the various sectors of the security sector of private policing. A key aspect of their work was to vet the backgrounds of applicants to ensure that undesirable persons (such as those with previous criminal records) could not obtain employment. The 2010 Coalition government intended to abolish the BSIA but it was temporarily reprieved pending further consideration of the manner in which the industry should be regulated in the future.

PRIVATIZATION

The private or commercial sector is involved in the delivery of other aspects of criminal justice service delivery. In England and Wales the adoption of the policy of privatization by governments headed by President Ronald Reagan (1981–89) and Prime Minister Margaret Thatcher (1979–90) led to the transfer of a number of criminal justice activities from the public to the private sectors. This included the running of prisons. In the US the first privately operated prison opened in 1984 in Hamilton County, Tennessee, and Wolds prison (opened in 1992 after Thatcher had been replaced by John Major) was the first privately managed prison to open in England and Wales.

In England and Wales, the operation of prisons became subjected to a process of 'contracting out' whereby bodies wishing to manage a prison could put forward bids to (initially) the Home Office. These bodies could be Her Majesty's Prison Service, which had historically run prisons, or organizations in the private sector and the contract to run prisons was put out to tender on a regular basis. This policy was subsequently extended through the Private Finance Initiative whereby contracts were awarded to private sector companies to design, build and manage new prisons (rather than existing ones as had previously been the case). The running of prisons by the private sector is set to expand under the 2010 Coalition government as these are cheaper to operate than those in the public sector, administered by HM Prison Service. A key problem with this process is that in order to mount a competitive bid, operating costs may be kept to a bare minimum at the expense of standards.

The policy of privatization was also developed in England and Wales through the policy of *contestability* in the early years of the twenty-first century. This entailed a mixed economy of service delivery by the state, private and voluntary sectors. This was especially applied to specific services utilized by the National Probation Service which became subjected to a process of competitive bidding between Probation Trusts, and the private and voluntary sectors. The transfer of public services to the private sector is now called 'outsourcing'.

Public involvement in the criminal justice system

Key idea

Members of the general public can also play an important part in the operations of the criminal justice system by volunteering in various aspects of its operations.

The personnel who staff the agencies of the criminal justice system are trained professionals. However, ordinary members of the general public can also perform a role in its operations by volunteering their services in key aspects of its work. In England and Wales, for example, individual members of the public can become involved in the criminal justice system by:

▶ serving as volunteer police officers (who are organized in the Special Constabulary) or as members of Neighbourhood Watch schemes

- serving on juries

- serving as magistrates

- serving in the youth justice system (for example, as members of Youth Offender Panels)

- serving on boards of visitors in the Prison Service.

Additionally, members of the public can join voluntary organizations which may participate in criminal justice activities. These include Rape Crisis Centres in England and Wales.

The involvement of members of the public in criminal justice affairs either as individuals or as members of voluntary organizations has been actively promoted by the 2010 Coalition government's 'Big Society' programme. One rationale for this is that volunteering is one way to bridge the gap in the provision of criminal justice services in an era of financial cutbacks when public sector organizations have experienced severe reductions in the level of public financing made available to them.

Dig deeper

Cavadino, M. and Dignan, J. (2007). *The Penal System: An Introduction*, 4th edn. London: Sage.

Joyce, P. (2012). *Criminal Justice: An Introduction*, 2nd edn. London: Routledge.

Joyce, P. and Wain, N. (2010). *A Dictionary of Criminal Justice*. London: Routledge.

Fact-check

1 In England and Wales the body that was set up by the 1985 Prosecution of Offences Act to conduct criminal prosecutions on behalf of the state was:

A The Director of Public Prosecutions

B The Police Prosecution Department

C The Crown Prosecution Service

D The Legal Services Commission

2 In England and Wales, which government department exercises responsibility for the Prison Service?

A The Ministry of Justice

B The Home Office

C The National Offender Management Service

D The National Probation Service

3 When the Coalition government took office in the United Kingdom in 2010, the annual expenditure on the criminal justice system was approximately:

A £100 million

B £1 billion

C £10 billion

D £20 billion

4 In England and Wales a key function of the National Parole Board is to:

A Determine which prisoners can be released under Home Detention Curfew

B Supervise the work of the National Probation Service

C Assess whether an offender who has been given a life sentence of imprisonment possesses no significant risk to the community and can be released from prison

D Supervise the administration of community penalties

5 In England and Wales the objective of rebalancing the criminal justice system sought to enhance the position of:

A Offenders

B Victims of crime

C Judges

D Magistrates

6 The term 'private policing' denotes:

  A Persons or organizations that deliver police services which operate in the private sector and seek to make a profit from their activities

  B Persons who are hired by property owners to protect their property

  C Policing that is performed by officers working undercover to ensure that their activities remain confidential

  D The British English term for what is termed 'private investigator' in the US

12

The police

The police carry out important functions within the criminal justice system. Their work includes seeking to prevent crime, detecting those who have broken the law, and conducting investigations that may form the basis of a subsequent prosecution. The police service has been described as the 'gatekeepers' of the criminal justice system in the sense that the work they perform is the first step in the process of bringing offenders to justice. In this chapter we will consider the role that the police perform in society. We will examine the functions that they carry out and the manner in which they perform them.

The role of the police

The police perform numerous roles in society. They are responsible for enforcing the law and taking action against those who break it. This task (which may require the police to detect who has been responsible for committing a crime) is the initial intervention against a lawbreaker that results in the subsequent occurrence of a number of actions being taken against him or her – it is in this sense that the police are the gatekeepers of the criminal justice system.

The police perform a vital function in civil society: 'the police service might be "the state in uniform", the pre-eminent visible embodiment of sovereignty and the rule of law (Rowe, 2008: 15). Their role 'can be defined by a set of activities and processes with a broad mandate to prevent, detect and control crime and disorder' (Grieve et al, 2007: 20).

Grieve, J., Harfield, C. and McVean, A. (2007). *Policing.* London: Sage.

Rowe, M. (2008). *Introduction to Policing.* London: Sage.

The police also maintain public order (a task sometimes referred to as 'order maintenance') and ensure that citizens are able to go about their everyday lives without fear of intimidation or harassment from those who would disrupt the lives of individuals or communities.

The physical presence of the police in our communities serves both to prevent crime and provide us with a sense of reassurance that is especially important in helping us overcome the fear of crime. The police may also perform a number of tasks not related to law enforcement but which are designed to help those who require assistance, no matter what form this takes. In England and Wales the latter role is referred to as the *service role* of policing and was traditionally seen as an important way through which public approval for the police could be secured.

The legitimacy of the police

A crucial issue that affects the ability of the police to operate in society is that of legitimacy – the police would be unable to perform any of their functions unless the general public accepted that they had a right to do so.

Legitimacy may be derived from one of two sources whereby the police are seen either as servants of the government (in which case legitimacy is conferred on the police from above) or as officials whose source of authority derives from the general public (in which case legitimacy is accorded from below). The former is referred to as a *Roman law* (or *Continental*) model of policing and the latter as a *common law* model of policing.

Within Roman law models, the police are typically controlled by and accountable to central government and use weaponry and other coercive methods to enforce their will, operating in a manner similar to that of the military. Their prime responsibility is to ensure the maintenance of the government by eliminating any threats that might be posed to it from politically motivated protests.

Within common law models, the police are typically subject to a degree of local control and accountability. They are a civilian force and routinely use non-militaristic methods to enforce their will. Their prime responsibility is to serve the public by tackling problems of concern to it, especially in connection with the prevention and detection of crime. They perform these tasks with the co-operation of the public by adopting an approach that is commonly referred to as *policing by consent*. We will consider this more fully in the following section in connection with the system of policing in England and Wales.

The development of policing by consent in England and Wales

Key idea

In England and Wales policing is underpinned by the principle of policing by consent: this means that the police actively seek the co-operation of the public in relation to the performance of their duties.

Professional policing (sometimes referred to as 'new' policing) in England and Wales commenced in 1829 when the Home Secretary, Sir Robert Peel, created the Metropolitan Police (now termed the Metropolitan Police Service). This system replaced a range of policing initiatives that formerly operated across London (including parish constables who served on an unpaid voluntary basis) with a force of officers who were paid a wage to perform police work. This professional system was subsequently adopted throughout England and Wales during the nineteenth century. Peel viewed his new police force as a more effective deterrent to crime than the prevailing system of capital punishment.

Initially, there was much opposition from the general public to the creation of professional police forces:

▶ Those at the lower end of the social ladder feared that the role of new police forces would be to control the way in which they conducted their lives and that they would thus be on the receiving end of aggressive police practices;

▶ Middle-class persons in the growing towns of nineteenth-century England were concerned that they would have to financially contribute towards the costs of a system of policing that had previously been provided more or less free of charge;

▶ Landowners queried whether this expenditure was necessary since traditional customs and habits in rural areas (especially deference to one's social superiors) kept the level of crime low;

▶ Persons from all social brackets feared that professional police forces posed a severe threat to the rights and liberties of the people since they may be used to further the political interests of the government by acting in a way similar to the police in late eighteenth- and early nineteenth-century France – a development that was sneeringly referred to as a 'Bourbon system of policing'.

It was thus necessary for those wishing to develop a professional system of policing throughout England and Wales to tread very carefully in order to counter the objections that have been referred to above. The principle of policing by consent was the method chosen to 'sell' the police to an otherwise sceptical general public.

THE UNDERPINNINGS OF POLICING BY CONSENT

In order to overcome potential resistance to the development of professional policing in England and Wales, it embraced a number of features which collectively underpinned the principle of policing by consent. These were:

▶ Methods of policing

The main task of the police was to prevent crime, and in the early years of professional policing it was assumed that the mere physical presence of a police officer patrolling a small geographic area on foot would be sufficient to achieve this purpose. There was no need, therefore, for them to unnecessarily involve themselves in the everyday life of the community as this might be regarded as unwarranted interference.

▶ Formalized procedures

The police were required to operate within the constraints imposed by the rule of law and apply formalized procedures against those who had broken the law as opposed to meting out responses which could be deemed to be unreasonably excessive.

▶ Police powers

Initially, the police were given no special powers with which to perform their duties. They were to rely on the common law powers possessed by all members of the general public. It was in this sense, especially, that the police were termed 'citizens in uniform' – they performed tasks that all members of the general public were empowered to perform if they so wished. The only difference was that the police were paid a wage to utilize these powers.

▶ Police weaponry

Initially, police officers were routinely armed only with a truncheon to be used for their personal protection in confrontational situations. The decision to not to provide the police with more substantial weaponry such as guns underpinned the concept of minimum force that governed the manner in which confrontational situations between the police and public should be handled.

▶ The service role of policing

This refers to the need for the police to perform duties that extended beyond those connected with law enforcement and crime and to befriend the community by providing aid and assistance to members of the public encountering any form of difficulty. This was an important way for the police to secure consent from all sections of the public.

▶ Recruitment

Initially, the police officers employed by professional police forces were drawn from the working class – many of them having previously been labourers: although this policy was partly governed by cost considerations (since working-class police officers would be paid less than persons drawn from a higher social bracket), it was also designed to construct the consent of working-class communities to the new system of policing. It was assumed that working-class police officers would police working-class communities in a more sympathetic way than would have been the case had policing been performed by middle-class persons. In the late twentieth century similar arguments were used in connection with the need for police forces to employ more officers from minority ethnic communities.

▶ The control of policing

Although the Metropolitan Police were controlled by central government through the Home Office (a situation that remained until the enactment of the 1999 Greater London Assembly Act whereby the role of the Home Secretary in London's policing was replaced by the Metropolitan Police Authority), elsewhere in England and Wales police forces were subjected to a considerable degree of local control that was initially exerted by those who controlled the machinery of local government. This situation ensured that policing addressed local concerns rather than following the requirements that were dictated by central government. We will consider this issue more fully in the following section.

Although these developments could not be expected to secure the universal consent of the public to the police, they did succeed in achieving a wider level of consent than had existed when professional policing was first introduced into England and Wales in 1829.

The above discussion also suggests that changes affecting the methods, procedures, powers, weaponry, service role, recruitment or control of policing might have the effect of eroding the principle of policing by consent. In the following section we will consider one of these in detail by examining policing methods.

Spotlight

A number of slang terms are used to describe British police officers. Initially, the term 'Peelers' was used as a reference to Home Secretary Robert Peel who created the Metropolitan Police force in 1829. Another is 'cop'. The rationale for this term is unclear, although one explanation centres on a document that a police officer carried and could produce if challenged by a member of the general public to prove that he was a 'constable on patrol'.

The methods of policing in England and Wales

Policing can be delivered in a number of ways. We refer to these as the 'methods of policing'. Although our discussion focuses on England and Wales, the methods that are discussed have been employed in a number of other countries.

Key idea

The roles performed by the police in connection with law enforcement, combating crime and order maintenance can be delivered in various ways. These include *preventive*, *reactive* and *proactive* methods.

Historically, police forces in England and Wales tended to favour a method referred to as 'preventive policing'. This took the form of a police officer being assigned to a small geographic area (which was termed a 'beat') which he would patrol on foot. It was assumed that the physical presence of a uniformed figure of authority in a locality would be sufficient to prevent crime and there was thus no need to undertake further actions or activities to stop crime from occurring. A key advantage of this method was that it helped to create a good relationship between police officers and the public and the nature of this relationship was portrayed in a television programme, *Dixon of Dock Green*, which was screened between 1955 and 1976.

The main disadvantage of preventive policing delivered in this way was that it required large numbers of police officers whose work was essentially boring. Accordingly, police forces began to move away from this method during the 1960s and embrace a different way to perform their role that was termed 'reactive' (or 'fire brigade') policing.

Reactive policing entailed the police responding to incidents after they had occurred rather than seeking to prevent them happening in the first place. Speed of response became the key criteria to determine the efficiency of policing and police patrol work became performed by officers in cars whose work entailed driving from one incident to another. Foot patrol became obsolete in the new police world of cars and two-way radios, although gains in efficiency were at the cost of the relationship between police and public. The police lost the close contact with the public that old-style preventive policing had provided and increasingly became seen as remote from the communities in which they operated.

> *The methods through which policing is delivered exert a considerable impact on the public's perception of the police service. During the 1970s, in England and Wales, police patrol work became underpinned by reaction to incidents as opposed to an attempt to prevent crime from happening. In connection with reactive policing, it was observed: 'The main benefit of this was that it provided tangible measurements, so that efficiency could be judged such as response times and arrest figures, and it enabled the police service to increase its output without the need to raise the number of officers who were employed. [...] It was also initially assumed that the increased efficiency that derived from reactive policing would improve the level of satisfaction held by the public towards the police. [...] However, any benefits were obtained at the expense of the police's relationship with the general public, especially in urban areas' (Joyce, 2011: 70).*
>
> Joyce, P. (2011). *Policing: Development and Contemporary Practice.*
> London: Sage.

The lack of knowledge by the police of the people in the areas in which they worked tended to result in police work being driven by stereotypical assumptions – that certain neighbourhoods were crime-ridden or that certain social groups were criminals. In England and Wales the association by the police of crime and minority ethnic groups resulted in the use of powers such as stop and search in a random manner in which the colour of a person's skin was associated with criminal wrongdoings. The resentment felt by those on the receiving end of such methods eroded the principle of policing by consent and was a major factor causing the inner-city riots in 1981 and prompted a rethink concerning the way in which policing was delivered.

The new style of policing that was promoted to rebuild the principle of policing by consent was that of *proactive* policing. This sought to prevent crime but required the police to undertake positive measures to achieve this objective. This might entail working with other agencies to seek a joint approach to combat crime (this was initially referred to as *multi-agency policing*, although we tend now to use the term 'partnership approach' to describe initiatives of this nature) and also involved restoring the contact between police officers and local communities. This aspect of proactive policing was commonly referred to as *community policing*. In most areas, proactive methods (especially community policing) were performed in addition to reactive policing methods rather than being a replacement of them.

A modern development of reactive policing is termed *zero-tolerance policing* (sometimes referred to as 'positive policing'). This entails a rigid and inflexible approach being taken to particular forms of crime, especially those that cause fear and apprehension in neighbourhoods. It was developed by the New York Police Department and aspects of this approach have been used in England and Wales.

Subsequent developments in the early years of the twenty-first century saw the further development of community policing into what became known as *neighbourhood policing*. This approach was promoted to combat the fear of crime by providing reassurance to communities that derived from the presence of a constant uniformed presence in its midst. This method of policing was universally adopted throughout England and Wales in the early years of the twenty-first century.

Contemporary methods of policing have drawn upon and developed initiatives that have been discussed above. The reliance on intelligence as the basis of police work has been developed by a number of methods that include *problem-oriented policing*. This approach was pioneered in America and entails police interventions being based on a prior analysis of information that typically derives from calls for assistance that have been received from the public. This analysis is conducted by local police officers who then formulate a plan of action to remedy the root causes of the problem which is frequently delivered by a multi-agency (or partnership) approach involving local government and other public agencies.

The control of policing

We have argued above that the question of who exercises control over policing has important consequences for the consent that is given to the police by the public.

Key idea

Police forces may be subject to the control of a number of stakeholders. These include central government, local government, senior police officers or a mixture of all three.

There are various options concerning the exercise of control over police work.

Control may be exercised by central government: as we have argued above, this tends to be a feature of police forces based on Roman law models of policing. Although this ensures that policing fulfils requirements that are judged to be of national importance, it may mean that the main purpose of policing is that of advancing the political objectives of the government (another way of expressing this is *politicizing* the police).

Alternatively, control may be exercised by senior police officers. For many decades (until the late twentieth century) policing in England and Wales came close to this model whereby the chief constables of each force exerted considerable control over police work, principally through their ability to determine the issues to which priority should be given. It was referred to as the doctrine of *professional autonomy* or *constabulary independence*.

The operational independence of the police in England and Wales has a long historical pedigree. The independence of the chief constable in determining such matters was summarized by Lord Denning as follows: 'No Minister of the Crown can tell him that he must, or must not, keep observation on this place or that; or that he must, or must not, prosecute this man or that one. The responsibility for law enforcement lies on him. He is answerable to the law and to the law alone' (Denning, 1968).

Denning, Lord (1968), judgment in the case of *R. v. Metropolitan Police Commissioner ex parte Blackburn* [1968] All E.R. 763.

The main advantage of this was that policing could be directed into areas of work that were judged to be important by a senior officer's professional judgement, uninfluenced by political or partisan considerations. The key difficulty was that police work could be driven by a chief officer's individual preferences or biases as opposed to addressing problems that were deemed important by large numbers of local people.

Finally, policing can be controlled by local people. There are various ways in which this involvement can be secured. Policing can be tied to the structure of local government, thus giving representatives of the people the ability to direct its activities. This was historically the situation in England and Wales during the nineteenth and much of the twentieth century. Alternatively, localities can elect an official whose remit is to exercise control over the police. This has been the case in England and Wales since November 2012 when directly elected Police and Crime Commissioners (one for each of the 41 police forces outside of London) took over the responsibilities for policing that had previously been exercised by police authorities.

One difficulty that arises when the control of policing is placed in any one of the three sets of hands referred to above is that those responsible for policing wield considerable power that is theoretically not subject to any form of external constraints. In England and Wales what was termed the 'tripartite system of police governance' was put forward as a solution to this problem.

The tripartite system of police governance in England and Wales

Key idea

In England and Wales the responsibility for police affairs is shared between three bodies – the Home Office, local government and chief constables. We refer to this three-way division as the 'tripartite system of police governance'.

The tripartite system of police governance was formalized by the 1964 Police Act. It entailed sharing the responsibilities for policing between three separate bodies – the Home Office, chief constables and (outside of London) police authorities. Under this Act:

- The Home Office was responsible for promoting the overall efficiency of the police service (the term 'service' embraces all 43 police forces in England and Wales);

- Chief constables were responsible for the operational direction and control of the individual police forces that they headed;

- Police authorities were given the role of securing the maintenance of an 'adequate and efficient' police force in the area over which they operated.

Additionally, the 1964 act created a structure of accountability based upon a system of checks and balances whereby some functions performed by one of the three partners sharing responsibility for police affairs could be subject to the scrutiny of the other partners and possibly be overturned. For example, under the 1964 legislation, a police authority could request its chief constable to produce a report on the policing of the area but this request could be vetoed by the Home Office.

There were several weaknesses with the tripartite system of police governance. The system of accountability was both complex and unwieldy. Further, it was impossible to provide a precise demarcation of responsibilities between the three parties and thus there were always grey areas that became a battleground for disputes between them.

From the perspective of central government, a further problem with the division of responsibilities for policing was that, although it made a heavy financial contribution towards the overall expenditure of each police force, it lacked the power to insist that this money was spent in a way that provided the best value for money or on functions that it deemed to be of importance.

The solution offered to the latter dilemma was to recast the tripartite system of police accountability in a way that gave the Home Office a greater degree of responsibility for determining the tasks of policing. This reform was implemented in the 1994 Police and Magistrates' Courts Act which gave the Home Secretary the ability to set national priorities which each police force was required to achieve and whose attainment would be assessed by a number of centrally devised performance indicators. Although this did not result in policing being totally dominated by central government, it did increase the power of the Home Office and this was further developed in the latter years of the twentieth century whereby police work was increasingly dominated by the need to achieve targets that were drawn up by the Home Office and other central government departments.

There were two problems with the imposition of a targets regime on policing in England and Wales:

1 Police forces were required to devote considerable resources to completing paperwork in order for central government (or central bodies within the police service such as Her Majesty's Inspectorate of Constabulary) to satisfy itself that targets imposed on police forces were being achieved;

2 Because police work was driven by the need to attain centrally imposed objectives, the localized needs and concerns of communities were being marginalized. One consequence of this was that public confidence in policing began to decline as people felt their problems were not being adequately addressed.

The remedy to both of these problems was provided by the Coalition government which took office in 2010. Centrally imposed targets were drastically reduced and the bureaucratic control that these had previously exerted over policing was replaced by local political control which entailed police authorities being replaced by one directly elected police and crime commissioner. This reform was implemented by the 2011 Police Reform and Social Responsibility Act.

Case study: Police and crime commissioners (England and Wales)

With the exception of London (where different arrangements applied), under the provisions of the 1964 Police Act, the involvement of local people in the policing of their communities was provided by police authorities composed of local councillors for the area covered by the police force and independent members who were chosen by a process of local nomination.

The 2010 Coalition government was sceptical of the extent to which this arrangement enabled local people to exert meaningful influence over the policing of their communities, and thus the 2011 Police Reform and Social Responsibility Act replaced each police authority with a police and crime commissioner who was directly elected by the people living in the area covered by the police force. The first elections took place in November 2012.

The main benefit anticipated by this reform was that local political control over policing would ensure that they responded to the issues that were of concern to local communities. This would increase public confidence in the police service.

However, police forces serve the populations of large geographic areas containing numerous communities, often with different concerns. It is difficult to see how one person can adequately reflect these concerns and ensure that all are addressed. The key danger is that politics may interfere with police work so that a police and crime commissioner will seek action to address the concerns of his or her supporters and marginalize those of communities composed of his or her political opponents.

This raises a further question of the extent to which police and crime commissioners will interfere with operational policing matters. Although the government stated its intention not to allow this to happen, the American experience of police commissioners (whether elected or appointed) suggests that it may occur, thus undermining the historic principle of constabulary independence which sought to ensure that policing would not be subject to outside control.

The structure and organization of policing

Key idea

Most countries have a variety of police forces that exist at national and local level and (in countries with a federal structure of government) at state level.

The issue of the control of policing is closely bound up with the structure of policing and the manner in which it is organized. In England and Wales the desire to enable local people to maintain some degree of control over policing meant that it was organized around local government. This remains the case today whereby counties form the basic unit of police administration, although the abolition of the Metropolitan Counties by the 1985 Local Government Act meant that the six police forces operating across these areas had no single local authority to which they are accountable.

In the US police forces are also structured around local government. The main units of administration are at city (or municipal) level, the first force founded being the Boston Police Department, formed in 1838. At county level police work is performed by sheriff's departments, sheriff's offices or the county police. The county police are mainly found in metropolitan counties: where no police force of this nature exists, law enforcement is discharged by sheriffs.

The US has a federal structure of government in which power is shared between the national government and the 50 states. Accordingly, police forces also exist at state level, the first force of which (the Pennsylvania State Police) was created in 1905. They operate under a variety of names that include Highway Patrol, State Patrol and State Police.

National police organization exists in England and Wales and in the US. In England and Wales the Serious Organized Crime Agency was created in 2005 to combat organized crime, and its remit extended across the entire United Kingdom. It will be replaced by the National Crime Agency in 2013.

In the US most aspects of law enforcement at the federal (or national) level are the responsibility of the Department of Justice and are performed by agencies that include the Federal Bureau of Investigation (FBI) and the Drugs Enforcement Agency (DEA).

Dig deeper

Brain, T. (2010). *A History of Policing in England and Wales from 1974: A Turbulent Journey.* Oxford: Oxford University Press.

Grieve, J., Harfield, C. and McVean, A. (2007). *Policing.* London: Sage.

Joyce, P. (2011). *Policing: Development and Contemporary Practice.* London: Sage.

Reiner, R. (2010). *The Politics of the Police*, 4th edn. Oxford: Oxford University Press.

Fact-check

1 In England and Wales, the tripartite system of police governance denotes that:

   A There are three ministers responsible for policing – the Home Secretary, the Justice Secretary and the Attorney General

   B The responsibility for the conduct of police affairs is shared by three parties – chief constables, police and crime commissioners and the Home Office

   C Police forces are organized into three tiers – national, regional and neighbourhood

   D There are three acts of Parliament that determine the control and accountability of the police – the 1984 Police and Criminal Evidence Act, the 1994 Police and Magistrates' Courts Act and the 2011 Police and Social Responsibility Act

2 In England and Wales the common law system of policing rests on the principle of:

   A Policing by consent

   B Policing by coercion

   C Policing by locally elected officials

   D Policing by the voluntary effort of the general public

3 In the US the policing agency that operates at federal (national) level is:

   A The Central Intelligence Agency

   B The United States Bureau of Justice

   C The Policing Agency of the United States of America

   D The Federal Bureau of Investigation

4 The term 'fire brigade' policing is used to describe:

   A Preventive policing

   B Problem-oriented policing

   C Reactive policing

   D Zero-tolerance policing

5 In England and Wales police authorities were replaced in 2012 with:

   A Sheriffs

   B Watch Committees

C The Big Society
  D Police and crime commissioners

6 In England and Wales, the key measure that relates to police powers is:
  A The 1964 Police Act
  B The 1984 Police and Criminal Evidence Act
  C The 1994 Police and Magistrates' Courts Act
  D The 2002 Police Reform Act

13

The courts

Courts provide the arena in which the guilt or innocence of those accused of having committed a crime are determined and, in the case of those convicted of a criminal offence, where sentence is passed. Courts are also concerned with judging other forms of disputes, perhaps where the state is party to judicial proceedings. This situation may arise if the legality of actions undertaken by the state are challenged by an aggrieved citizen. This chapter examines the role performed by domestic courts and those with international jurisdiction (such as the European Court of Human Rights), the manner in which they are organized, and the key personnel responsible for their operations.

The organization of criminal courts in England and Wales

Key idea

Criminal courts are organized in a hierarchical fashion that reflects the seriousness of cases that are tried before them and the ability of higher courts to review the sentencing decisions made by the lower ones.

Criminal courts are organized in a hierarchical fashion whereby the least serious criminal offences are heard by lower-tier courts and the more serious cases are tried by higher-level ones. This organization also enables the sentencing decisions reached by one court to be examined by another court further up the judicial hierarchy. These courts are referred to as 'appellate courts'.

The court structure in England and Wales

In England and Wales the vast majority of criminal cases (in excess of 90 per cent of the total number) are heard in magistrates' courts. These are responsible for trying summary offences and the powers of magistrates are limited to the ability to impose a fine of £5,000 and/or a prison sentence of no more than six months. The more serious criminal cases (those that are triable on indictment) are heard in a Crown Court. These are presided over by a judge and the decision as to whether a defendant is guilty or not guilty of the crime of which he or she is accused is made by a jury. Some offences (those that are triable either way) can be heard in either a magistrates' or a Crown Court and it is up to the defendant to decide in which type of court the trial should take place.

In England and Wales, the vast majority of criminal cases are heard in magistrates' courts:

'Virtually all criminal court cases start in the magistrates' courts. The less serious offences are handled entirely in magistrates' courts, with over 90 per cent of all cases being dealt with in this way. The more serious offences are passed on to the Crown Court, either for sentencing after the defendant has been found guilty in the magistrates' court, or for full trial with a judge and jury' (Ministry of Justice, 2011: 62). In 2010:

▶ 'an estimated 1.68 million defendants were proceeded against in criminal cases in the magistrates' courts;

▶ 180,000 trials were recorded in the magistrates' courts;

▶ some 153,900 cases were disposed of by the Crown Court;

▶ there were approximately 43,300 trial listings in the Crown Court' (Ministry of Justice, 2011: 2 & 3).

Ministry of Justice (2011). *Judicial and Court Statistics 2010*. London: Ministry of Justice.

If a person is found guilty of a criminal offence, the sentence that is handed out can be subject to a review by what is termed an 'appellate court'. The Crown Court can act in this capacity in relation to the sentences of magistrates' courts and the sentencing decisions of the Crown Court may be reviewed by the Court of Appeal.

Above the Court of Appeal is the Supreme Court. This was established under the provisions of the 2005 Constitutional Reform Act and replaced the role that had previously been performed by the Law Lords who served on the Judicial Committee of the House of Lords. The Supreme Court is the highest court of appeal regarding criminal cases that have been heard in England, Wales and Northern Ireland. It also has jurisdiction over Scottish civil cases.

Although a sentenced defendant was historically the most likely party to a criminal prosecution to appeal against a sentencing decision (on the grounds either he or she was not guilty or that the sentence passed was overly severe), since the enactment of the 1988 Criminal Justice Act the prosecution also has the ability to do this in cases where the sentence passed is regarded as unduly lenient.

Under this procedure, the Crown Prosecution Service (acting perhaps at the request of a victim of the crime) can ask the Attorney General to refer the matter to the Court of Appeal. The ability to do this is confined to all cases that can be heard in the Crown Court and a limited number of offences which are triable in either a magistrates' court or the Crown Court. The Court of Appeal then reviews the sentence and can increase the sentence if it agrees that the initial sentence was unduly lenient.

And if things go wrong?

Key idea

A mistake by a court that results in a person being wrongfully convicted is known as a 'miscarriage of justice'.

Although the Court of Appeal and the Supreme Court are able to remedy mistakes made by lower tier courts, it remains possible that errors can be made, in particular when a person is convicted of a crime that he or she did not commit. We refer to this as a 'miscarriage of justice'.

Case study: Miscarriages of justice – the case of Stefan Kiszko

The introduction of the Criminal Cases Review Commission to examine alleged miscarriages of justice in England and Wales occurred against the background of a number of cases of persons being wrongfully convicted of a crime they did not commit. One of these cases was that of Stefan Kiszko.

In 1975 the murder and sexual assault of a young schoolgirl caused national concern which encouraged the police to secure a speedy arrest and conviction of the offender. The suspect they felt responsible for this murder was a tax clerk, Stefan Kiszko.

He was a social misfit and had the mental and emotional age of a 12-year old. Under intense police questioning (with no solicitor present) he confessed to the crime in the belief that having done so he would be allowed to go home to his mother. Although this confession was later withdrawn, he was tried for the crime and received a life sentence for murder in 1976.

There were several issues that made the conviction unsafe – for example, had he committed the crime, the defence of diminished responsibility could have been made. More significantly, however, was the prosecution suppression of evidence that proved his innocence. Samples taken from the crime scene contained samples of sperm: Kiszko was infertile and could not produce sperm. The prosecution knew this at the outset, but failed to disclose it to the defence.

Kiszko's mother campaigned tirelessly for his release and in 1992 he was released from custody by the Court of Appeal which accepted that forensic evidence clearly demonstrated that he could not have committed the crime for which he had served 16 years in prison.

Hardly any of those responsible for Kiszko's conviction (which one MP described as 'the worst miscarriage of justice of all time') were willing to offer any apologies to him, the main exception being the family of the murdered girl. He died in 1993 aged 41 and his mother died shortly afterwards.

In 2007 DNA technology (which was not available in the 1970s) was used to convict the rightful killer of the murdered schoolgirl.

In an attempt to provide against miscarriages of justice, the Criminal Cases Review Commission (CCRC) was established by the 1995 Criminal Appeal Act to investigate suspected problems of this nature that have arisen in England, Wales and Northern Ireland with regard to either the sentence awarded by a court or the verdict that was reached. In cases where the CCRC believes an injustice has occurred, the case is referred back to the Court of Appeal for further consideration.

The personnel of the criminal courts in England and Wales

Key idea

In England and Wales courts are staffed by personnel termed 'magistrates' and 'judges'.

The lower-tier courts in England and Wales are staffed by magistrates. Most of these are members of the general public who volunteer their services to perform judicial work and are termed the lay magistracy. There are around 30,000 of these in England and Wales, and criminal cases are usually heard before what is termed a 'bench' of three magistrates.

In addition to the lay magistracy, there are a relatively small number of full magistrates. These are now termed 'district judges (magistrates' courts)'. Unlike lay magistrates, these are paid a salary (the old name for them being 'stipendiary magistrates'). They are required to be legally trained and only one of them is needed in order to try a criminal case.

Crown Courts and the higher appellate courts are staffed by judges. These are selected from experienced members of the legal profession. Historically, judges came from the ranks of barristers, but now solicitors are also able to serve in this judicial role. Judges are organized in a hierarchical fashion: the most junior ones are known as recorders and the most senior are the justices of the Supreme Court.

Historically, the appointment of judges heavily relied on the 'old boys' network' whereby existing judges had a considerable ability to influence the appointment process which was conducted by the Lord Chancellor's Department (which is now known as the Ministry of Justice). This tended to mean that the typical judge was white, male, middle class, educated at public school and at Oxford or Cambridge Universities. The socially unrepresentative nature of the judiciary was subsequently tackled by a number of reforms which included vacancies being advertised and candidates being required to formally apply for appointment. A key reform was contained in the 2005 Constitutional Reform Act. This established a Judicial Appointments Commission for England and Wales whose role was to recommend candidates for judicial appointments to the Lord Chancellor.

The court structure in the US

Key idea

The structure of courts in the US consists of two different systems that reflect the federal nature of the American system of government whereby power is divided between the federal (or national) government and the 50 states.

In the US criminal courts exist at federal (national) level and also at state level. The jurisdiction of federal courts is set out in Article Two of the American Constitution and includes criminal offences deemed to be federal in nature.

Criminal (and also civil) matters that are subject to federal jurisdiction are dealt with by district courts: each state has at least one of these. They are presided over by a judge and juries may also be used. US circuit courts of appeal act as appellate courts to determine appeals against sentencing decisions of district courts that are based on an allegation of a mistake of law (although the prosecution cannot appeal against a verdict of not guilty by the lower-tier court).US circuit courts of appeal are organized into regional circuits and are presided over by a panel of judges (usually numbering three).

The highest court of appeal in the US is the US Supreme Court and its key role is to provide the definitive interpretation of the American Constitution when its provisions have become the subject of legal wrangle. It also hears appeals against decisions reached by US circuit courts of appeal and also decisions made by a supreme court of one of the states. Aggrieved parties petition the Supreme Court for their case to be heard. It is presided over by the Chief Justice of the United States and eight associate justices.

The court system used by the 50 states is subject to wide variation. Trial courts of general jurisdiction (which use a variety of names including 'circuit courts' and 'superior courts') hear both criminal and civil cases. They are presided over by a judge, and juries are not commonly used. These lower-tier courts operate alongside state courts of limited jurisdiction that deal with matters that include juvenile crime and minor traffic offences.

In many states, the next level courts are intermediate appellate courts. These hear appeals based on procedural matters or alleged errors of fact made by the lower-tier court (although the prosecution cannot appeal against a not guilty verdict). Cases are heard by a panel of two or three judges.

The highest court in each state is often termed a supreme court. It acts as an appellate court for appeals against decisions reached by state circuit courts and (in states that have them) state intermediate appellate courts that are based upon an alleged error of law. Cases are heard by a panel of judges whose number varies from three to nine.

Courts with international jurisdiction

Key idea

Individual nation states may also be subject to the operation of courts that have international jurisdiction. In Europe these include the European Court of Human Rights and the European Court of Justice.

The courts which function within one country are referred to as domestic courts. In addition to these, there are courts that exercise jurisdiction over a number of countries. We will consider the operations of two of these courts that affect the criminal justice system in England and Wales.

THE EUROPEAN COURT OF JUSTICE (ECJ)/THE COURT OF JUSTICE

This court was established in 1952 and its main purpose is to ensure that European Union (EU) law is adhered to within member countries. Disputes between states, between the EU and member states, between individuals and the EU, or between the institutions of the EU are all referred to this court. It has the power to declare unlawful any national law that contravenes EU law and also has the power to fine companies in breach of this legislation. The 2009 Treaty of Lisbon renamed the ECJ the 'Court of Justice'.

THE EUROPEAN COURT OF HUMAN RIGHTS (ECHR)

In 1950 the Council of Europe (whose membership is wider than that of the EU, with which it should not be confused) drew up the European Convention on Human Rights. This is enforced by the European Court of Human Rights (ECHR) which was reorganized in 1988 (a reform that entailed the new court incorporating the work previously performed by the European Commission of Human Rights). It is based in Strasbourg.

The ECHR investigates complaints concerning breaches of human rights that may be made by signatory states or their citizens. Decisions of the ECHR are binding on member states, unless the court's opinion is advisory, related to an interpretation of the Convention or its Protocols. However, the only penalty that can be exacted for non-compliance is expulsion from the Council of Europe.

The 1998 Human Rights Act enabled domestic courts to enforce the European Convention on Human Rights. However, the ECHR may still adjudicate complaints if the domestic procedure provides an ineffective remedy to the complaint.

The role of the European Court of Human Rights is to enforce the European Convention on Human Rights which entered into force in 1953. 'The Convention was the first international human rights instrument to aspire to protect a broad range of civil and political rights both by taking the form of a treaty legally binding on its High Contracting Parties and by establishing a system of supervision over the implementation of the rights at the domestic level' (Gomien, 2005: 12).

Gomien, D. (2005). *Short Guide to the European Convention on Human Rights*, 3rd edn. Strasbourg, Council of Europe Publishing.

Constitutional courts

Key idea

The role of constitutional courts is to ensure that a country's basic law, enshrined in a constitution, is upheld by national and (where they exist) subnational governments such as the American states. They exercise this role through the process of judicial review.

A constitution establishes a framework or a structure within which a country's system of government is conducted. It provides for the division of responsibilities between the executive, legislative and judicial branches of government and, in federal states, sets out the respective responsibilities of the national and state governments. It also generally establishes the rights that citizens in a country can expect to exercise.

Courts whose remit is to adjudicate disputes arising from the constitution are referred to as constitutional courts. Typically this involves determining whether a piece of legislation passed by a country's national government conflicts with the constitution. In countries with federal structures of government (such as the US or Germany) this may also involve scrutinizing the actions of state governments. In the US actions undertaken by the President in the form of executive orders are also subject to the process of judicial review.

If a constitutional court determines that the action that it has examined is in breach of the constitution, it is declared 'unconstitutional', the effect of which is to overturn the act which is thus rendered 'null and void'.

Constitutional courts may be totally separate from the mainstream judicial system as is the case in France where work of this nature is performed by the Conseil constitutionnel. Its main role is to determine whether laws that have been approved by the French Parliament are constitutional before being formally enacted by the President. Additionally, since 2010 an individual citizen who is party to judicial proceedings may also apply for a decision as to whether the law related to the case is constitutional.

Alternatively, this work may be carried out by courts performing other duties within the criminal justice process. In the US the Supreme Court is an example of this. It hears appeals relating to both civil and criminal cases and also acts as a constitutional court.

THE AMERICAN SUPREME COURT

The American Supreme Court consists of nine judges who are appointed by the President of the United States, subject to confirmation by the Senate. They hold office 'during good behaviour', which is generally taken to mean that they can serve for the remainder of their lives unless they voluntarily choose to retire. They may be removed by the process of Congressional impeachment, but this would need approval from both Houses of Congress and has never happened. Their role as a constitutional court is performed when cases are referred to them on appeal either from the highest courts of appeal in a state or from the federal court of appeal.

The power of the Supreme Court includes being able to declare null and void laws passed by Congress. This role was not explicitly specified in the Constitution and was asserted for the first time by Chief Justice John Marshall in the 1803 decision *Marbury* v. *Madison*. This initiated the process of judicial review and has been exercised ever since. It also embraces scrutiny of actions taken by the President and by the states.

Spotlight

The American Supreme Court consists of nine justices. Its role to interpret the Constitution gives it the power to declare acts passed by Congress as unconstitutional, thus rendering them null and void. In the 1930s the Supreme Court's opposition to President Roosevelt's New Deal measures led him to contemplate introducing legislation that would increase the number of justices to 15 in order to outvote his opponents. However, this course of action was not required since in 1937 one of the judges who had previously opposed legislation of this nature decided henceforth to back it – hence the phrase 'the switch in time that saved nine'.

Judicial review provides the court with a considerable degree of political power, and decisions that it made in the 1950s and 1960s were influential in establishing the civil rights of black Americans. Its judgments can effectively be overturned by amending the Constitution, but this is unlikely to occur. Since 1789 there have been only 27 amendments made to this document and ten of these – collectively referred to as the Bill of Rights – were inserted in 1791.

Judicial review in England and Wales

Key idea

In the United Kingdom, the process of judicial review is more limited than in countries with codified constitutions. The political concept of the sovereignty of Parliament also places limits on the power that the judiciary can wield over the legislative branch of government.

The UK does not have a codified constitution in the sense of there being one document containing all information concerning the operations of government. Here, the process of judicial review is much more limited than it is in the US, being confined to determining whether a decision that has been taken by a relevant body strictly conforms to the law. This process cannot determine the merits of the decision, but only whether the correct procedures were followed in reaching it.

In the UK the doctrine of the sovereignty of Parliament prevents legislation being annulled by the judiciary. However, the enactment of the 1998 Human Rights Act enhanced the power of the judiciary by giving them the ability to judge legislation in accordance with the provisions of the European Convention on Human Rights that was now embodied into UK law.

Under the new procedure, judges of the Supreme Court (formerly the Law Lords) are able to draw Parliament's attention to the fact that an existing or proposed piece of primary legislation contravenes the European Declaration of Human Rights. It does this through the mechanism of a *declaration of incompatibility*. Although this action does not annul the legislation in question, ministers are then authorized to use a simplified process to remove the incompatibility if they choose to do so.

> In addition to dealing with criminal offences, the courts also perform the function of judicial review: 'Judicial review in the UK comprises an assessment of a decision made by a public body (which includes government departments, local authorities, tribunals, or any other organization that exercises a public function). [...] The basis on which judicial intervention is founded is the doctrine of ultra vires which suggests that a public body has acted beyond its authorized limits. [...] In countries that possess codified constitutions, the judiciary are responsible for ensuring that the constitution is upheld. Senior courts (such as the American Supreme Court or the French Conseil Constitutionnel) perform this function' (Joyce and Wain, 2010: 112–13).
>
> Joyce, P. and Wain, N. (2010). *A Dictionary of Criminal Justice*. London: Routledge.

Case study: The judiciary and internment

The manner in which judicial review in connection with human rights issues operates is illustrated in connection with internment.

Internment is defined as 'indefinite detention without trial'. It means that a person suspected of a crime can be indefinitely placed in a prison or similar custodial regime without having first been tried and convicted of an offence. This power was introduced in the United Kingdom by the 2001 Anti-terrorism, Crime and Security Act as an exceptional measure through which to combat terrorism and which applied only to foreign nationals. This was cited by the government as the 'emergency' that justified it opting out (the technical term is derogation) of the European Convention on Human Rights which would in normal circumstances prevent a government performing an action of this nature. By December 2004, 14 men had been detained in this fashion.

Various legal challenges were mounted to internment, which included assertions that the process was discriminatory in that it treated foreign nationals in a manner different to that of British subjects (who could not be interned).

These culminated in appeals by nine detainees being heard before the Law Lords in December 2004. They ruled (by a majority of 8 to 1) that the decision by the government to opt out of Article 5 of the European Convention on Human Rights was a disproportionate response to the threat of terrorism, which did not constitute a state of public emergency. One of the judges, Lord Hoffman, stated that 'the real threat to the life of the nation [...] comes not from terrorism but from laws such as these'. Another, Lord Nicholls, argued that 'indefinite imprisonment without charge or trial is an anathema in any country which observes the rule of law'.

This judgment that the government's actions were incompatible with the protection that the European Convention on Human Rights afforded to those accused of crime forced the government to rethink its approach to terrorism. Internment without trial was ended and in its place the 2005 Prevention of Terrorism Act inserted control orders which placed stringent conditions affecting issues such as residence and travel on foreign nationals suspected of involvement with terrorism.

Administrative courts

Key idea

A key role performed by administrative courts is to adjudicate disputes between the citizen and the state, including government departments and other forms of public agencies.

Administrative law is a branch of public law that is concerned with resolving disputes between citizens and the state. This law may be administered by the courts that operate within the mainstream judicial system or by a process that is separate from this.

In England and Wales challenges mounted by the general public to the actions or operations of the executive branch of government may be heard in the courts or by a separate system that makes use of tribunals. Additionally, complaints relating to maladministration (that is, that a decision was reached based on the use of incorrect procedures) may be submitted to ombudsman that operate at the levels of central and local government.

In the US administrative law is administered by Administrative Law Judges (ALJs) and their role is to resolve disputes between a government agency and a member of the public affected by that decision. They operate at both federal and state level:

▶ At federal level, their operations are regulated by the 1946 Administrative Procedure Act and their appointments do not require the confirmation of the Senate. Each agency has a separate set of ALJs that are attached to them. They are regarded as part of the executive branch of government rather than the judicial branch.

▶ At state level, ALJs are regulated by state law. States vary as to whether separate agencies have a discrete set of ALJs or whether they can operate across all state agencies.

Germany and France are examples of countries where a separate judicial process exists to adjudicate disputes that relate to disagreements between individuals and the operations of the state, including allegations that illegal actions were undertaken by ministers, civil servants and public bodies. The administrative court structure is headed by the Conseil d'état, below which are the *cours administratives d'appel* whose role includes handling appeal from the *tribunaux administratifs* that operate within their jurisdictions.

Dig deeper

Gibson, B. and Watkins, M. (2009). *The Magistrates' Court: An Introduction.* Hook, Hampshire: Waterside Press,

Griffith, J. (2010). *The Politics of the Judiciary*, 5th edn. London: Fontana.

Woodhouse, D. (2004). 'The Constitutional and Political Implications of a United Kingdom Supreme Court', *Legal Studies* 24(1–2): 134–55.

Fact-check

1 An appellate court is one that:
   A Heard accusations relating to the theft of fruit and vegetables in the sixteenth century
   B Hears appeals against judgments handed out by lower-tier courts
   C Constitutes a country's final court of appeal in criminal matters
   D Has limited powers of jurisdiction (such as a magistrates' court in England and Wales)

2 In the US justices of the Supreme Court are appointed by:
   A Congress
   B The President of the United States
   C State Bar Associations
   D Existing justices of the Supreme Court who fill vacancies as they arise

3 In England and Wales approximately what proportion of criminal trials are conducted in magistrates' courts?
   A 50%
   B 60%
   C 80%
   D 90%

4 Members of the Appellate Committee of the House of Lords were more commonly known as:
   A Peers
   B Law Lords
   C Privy Councillors
   D Lord Justices of Appeal

5 In the US the procedure by which the Supreme Court can overturn an act because it conflicts with the Constitution is known as:
   A Judicial review
   B Judicial interpretation
   C Judicial law-making
   D Judicial independence

6 In England and Wales allegations relating to miscarriages of justice are referred to:

A The Home Office

B The Independent Police Complaints Commission

C The Criminal Cases Review Commission

D The monarch (who may issue a royal pardon)

14

Trial procedure

This chapter considers the way in which those accused of committing a crime are dealt with by the courts. It examines the prosecution process, the safeguards that seek to ensure that those accused of having committed a crime are fairly dealt with by the courts, and the manner in which trials are conducted and a defendant's innocence or guilt is determined. It also evaluates the strengths and weaknesses of the system of trial by jury which forms an important aspect of trial procedure in countries that include the UK and USA.

Prosecuting authorities

Persons who are suspected of having committed a crime and who have been formally charged with a criminal offence will be prosecuted. The mechanism through which this is carried out is a trial before a court of law.

The procedures involved in the prosecution of crimes vary from country to country. The starting point concerns the authorities who have the responsibility to decide whether an alleged criminal offence should be prosecuted.

Key idea

The agency that is responsible for initiating and conducting prosecutions varies from one country to another. In England and Wales prosecutions are the responsibility of the Crown Prosecution Service.

In England and Wales the initiation of a criminal trial was historically underpinned by common law, whereby it was up to the victim (or a relative) to initiate criminal proceedings. The creation of the office of the Director of Public Prosecution (DPP) in 1879 introduced a system of public prosecution in which trials were the responsibility of the police and conducted in the name of the state. In recognition of the role of the police, magistrates' courts were often termed 'police courts'.

The 1985 Prosecution of Offences Act separated the tasks of investigating crime and prosecuting it and allocated tasks relating to prosecution to a new body, the Crown Prosecution Service (CPS). This agency commenced work in 1986. It is headed by the DPP and the Attorney General is responsible to Parliament for its operations. It currently employs around 8,000 personnel, of which approximately 3,000 are legal practitioners (usually solicitors).

Under the procedure that has been adopted since 1986, the police investigate a crime and, if they feel the case merits a prosecution, will forward a file to the CPS that contains evidence that was unearthed during their investigation. This file is then reviewed by a solicitor who works for the CPS who has had no prior involvement with the case and is thus able to make a dispassionate but professional review of the evidence.

Having reviewed the file of evidence, the CPS may disagree with the police that the matter should be the subject of a prosecution. The technical term we give to this decision is 'discontinuance'. By the late twentieth century over 10 per cent of cases sent to the CPS by the police were not proceeded with. If the CPS agrees with the police that the matter should be prosecuted, they will determine what the precise charge should be. In most cases the police will already have charged the suspect but it is up to the CPS whether they stick to this charge or prosecute the offender for a different offence. Decisions of this nature are guided by an official document – *The Code for Crown Prosecutors*.

The final role of the CPS is to conduct prosecutions. Trials in magistrates' courts are commonly conducted by solicitors who work for the CPS. Trials in the Crown Court are usually conducted by barristers who are brought in by the CPS, although since the late twentieth century it has employed some barristers to carry out this work.

Key idea

In the US decisions relating to prosecutions are the responsibility of district attorneys at state level and US attorneys concerning federal cases heard by the US Supreme Court.

The conduct of criminal prosecutions in the US reflects its federal political structure in which power is divided between the 50 states and the national (termed 'federal') government.

At state level, the task of initiating a prosecution is conducted by district attorneys. These officials are responsible for reviewing arrests made by the police, making charging decisions based on their interpretation of the law and representing the state in criminal cases that come before the courts. These were initially appointed to their office, but trends that commenced during the 1830s resulted in these officials being elected to office by local voters. The power of district attorneys grew considerably in the nineteenth century, most notably in the amount of discretion they possessed in connection with deciding whether a particular case should be prosecuted or whether, having initiated a prosecution, it should be discontinued. This discretion exerts a considerable influence over police work – the police appreciate that there is no point in spending time and money investigating a crime when it is known in advance that the district attorney will refuse to prosecute the case.

> *District attorneys wield considerable power in the American criminal justice process: 'as an elected official given discretionary power by the constitution or by state statutes, his decisions were virtually unreviewable. This freedom of choice was, in the end, what set him apart from all other members of the criminal justice system' (Jacoby, 1980: 38).*
> Jacoby, J. (1980). *The American Prosecutor: A Search for Identity.* Lexington, MA: Lexington Books.

At national (or federal) level, US attorneys exercise responsibility for trials which are heard in the US Supreme Court. These officials are appointed to office by the President of the United States, subject to confirmation by the Senate.

Proceeding with a prosecution

Key idea
There are procedures whereby the desire of a prosecutor to try a person for a criminal offence can be overruled.

When a prosecuting authority such as the CPS in England and Wales or a district attorney in the US have taken the decision that the suspect of a criminal offence should be prosecuted, the case will usually proceed to court.

However, there may be additional hurdles to overcome before a trial takes place.

In England and Wales magistrates had the historic ability to throw out a case which was brought by a prosecuting authority. This had the effect of discharging the defendant. The procedure through which this process was conducted was termed 'committal proceedings', at which the strength of the evidence against a person accused of a crime could be tested in a judicial forum.

The role of the magistrates was to determine whether sufficient evidence existed to warrant the case being formally tried in a magistrates' court or Crown Court. This procedure had the effect of elongating a criminal trial and the 1998 Crime and Disorder Act abolished committal proceedings in relation to indictable offences which (when this aspect of the legislation was implemented in 2001) henceforth went directly to a Crown Court. The role of the magistrates in relation to indictable offences became that of determining whether the accused person should be released on bail or remanded in custody until the Crown Court trial could take place.

In the US the decision whether a prosecution that a district attorney wished to mount should proceed to trial can be made by a grand jury. The role of the grand juries (whose origins date from twelfth-century English practice and are provided for in the Fifth Amendment to the US Constitution) is to consider the evidence that has been gathered by the prosecution and determine whether it is sufficient to justify a charge followed by the case proceeding to trial. If the grand jury considers that a trial is appropriate, the defendant is then indicted (that is, formally charged) for the offence which he or she has been accused of committing. The indictment is a document that specifies the charges that will be brought against the accused person.

Although the purpose of grand juries was to defend the citizen against the abuse of power by government, there is a tendency for these bodies to support the desire of the district attorney to prosecute. Additionally, a ruling by the Supreme Court (*Hurtado* v. *California* [1884]) made it optional for states to use them and some have replaced grand juries with preliminary hearings that are held before a judge.

Grand juries also exist in relation to a number of federal (or national) criminal offences and have to be used unless the defendant waives this right. In 1970 special federal grand juries were introduced to deal with organized crime and corruption.

The rights of defendants accused of a criminal offence

Key idea

There are a number of safeguards to ensure that persons accused of a criminal offence are treated fairly by the state and the legal process.

Persons who are accused of a criminal offence are provided with a number of safeguards regarding the manner in which criminal proceedings should be conducted. These are contained in constitutions and legislation that apply to individual nations and the principles that underpin them, such as the rule of law. They are additionally to be found in regional systems of international law that apply to specific regions of the world (one example of this being the European Convention on Human Rights that has been in force since 1953) and international law with worldwide application (that may be promoted by the United Nations in the form of conventions).

Some of the main safeguards that apply to a person accused of a criminal offence that are present in liberal democratic countries are as follows:

► Citizens can be punished only by the state applying formalized procedures (in the US the Fifth and Fourteenth Amendments to the Constitution refer to this as 'due process of law');

► The right to speedy adjudication of the crime of which a person is accused;

► The right of the defendant to know what charge is being brought and the rationale for this;

► The right of a person accused of a crime to be legally represented in the pre-trial and trial periods. In England

and Wales the system of legal aid was introduced in 1949 to secure the latter objective;

► The right to a fair trial: this has implications for what the media are allowed to say about a defendant in the period leading up to a trial;

► All citizens who are judged to have committed a wrongdoing will be treated in the same way – nobody is 'above the law';

► The right of an accused person not to incriminate him- or herself;

► The need for the prosecution to prove the guilt of an accused person (rather than the accused person being required to prove his or her innocence);

► The application of the rule of double jeopardy (whereby a person acquitted of a criminal offence cannot be subsequently retried for that offence).

However, these defences are subject to considerable variation from one country to another. In the US, for example, the Fifth Amendment to the Constitution establishes an absolute prohibition on the retrial of a person who has been acquitted of a criminal offence subject to state or federal jurisdiction. This does not, of course, prevent that person being tried for a different offence.

In America, the safeguard against self-incrimination is guaranteed by the Constitution: 'the Fifth Amendment of the United States Constitution assures the individual the right to refuse to incriminate himself by his own testimony in a criminal proceedings. The right against self-incrimination is available in any proceeding, criminal or civil, administrative or judicial, investigatory or adjudicatory, and protects any disclosures which could be used to incriminate the individual in any future criminal proceeding' (Collins, 1988: 65–6). Persons exercising this right are said to 'plead the Fifth'.

Collins, C. (1988). 'The Right against Self-incrimination and the Production of Corporate Papers: *Braswell v. United States*', *Journal of Civil Rights and Economic Development* 4: 65–78.

In England and Wales, however, the absolute prohibition on double jeopardy was removed by the 2003 Criminal Justice Act which permitted an acquitted person to be retried for the same offence if, following the trial, new and compelling evidence came to light.

Similarly, the right of a person accused of a crime or appearing as a witness to refuse to answer questions on the grounds that this might incriminate him- or herself is enshrined in the Fifth Amendment to the Constitution, thus providing a legal basis to the right of silence. In the UK the right was qualified by the 1994 Criminal Justice and Public Order Act whereby a jury may (if it wishes) draw inferences when an accused person presents evidence in court based on information which he or she had refused to provide in answer to questions put earlier by the police.

Plea bargaining

Key idea

The final decision as to what a person accused of a crime will be formally charged with may be subject to a process of negotiation. We refer to this process as 'plea bargaining'.

Plea bargaining entails a lighter sentence being given for a plea of guilty by a defendant. There are two stages in the prosecution process where this process can occur – at the charging stage or following charge when the case proceeds to court.

PLEA BARGAINING AT THE CHARGING STAGE

The discretion that is available to prosecutors makes it possible to bargain with the defence on the precise charge that will be placed before the courts. This procedure will typically take the form of a deal whereby the prosecution downgrade the charge to a less serious one in return for the defendant agreeing to plead guilty to it. This will bring financial savings to the state and is explained by the fact that a specific crime is often capable of being interpreted in different ways.

In England and Wales, for example, the CPS may initially wish to charge a defendant with a crime that has to be heard in a Crown Court to which the defendant will plead not guilty, thus triggering what is likely to be an expensive trial before a judge and jury. However, the CPS may settle for a plea of guilty to a lesser but related charge that can be heard in a magistrates' court. The problem with this procedure is that the victim of the crime may feel cheated of justice if the penalty handed out by the court seems insufficient in relation to the harm that has been caused.

PLEA BARGAINING FOLLOWING CHARGING

Plea bargaining may also occur after the charging stage when a case is placed before the courts. At this stage, plea bargaining involves judicial personnel and the main objective is to secure an early plea of guilty. This speeds up the trial process by reducing the number of required hearings, thereby saving money.

Case study: Plea bargaining in England and Wales

Although plea bargaining is an accepted aspect of the American criminal justice system, in England and Wales it traditionally existed only on an informal basis. In 1970 Lord Chief Justice Parker put forward the 'Turner Rules' governing plea bargaining which insisted that the defendant should be free to make up his or her mind regarding how to plead and insisting that judges in open court should not give any indication of the variation in sentence that would derive from pleas of guilty or not guilty. However, it remained possible for barristers to seek this information from the judge privately, in chambers.

The 1994 Criminal Justice and Public Order Act (the relevant provisions of which were subsequently replaced by the 2000 Powers of the Criminal Courts (Sentencing) Act) sought to introduce a formalized system of plea bargaining following charging. This was referred to as 'sentence discount for a timely plea of guilty' and sought to make the process of plea bargaining more transparent than would be the case if private arrangements between defence, prosecution and magistrates or judges were entered into behind closed doors, outside the arena of the court.

The 2003 Criminal Justice Act created the Sentencing Guidelines Council whose responsibilities included issuing sentencing guidelines regarding discounts for pleas of guilty. Additionally, this legislation allowed a magistrate dealing with an offence that was triable either way to give an advanced indication as to whether a sentence delivered in response to a guilty plea would be custodial or non-custodial. Building upon this reform, a formalized system of plea bargaining in Crown Courts was developed by the Court of Appeal in the Goodyear case (*R.* v. *Goodyear* [2005]) which established a framework that enabled a judge, when requested by the defence, to give an indication in open court as to the maximum sentence for a guilty plea when this was immediately entered.

Reforms that further advanced the principle of plea bargaining were also contained in the 2005 Serious Organized Crime and Police Act which placed on a statutory basis formal agreements between the prosecution and defence whereby defendants who aided a prosecution (for example by supplying evidence or giving assistance to the law enforcement agencies) would receive credit from the court in the form of a lighter sentence.

There are, however, problems with this procedure. It can result in serious crimes being dealt with too leniently or, alternatively, it might be argued that increasing the pressure on defendants to plead guilty may result in miscarriages of justice if innocent people feel constrained to plead guilty to avoid a harsher sentence which may be inflicted upon them if they fear that their plea of not guilty will be rejected by the court.

Trial procedure

Key idea

Criminal trials are conducted according to formal rules and procedures. These include rules of evidence which are important to countries such as England and Wales and the US that have adversarial legal systems.

The purpose of a trial is to determine the guilt or innocence of a person accused of committing a crime. There are two main ways whereby this can be determined.

Countries that include England and Wales and the US use the *adversarial legal system*. This has its origins in the procedure of trial by combat and entails two parties (the prosecution and the defence) seeking to establish the truth of the case they are presenting (which may entail undermining the evidence that is presented by the other party to the case). The courtroom thus becomes a forum akin to that of a battleground in which two parties fight each other to prove the case that they are presenting. The court acts as an impartial body that hears both sets of arguments, referees the contest to ensure that both sides operate according to established rules and procedures, and ultimately determines which version of events is the most convincing.

Spotlight

The system of adversarial justice that is used in Britain and the US originates from the English practice of trial by battle (or combat). This entailed nobles fighting each other to establish innocence and guilt (a noblewoman could choose a champion to fight on her behalf). Trial by battle was outlawed in the late Middle Ages.

The alternative to an adversarial legal system is an *inquisitorial legal system*. In systems of this nature, the court plays an active part in the investigation of an alleged offence. In France, for example, this function is carried out by a legal official known as the *juge d'instruction* (investigating judge) who acts in accordance with instructions given by the prosecutor's office. In order to discharge this function, the judge will question suspects and witnesses and may direct further investigations by the police. The aim of this process is to gather all relevant facts in order to determine whether a trial should be ordered. In France the inquisitorial legal system is used in only a minority of criminal cases and any trial that subsequently takes place operates according to adversarial legal system principles.

RULES OF EVIDENCE

Criminal trials must be conducted according to established rules and procedures. Rules of evidence are an important aspect of this in countries such as England and Wales and the US that have adversarial legal systems.

Rules of evidence determine what evidence is admissible and can be presented before a court of law for the consideration of those who act as triers of fact (which in a case brought before a Crown Court in England and Wales is the jury). In the case of evidence that is disputed, the trial judge will send the jury away and the defence and prosecution will put forward arguments for and against the evidence being presented in open court. This procedure is known as 'voir dire', and if, having heard the arguments, the judge determines that the evidence is inadmissible, the jury will be unaware of its contents.

Other aspects of trial procedure that are covered by rules of evidence include the summoning of witnesses or the production of documents that relate to the case, the way in which witnesses are questioned, and the prohibition of hearsay evidence (that is, evidence founded on rumour or gossip).

TRIAL BY JURY

Key idea

The right to trial by jury is often viewed as a fundamental civil liberty in liberal democratic countries such as England and Wales and the US. There are both advantages and disadvantages to this system.

The ability of a defendant to have his or her case heard by a panel drawn from ordinary members of the public is an important right in a number of countries. This procedure is sometimes termed 'trial by one's peers' (or 'one's social equals'). Their role is to act as triers of fact – that is, they listen to the evidence which is presented by the prosecution and defence and when both sides have concluded presenting their respective cases, they determine the innocence or guilt of the defendant. They do this by delivering a verdict which is read out in open court.

Case study: The jury system in England and Wales

In England and Wales juries consist of 12 persons who are randomly chosen from names included on the electoral register (which is drawn up by local authorities and contains the names of all persons who are eligible to vote in election contests). The selection is carried out by a national Jury Central Summoning Bureau which was set up in 1999.

Historically, certain categories of persons were disqualified from jury service, others were ineligible to serve, and some were excused as of right. However, the 2003 Criminal Justice Act removed most of these categories in an attempt to make jury service a civic duty for which most members of society were eligible.

Traditionally, the universal agreement of all 12 jurors was required to reach a verdict. However, the 1967 Criminal Justice Act permitted the outcome of a trial to be determined by a majority verdict, provided that no more than two jurors dissented from the majority opinion: in other words, a verdict of guilty or not guilty could be determined by a vote of 10 to 2.

A trial by jury is more expensive than a summary trial that takes place in a lower-tier court (such as a magistrates' court in England and Wales) where juries are not used. For this reason, governments in the United Kingdom have been trying for several years to restrict the right of trial by jury to the most serious offences and reduce the number of offences that are triable either way (that is, the offence may be heard in either a magistrates' court or a Crown Court and the defendant may choose where the case should be heard). However, any reform that seeks to limit the right of trial by jury will be resisted on the grounds that it undermines the historic civil liberties of UK citizens and thus far only very limited progress has been made in implementing this objective.

Juries possess a number of advantages. They enable ordinary members of the public to play a part in legal procedures and also ensure that the state cannot act in an oppressive manner towards its citizens, which might be the case if a trial was conducted before a judge alone. This is especially important in cases involving matters to which the state is a party – for example when the state's desire for official secrecy clashes with the public's right to know. Additionally, a jury can enable judicial outcomes to be influenced by popular conceptions of what constitutes right and wrong behaviour. They may do this by pronouncing a verdict of 'not guilty' in the face of overwhelming evidence to the contrary. Although this indicates that a jury's verdict may not always be based on an objective consideration of facts that are presented in a trial (and may also result in injustices – an issue we consider below), it may encourage governments to change the law and bring it in line with the popular consensus concerning acceptable and unacceptable behaviour.

However, there are also disadvantages associated with the jury system. They may not be socially representative, which could result in some sections of society dominating the composition of juries to the detriment of others, such as the working class or minority ethnic groups. Should this happen, the verdicts of juries may lack legitimacy among communities who feel excluded from participation in juries.

Trial by jury is an important aspect of trial procedure in the United Kingdom and in the US. However, it has advantages and disadvantages.

A key advantage of this procedure has been stated to be that the jury 'represents a uniquely subtle distribution of official power, an unusual arrangement of checks and balances. It represents also an impressive way of building discretion, equity, and flexibility into a legal system. Not the least of the advantages is that the jury, relieved of the burden of creating precedent, can bend the law without breaking it.' (Kalven and Zeisel, 1966: 498).

The collective nature of decision-making from persons of varied social backgrounds has also been regarded as an attribute of trial by jury: 'it is to be expected that the amalgam of personal and social attributes that make up a jury will produce verdicts that reflect that unique social mix rather than the broad social characteristic of the individuals concerned' (Baldwin and Kinsey, 1979:104–5)

A key disadvantage is that jurors may depart from the evidence presented in a trial and allow other factors to influence their verdict: 'the ability to pronounce a verdict of "not guilty" in the face of overwhelming evidence to the contrary may result in injustices which bring the legal system into disrepute. In America, a jury's acquittal of Los Angeles police officers who had severely attacked the black American Rodney King in 1992 resulted in riots against the obvious manifestation of racial bias behind this verdict' (Joyce, 2006: 237).

Baldwin, J. and Kinsey, M. (1979). *Jury Trials*. Oxford: Clarendon.

Joyce, P. (2006). *Criminal Justice: An Introduction to Crime and the Criminal Justice System*. Cullompton, Devon: Willan Publishing

Kalven, H. and Zeisel, H.(1966). *The American Jury*. New York: Little, Brown.

We have already mentioned that a jury may sometimes take into account issues other than the factual evidence presented in a trial when considering their verdict. Although we have argued that benefits can arise from such a course of action, it also poses considerable dangers – a jury's decision may, for example, be founded on factors such as racial, gender or homophobic prejudice and result in the innocent being punished or the guilty let off. Other factors may also sway a jury's verdict such as the performance of lawyers, the jurors' lack of knowledge concerning the law or court proceedings, or their inability to understand the evidence that is presented during the trial.

THE BURDEN OF PROOF

In order for a person to be judged guilty of the offence of which he or she has been accused, it is necessary for those who act as triers of fact to be satisfied beyond a reasonable doubt that the case put forward by the prosecution is accurate. This term is not necessarily an easy one to apply and the trial judge will give the jury advice as to how they should apply it in relation to the case with which they have been concerned.

Dig deeper

Ashworth, A. (2010). *Sentencing and Criminal Justice*, 5th edn. Cambridge: Cambridge University Press.

Easton, S. and Piper, C. (2008). *Sentencing and Punishment: The Quest for Justice*, 2nd edn. Oxford: Oxford University Press.

Hastie, R. (ed.) (1994). *Inside the Juror: The Psychology of Juror Decision Making*. Cambridge: Cambridge University Press.

Walker, N. and Padfield, N. (2011). *Sentencing: Theory, Law and Practice*, 3rd edn. Oxford: Oxford University Press.

Fact-check

1 In the US a grand jury:

  A Is composed of important people such as elected politicians and persons nominated by the President of the United States

  B Determines the guilt or innocence of a person accused of committing a criminal offence

  C Decides if there is sufficient evidence to justify committing an accused person for trial

  D Is used only in connection with federal (national) criminal trials

2 The legal system used in the UK and the US whereby defence and prosecution lawyers compete against each other to prove the truth of their case is known as:

  A Adversarial justice

  B Inquisitorial justice

  C Trial by combat

  D Winner takes all justice

3 The term 'double jeopardy' refers to:

  A A person being tried for more than one criminal offence

  B A belief that an offender who has committed one crime has carried out others

  C The inability to retry a person for a criminal offence for which he or she has previously been acquitted

  D The ability of a trial judge to add an additional sentence to that imposed on a convicted offender who has refused to co-operate with the trial

4 In England and Wales for an offender to be convicted of a criminal offence, it is necessary for the prosecution to prove guilt:

  A To the satisfaction of the judge

  B According to guidelines laid down by the Sentencing Panel for England and Wales

  C On the balance of probabilities

  D Beyond a reasonable doubt

5 Plea bargaining is a system whereby:

A The judge threatens to pass a severe sentence unless the accused person admits to his or her guilt

B The defence and prosecution come to an arrangement regarding a plea of guilty in order to secure a lenient sentence

C The defence puts pressure on witnesses not to turn up to a trial in order to get the case thrown out of court

D The defence refuses to enter a plea of guilty or not guilty

6 Rules of evidence consist of:

A Guidelines to lawyers concerning how they may present a case to the courts

B Guidelines to a jury concerning how they should weigh up the evidence that has been presented in a trial

C Guidelines to judges as to how they should preside over a trial

D Guidelines as to what kind of evidence is admissible in a trial

15

Prisons

This chapter considers the development of prisons and the role that they perform in the criminal justice system. In particular, it considers the tensions that exist between the view that prisons should be institutions that seek to bring about the reform and rehabilitation of offenders and the belief that their key function is to punish those who have broken the law. These conflicting perspectives exert a profound impact on the prison environment and reflect the changing purposes of punishment across historical time periods.

The development of prisons – early nineteenth-century reform

Key idea

Considerable attention was devoted to the role that prisons could perform in the latter years of the eighteenth century. In England and Wales, reform was promoted by evangelical reformers and those inspired by the views of classicist criminology.

In England and Wales prisons were historically regarded as institutions that were responsible for holding those who had committed a crime pending sentence. Until the early years of the nineteenth century the penalty for most criminal offences in England and Wales was execution, although this was frequently commuted to transportation, initially to America and latterly to Australia and Tasmania. This procedure was ended in 1852.

However, towards the end of the eighteenth century ideas were developed that suggested prisons could perform additional roles that included bringing about the reform of those who had committed crime. In England and Wales there were two contrasting ways whereby this objective could be achieved.

Prison reformers such as Elizabeth Fry and John Howard were driven by religious impulses. They believed that a prison regime could be developed so that a criminal would reflect on his or her behaviour and, with the aid of religious instruction, would lead a law-abiding life in the future. The reliance on religion to transform the behaviour of criminals led to this approach being referred to as *evangelical* reform.

The views of other prison reformers in this period were influenced by classicist criminology (an approach we have considered in Chapter 3). This secular (or non-religious) approach viewed crime as an irrational act and saw the role of prisons as institutions that would transform those who had acted in this way into persons who would behave in a rational – and law-abiding – manner in the future. Jeremy Bentham was a leading advocate of this aspect of prison reform.

Case study: Jeremy Bentham and the panopticon

Jeremy Bentham was an important influence in the development of classicist criminology in Great Britain. One of his concerns was to use prisons to bring about the reform of inmates, thus transforming them into useful members of society – he viewed them as mechanisms 'to grind rogues honest'.

In 1791 he wrote a three-volume work, *The Panopticon*, in which he put forward a blueprint for the design of prisons in order for them to be able to bring about the transformation of the behaviour of offenders. Central to his idea was the principle of surveillance whereby an observer was able to monitor prisoners without them being aware when they were being watched. What was termed an 'invisible omniscience' secured the constant conformity of inmates since they were unable to know when their actions were being observed.

To achieve this function, Bentham proposed that prisons should be designed with a central tower which housed the observers from which rows of single cells arranged in tiers and separate blocks would radiate. These cells would be isolated from each other. He promoted this design in Millbank Penitentiary. Pentonville Prison (opened in 1842) was also influenced by this concept.

Spotlight

Jeremy Bentham was a prominent English prison reformer. He was concerned that the citizens of London should not be required to contribute money towards the construction of a monument in his memory after his death. Instead, he arranged to have his body stuffed and put on public display. We can still see him today in a glass case contained in the entrance hall of King's College London.

Other countries followed a similar path. In the US the penitentiary was developed in the early 1800s as an institution that was designed to bring about the reform of criminals. This role was especially inspired by religious sentiments.

Prison regimes

Two models guiding the character of prison regimes were developed in the early part of the nineteenth century – the *separate system* and the *silent system* – these were systems of prison discipline. Both were used in American and British prisons and the term 'solitary model' or 'solitary system' is also used to describe both of them.

Key idea

For much of the nineteenth century, those convicted of crime were subjected to harsh prison conditions. Various types of prison regimes were developed in this period to ensure that those convicted of a crime would experience a harsh environment while they were imprisoned.

The separate system was developed in the US (the first prison using the regime and the style of architecture that supported it being the Eastern State Penitentiary in Philadelphia, Pennsylvania, in 1829) and entailed prisoners being placed in solitary confinement during the early part of their sentence. This procedure was designed to make a prisoner reflect on the behaviour that had led to this situation and thus become susceptible to religious ideals delivered by the prison chaplain that would result in him or her reforming their ways. However, the separate confinement of prisoners had long-term psychological effects which resulted in some regimes that used it reducing the period of separate confinement.

The silent system was developed in Auburn Prison, New York, in the early decades of the nineteenth century. This regime forbade all forms of communication between prisoners – one reason for this being to stop the spread of crime arising from prisoners learning tricks of the trade from each other. However, the system did not preclude communal activities such as taking exercise or eating. In Britain, the silent system required prisoners to pass their time by performing monotonous activities such as working the treadmill. In the US, however, prisoners were also released each day to perform labour in factories or fields.

Late nineteenth-century prison reform

Key idea

In England and Wales, the Gladstone Report (1895) heralded a move away from harsh prison conditions and initiated the rehabilitation of offenders as a key role to be played by these institutions.

In England and Wales the reduced use made of the death penalty during the nineteenth century meant that imprisonment became a more widely used response to crime. This period also witnessed a shift away from rehabilitation towards that of custodial regimes in which the secure confinement of inmates was the main consideration.

Deterrence held sway in Britain after the 1860s and was characterized by harsh conditions and severe punishments whereby disobedience was subject to physical forms of punishment that included flogging and solitary confinement. Conditions were made unpleasant in order to deter offenders from returning. Although the goal of reform was not totally abandoned, its accomplishment was primarily to be accomplished by instilling the work ethic and other positive values as opposed to addressing the root causes of criminal behaviour. This philosophy underpinned the 1864 Penal Servitude Act.

A new approach regarding the role of prisons in England Wales was initiated by a report written by Herbert Gladstone in 1895 which argued that offenders were sent to prison *as* punishment and not *for* punishment. This view suggested that the deprivation of liberty constituted sufficient punishment and the report went on to argue that the role of prisons was to bring about reform of offenders so that they would leave prisons better persons than they had been when they were originally convicted. Many of its provisions were incorporated into the 1898 Prison(s) Act and it prompted the abandonment of some of the harsher aspects of the prison regime that included the crank and the treadmill.

In England and Wales the rehabilitative ideal governed the role of prisons for much of the twentieth century. This owed its origins to a late nineteenth-century report that argued: 'We start from the principle that prison treatment should have as its primary and concurrent objectives deterrence and reformation.' The latter was designed to ensure that prisoners would be sent out 'better men and women, physically and morally, than when they come in' (Departmental Committee on Prisons, 1895).

Departmental Committee on Prisons (1895). *Report from the Departmental Committee on Prisons* (The Gladstone Report). London: HMSO, Sessional Paper 1895, c. 7702.

The emphasis on prisons as institutions to bring about the reform of prisoners gave rise to the *rehabilitative ideal* (sometimes referred to as the treatment model) becoming the underlying philosophy guiding the work of prisons. Their role was to focus on treatment to change the habits and values of offenders and enable them to be rehabilitated.

In the US the rehabilitative ideal that was initiated in the early years of the nineteenth century was further developed during the 1870s by the introduction of the indeterminate sentence which provided an offender with an incentive to reform and by further reforms that were introduced during the twentieth century which resulted in prisons being relabelled as 'correctional institutions' during the 1950s. This prompted the introduction of a wide range of treatment programmes within prisons over the following 20 years that were designed to reform offenders.

The move away from rehabilitation

Key idea

In the latter decades of the twentieth century there was a move away from prisons as rehabilitative institutions in both the UK and the US. Instead, the main role of prisons became that of punishing offenders.

In England and Wales the rehabilitative ideal guided the nature of the prison regime for much of the twentieth century. However, although prisons did provide such support (including education, vocational training and treatment programmes), it was not consistently of a standard high enough to alter the habits of many convicted prisoners, many of whom continued with a life of crime upon their release from prison.

The view that prisons were failing to attain the objective of rehabilitation prompted a rethink as to what alternative purposes they might serve.

> *The view that prisons were not bringing about the rehabilitation of offenders was forcibly put forward in an article written by Martinson (1974) which posed the question as to whether studies that examined the effectiveness of treatment programmes delivered in prisons revealed the fact that 'nothing works'. This formed the basis of a fundamental rethink as to the role that prisons should perform – 'the Nothing Works doctrine [...] has shaken the community of criminal justice to its root. [...] widely assorted members of the criminal justice field are briskly urging that punishment and incapacitation should be given much higher priority among criminal justice goals' (Adams, 1976: 76).*
>
> Adams, S. (1976). 'Evaluation: A Way out of Rhetoric', in R. Martinson, T. Palmer, and S. Adams (eds), *Rehabilitation, Recidivism, and Research*. Hackensack, NJ: National Council on Crime and Delinquency.
>
> Martinson. R. (1974). 'What works? – Questions and Answers about Prison Reform', *The Public Interest* 35 (Spring): 22–54.

In the latter years of the twentieth century the rehabilitative model was challenged by a new approach towards sentencing that emphasized the goal of retribution – the main aim of punishment was to give offenders their 'just deserts'. This approach was based upon the *justice model* which originated in the US during the 1970s. Its main features were to advocate replacing indeterminate sentences with determinate ones, protecting the rights of those suspected of crime through the application of due process principles, ending judicial and administrative discretion and inconsistency in sentencing decisions, and seeking to ensure that punishment was proportionate to the crime that had been committed.

Although many of the key features of the justice model appealed to liberal reformers, its main attraction was to conservatives who sought to limit judicial discretion as they believed it was responsible for leniency towards offenders – the emphasis on punishing a criminal for the offence that had been committed enabled an offender's circumstances to be marginalized when a sentence was passed. Accordingly, aspects of the justice model were incorporated into a more general law and order ideology that sought to 'get tough' with criminals. Prisons thus became the central focus of penal strategies in England and Wales and the prison population steadily rose. Between January 1994 and May 1997 it increased from 50,000 to 60,000. This was due to a new sentencing philosophy rather than an increase in crime. One important consequence of this was overcrowding within prisons.

Changes of a similar nature occurred in the US during the 1970s. Between 1975 and 1989 the annual prison population of the United States rose from approximately 240,000 to 683,000, an increase of around 180 per cent. An important development in this period affected the system of parole whose role was challenged by the reduced use that was made of indeterminate sentences and increased public scepticism concerning the effectiveness of rehabilitation.

Rehabilitation within prisons

It has been argued above that one role of prisons is to bring about the rehabilitation of offenders. The importance attached to this objective varies across historical periods, but even when other aims (such as retribution) become the main aims of imprisonment, the desire to bring about rehabilitation remains a goal, even if subordinate to other objectives.

In this section we will consider two issues – how rehabilitation can be achieved and what problems prisons encounter when attempting to deliver this objective.

Key idea

Rehabilitation within prisons can be achieved by treatment programmes or by the provision of education and vocational training courses that are designed to ensure that offenders are equipped with the skills to lead law-abiding lives upon release.

REHABILITATION PROGRAMMES

One way in which prisons can seek to secure the rehabilitation of offenders is to offer programmes that seek to tackle the root causes of their offending behaviour. These may include programmes to tackle alcohol and substance abuse, programmes designed to aid the control of anger, and more specialized programmes directed at specific forms of offending behaviour such as sexual offending. These are collectively referred to as 'cognitive behavioural programmes', one example of which in England and Wales is the Sex Offender Treatment Programme (SOTP) that seeks to challenge the excuses and behaviour that underpin this form of offending behaviour and provides offenders with an understanding of the impact of their crimes on the victim. However, specialist programmes of this nature are costly and this may limit the numbers of inmates who are able to benefit from them. We will consider these more fully in Chapter 18 in connection with recidivism.

In addition to programmes that seek to tackle the causes of offending behaviour, prisons also aim to provide inmates with skills that will equip them on release to find employment and thus turn away from crime. Programmes offering educational facilities and vocational training are especially important in delivering this goal. The effectiveness of programmes of this nature is, however, undermined by a number of problems. In the UK these include overcrowding of prisons (which imposes limits on the number of prisoners able to participate in them) and the nature of work that can be offered. Additionally, a large proportion of prison sentences are too short to enable programmes of this nature to add significantly to the skills of an offender.

REHABILITATION AND THE PRISON ENVIRONMENT

Key idea

The nature of the prison environment may be incompatible with the goal of rehabilitation. The conditions experienced by individuals within prisons may undermine this objective.

The environment within prisons may not be appropriate to securing the rehabilitation of offenders. Rehabilitative work is often carried out in a regime dominated by security considerations – a problem aggravated in the UK by prison overcrowding. The stigma of having been a prisoner may also make it difficult for a prisoner to obtain work upon release, even if new skills were acquired during the period of imprisonment. This may mean that prisoners will use their time in prison to build contacts with the criminal underworld and learn skills that will better equip them for a criminal career upon release. It is in this sense that prisons have been described as 'universities of crime'.

Imprisonment has a poor record in securing the reform and rehabilitation of offenders and (in conjunction with the high costs of imprisonment that amount to around £40,000 per year for each prisoner in England and Wales) this has been used as an argument to suggest that prisons do not 'work': 'Nobody regards imprisonment in itself as an effective means of reform for most prisoners. [...] it can be an expensive way of making bad people worse' (Home Office, 1990: para. 2.7).

However, the same publication argued that prison could be successful in other ways: 'For most offenders prison has to be justified in terms of public protection, denunciation and retribution' (Home Office, 1990: para. 2.7). These alternative functions of imprisonment underpinned the penal policy of the Conservative Home Secretary Michael Howard. He declared: 'Let us be clear. Prison works. It ensures that we are protected from murderers, muggers and rapists, and it makes many who are tempted to commit crime think twice' (Howard, 1993).

Home Office (1990). *Crime, Justice and Protecting the Public*. London: HMSO, Cm 965.

Howard, M. (1993). Speech to the Conservative Party Conference, 6 October.

The prison environment may also exert long-term consequences on the subsequent behaviour of those who are subject to it. Studies in the sociology of imprisonment emphasize how the nature of imprisonment may result in a range of psychological disorders that include anxiety, depression and withdrawal – factors that are not compatible with self-improvement. A number of prisoners enter prisons with mental health problems which may be aggravated by further aspects of psychological deterioration that occur during the period of confinement. The need to adapt to a regime that is frequently violent may also result in prisoners becoming brutalized and returning to their communities upon release potentially more dangerous persons than they were when they received a custodial sentence.

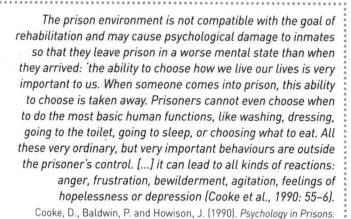

The prison environment is not compatible with the goal of rehabilitation and may cause psychological damage to inmates so that they leave prison in a worse mental state than when they arrived: 'the ability to choose how we live our lives is very important to us. When someone comes into prison, this ability to choose is taken away. Prisoners cannot even choose when to do the most basic human functions, like washing, dressing, going to the toilet, going to sleep, or choosing what to eat. All these very ordinary, but very important behaviours are outside the prisoner's control. [...] it can lead to all kinds of reactions: anger, frustration, bewilderment, agitation, feelings of hopelessness or depression (Cooke et al., 1990: 55–6).

Cooke, D., Baldwin, P. and Howison, J. (1990). *Psychology in Prisons*. London: Routledge.

Perceived (or actual) injustices experienced by prisoners may also undermine the objective of rehabilitation and result in them channelling their energies into rebellion rather than self-improvement. These injustices may take several forms – the nature of prison discipline, the facilities that are available within institutions or the way complaints by prisoners are responded to. Rebellion takes the form of prison disorders or riots. A riot and siege at Strangeways prison, Manchester, in 1990 stretched over 25 days and resulted in Lord Woolf being asked by the government to publish a report on these events and the future direction of prison policy in Britain. He argued in his report (published in 1991) that a balance needed to be struck in prisons between security, control and justice. He argued that the latter required that prisoners should be treated fairly and humanely.

Dig deeper

Jewkes, Y. (2007). *Handbook on Prisons*. Cullompton, Devon: Willan Publishing.

Matthews, R. (1995). *Doing Time: An Introduction to the Sociology of Imprisonment*. Basingstoke: Macmillan.

Ramsbotham, D. (2005). *Prisongate – The Shocking State of Britain's Prisons and the Need for Visionary Change*. London: The Free Press.

Fact-check

1 In a prison that used the separate system what were prisoners not allowed to do:

A Communicate with the guards

B Communicate with each other

C Communicate with their families

D Communicate with ex-offenders upon their release

2 In England and Wales the 1895 Gladstone Report helped to promote:

A Prisons as rehabilitative institutions

B Prisons as institutions whose main function was to punish prisoners

C The principle referred to in the report as positive custody

D The development of more severe prison regimes to prevent escapes

3 The phrase 'prison works' was promoted by which United Kingdom Home Secretary:

A Sir Robert Peel

B William Whitelaw

C Michael Howard

D Jack Straw

4 One important feature of the justice model was:

A To ensure that victims of crime receive justice from the criminal justice system

B To ensure that an offender's background was given full consideration by the court

C To ensure that a sentence reflected the seriousness of the crime that had been committed

D To ensure that offenders received the full sentence that was imposed by the court

5 Approaches used in prison that seek to tackle the causes of offending behaviour are known as:

A Rehabilitation programmes

B Cognitive behavioural programmes

C Correctional programmes

D The justice model

6 What is the approximate cost of a custodial sentence in England and Wales?

A £20,000 per year

B £30,000 per year

C £40,000 per year

D £50,000 per year

16

Youth crime and youth justice systems

Historically, children who broke the law were treated in the same way as adult offenders. However, the belief that young people could not totally be held responsible for their actions underpinned developments that established separate systems of youth justice. This chapter examines the system that deals with crime committed by those below the age of 18. It considers the philosophy that underpins a separate system of juvenile justice and the manner in which such systems operate. It also considers how specific types of misbehaviour associated with young people especially – such as antisocial behaviour – are dealt with by the criminal justice system.

Key idea

A youth justice system deals with crime that is committed by young persons who have reached the age of criminal responsibility but who are below the age of adults.

A child cannot be charged with a criminal offence until he or she has reached the age of criminal responsibility. This is the age at which a child is deemed to know right from wrong and can thus be held accountable for criminal actions that have been undertaken. This age varies from one country to another: in England and Wales it is ten years of age (a limit introduced by the 1963 Children and Young Persons Act) but in other countries is higher.

In the US the age of criminal responsibility is determined by each state and ranges from 6 to 12 years. It is 12 years in the Irish Republic and Holland, 13 years in France, 14 in Germany, Spain, Italy and Denmark and 15 in Finland, Iceland and Norway.

Additionally, the presumption of *doli incapax* historically applied in England and Wales whereby it could not automatically be assumed that children aged between 10 and 13 who had committed a criminal offence were responsible for their actions. Accordingly, the task of the prosecution initially was to prove that the child did know right from wrong and was thus aware of the consequences of his or her actions and could be placed on trial for them. This presumption was abolished by the 1998 Crime and Disorder Act and henceforth it became the role of defence lawyers to prove that a child was incapable of determining whether an action was right or wrong and could thus not be held responsible for criminal actions that had been committed.

Historically, in many countries children were regarded as 'small adults' and, if they committed a crime, were dealt with in the same way as an adult offender and were subject to the same punishments: in England and Wales, for example, children below the age of 14 could be imprisoned and the death penalty could be applied to children and young persons until the enactment of the 1908 Children Act. During the twentieth century, a separate system of juvenile justice was developed and subsequently offenders between 10 and 18 years of age were placed under a number of different categories to which different types of punishments could be applied. The 1933 Children and Young Persons Act classified persons below the age of 14 as 'children' and those aged 14 to 17 as 'young persons'. Those aged 18 to 20 are often referred to as 'young adults', although this designation is not derived from legislation. For convenience, in this chapter we will use the term 'juvenile offender' in connection with those aged 10 to 17.

The development of the youth justice system in England and Wales

A small number of important initiatives took place in the nineteenth century to specifically cater for juvenile offenders. These included the 1838 Parkhurst Act that provided a state-run prison facility for juvenile offenders. However, the main developments took place in the twentieth century. These were:

▶ **The 1907 Probation of Offenders Act:** This measure placed probation work on a statutory footing, and probation officers were given specific responsibilities in connection with juvenile offenders;

▶ **The 1908 Children Act:** This legislation created a separate system of juvenile courts to deal with young offenders. They were modelled on a system that was pioneered in Chicago in 1899. These were renamed Youth Courts by the 1991 Criminal Justice Act and handled criminal offences carried out by those aged 10 to 17;

▶ **The 1908 Crime Prevention Act:** This measure created a new form of custodial regime for offenders aged 16 to 20 (raised to 21 in 1936) that was called a 'borstal'. Borstals operated according to a strict disciplinary regime within which offenders learned a craft or trade that would enable them to find employment when they were released. These were renamed Youth Custody Centres by the 1982 Criminal Justice Act and subsequently Young Offender Institutions by the 1988 Criminal Justice Act. These cater for those aged 15 to 21;

▶ **The 1948 Children and Young Persons Act:** This legislation created Detention Centres to cater for persistent young offenders aged 15 to 17 and a non-custodial sentence which required less serious juvenile and young adult offenders to attend Attendance Centres for brief periods during which time they would engage in physical training and constructive hobby programmes;

▶ **The 1998 Crime and Disorder Act:** This measure placed multi-agency (or partnership) work on a statutory basis which, in connection with juvenile crime, entailed the creation of Youth Offending Teams. The act also created a number of new court orders which aimed to combat youth crime by early interventions directed at juvenile criminals or their families;

▶ **The 1999 Youth Justice and Criminal Evidence Act:** This legislation introduced restorative justice into the state's response to juvenile crime through the mechanism of a referral order issued by a youth court;

▶ **The 2008 Criminal Justice and Immigration Act:** This amalgamated a number of existing community sentences related to juvenile crime (such as curfew orders and supervision orders) into a generic youth rehabilitation order. This contained a number of sanctions (termed 'requirements') and courts were able to impose as many of these on a young offender as they felt appropriate.

Youth Offending Teams (YOTs) and Youth Offender Panels (YOPs)

Key idea

YOTs and YOPs perform important roles in the contemporary operations of the youth justice system in England and Wales.

YOTs and YOPs were important initiatives introduced by the 1997–2001 Labour government that underpin the operations of the contemporary youth justice system in England and Wales.

In 1996 a report by the Audit Commission entitled *Misspent Youth* offered a number of criticisms of the existing way in which the juvenile justice system operated. One of these was that the agencies that dealt with young people were insufficiently co-ordinated and a situation in which each pursued its own ends could add to the burdens placed on other agencies. For example, a school that excluded troublesome children might create problems for the local police that arose from youths hanging around on street corners with nothing constructive to do.

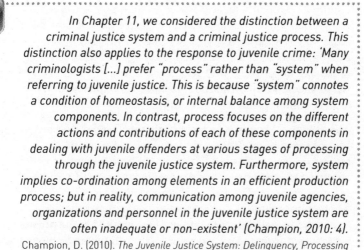

In Chapter 11, we considered the distinction between a criminal justice system and a criminal justice process. This distinction also applies to the response to juvenile crime: 'Many criminologists [...] prefer "process" rather than "system" when referring to juvenile justice. This is because "system" connotes a condition of homeostasis, or internal balance among system components. In contrast, process focuses on the different actions and contributions of each of these components in dealing with juvenile offenders at various stages of processing through the juvenile justice system. Furthermore, system implies co-ordination among elements in an efficient production process; but in reality, communication among juvenile agencies, organizations and personnel in the juvenile justice system are often inadequate or non-existent' (Champion, 2010: 4).

Champion, D. (2010). *The Juvenile Justice System: Delinquency, Processing and the Law.* New Jersey: Prentice Hall, 6 ed.

The solution to the lack of co-ordination by agencies that dealt with young people was the creation of YOTs under the provisions of the 1998 Crime and Disorder Act. This required a number of agencies that included the police, probation officers, social workers and education and health staff to formally co-ordinate their activities using local government as their organizational framework. To do this, personnel would be seconded to the YOT from the participating agencies and work under the direction of a YOT manager. The role of the YOT includes developing and supervising intervention programmes to combat youth offending (including community sentences imposed by the courts), determining whether intervention is required in the cases of juvenile offenders who have received final warnings from the police and preparing pre-sentence reports and other information required by the courts in connection with criminal proceedings against juveniles. Under exceptional circumstances, intervention of a non-punitive kind can be directed at children below the age of ten.

The 1999 Youth Justice and Criminal Evidence Act required a Youth Court to issue a referral order to a first-time offender aged 10 to 17 who pleaded guilty to an offence that did not require a custodial sentence. This legislation gave statutory recognition to restorative justice (a principle we will consider more fully in Chapter 17). The referral order replaced the existing sentence of a conditional discharge and had the effect of passing the offender over to a Youth Offender Panel (YOP) whose membership included representatives drawn from the local community and a member of the YOT.

The YOP would convene a meeting that included the offender, his or her family, and either the victim(s) or a community representative which would draw up (and subsequently monitor an offender's compliance with) a programme termed a youth offender contract. This had to contain reparative provisions and whose main intention was to prevent reoffending behaviour. Successful completion of the programme resulted in the offence being wiped from the official record – the official terminology being that the offence was regarded as a spent conviction under the terms of the 1974 Rehabilitation of Offenders Act. This means that it does not have to be subsequently declared save under exceptional circumstances.

An important issue relating to combating juvenile crime is at what stage should intervention by the state be initiated.

Social methods of crime prevention (that are referred to in Chapter 4) are often used in connection with preventing juvenile offending by seeking to identify those who might commit crime and intervene before this potential can be realized. 'Offending by young people is associated with a range of risk factors including inadequate parental supervision; aggressive or hyperactive behaviour in early childhood; truancy and exclusion from school; peer group pressure to offend; unstable living conditions; lack of training and employment, and drug and alcohol abuse. These factors can be used to target measures to prevent crime by identifying areas where young people are at risk' (Audit Commission, 1996: 57).

Audit Commission (1996). *Misspent Youth.* Abingdon: Audit Commission Publications.

The youth justice system in America

Key idea

As in England and Wales, a separate system for dealing with young offenders also exists in the US.

In the US a separate system exists to deal with offences committed by those below the age of 18. Historically, a young person would be tried within the same system that applied to adult offenders. In 1899 Chicago pioneered a separate court to deal with young offenders under the age of 16 and other states followed suit either by establishing specific juvenile courts (sometimes called 'family courts') or by providing for cases involving juvenile offenders to be heard in separate sessions of the regular courts. Juries are not involved in proceedings of this nature. Offenders below the age of 18 years are regarded as delinquent rather than criminal and in many states this differentiation is upheld by the plea of 'delinquent' or 'not delinquent' (rather than 'guilty' or 'not guilty') that is entered at the outset of the trial of juvenile offenders and (when an offence is proved) by the use of the term 'adjudicated delinquent' as opposed to 'convicted'.

Young offenders may be handed out conditional dispositions by a juvenile court which typically consist of probation. Youths on probation may be required to meet conditions imposed on them as part of their sentence such as alcohol or drug counselling or therapy and psychological counselling. Reparation to victims of crime may also be imposed on youths who have committed property offences. The 1968 Juvenile Delinquency Prevention and Control Act made federal funding available for local schemes designed to divert juveniles from crime and custodial regimes were historically focused on reforming the habits of offenders.

Historically, children who committed crimes that warranted a custodial sentence would be sent to adult prisons. However, during the early years of the nineteenth century reformatories were pioneered to specifically cater for juvenile offenders which emphasized the goal of rehabilitation. The first of these was the New York House of Refuge that was established in 1824 and similar facilities were subsequently set up in other states. The 1974 Juvenile Justice and Delinquency Prevention Act gave financial incentives to states to separate adult and juvenile offenders, with the latter being housed in juvenile correctional facilities or state training schools.

The focus of the American youth justice system was initially on the rehabilitation of offenders. However, concerns regarding rising juvenile crime rates towards the end of the 1980s resulted in a more punitive approach which included allowing states to formally try juveniles as adult offenders for some violent crimes and increased numbers of juvenile offenders were placed in custodial regimes. Execution of juvenile offenders also remains a sentencing option, even if it is used rarely.

Case study: The Scottish youth justice system

A distinct system is used in connection with juvenile crime in Scotland where offending by young people below the age of 16 is primarily treated as a welfare issue. The procedure was introduce by the 1995 Children (Scotland) Act and is now governed by the 2011 Children's Hearings (Scotland) Act which created a non-departmental public body – Children's Hearings Scotland – and a National Convenor of Children's Hearings Scotland to supervise the new arrangements.

Offenders aged 8 to 15 are referred by the police to the Children's Reporter Administration which determines whether to refer the matter to the Children's Hearings System which is conducted by a Children's Panel. Hearings provide a mechanism whereby a multi-agency approach can be brought to bear on addressing the causes of the child's offending behaviour. The 2011 Act replaced the existing 32 local Children's Panels with a single national panel which recruits local members. As a result of the hearings, the panel can decide to take no further action or it may impose a Supervision Requirement to which a wide range of conditions can be attached.

Since the raising of the age of criminal responsibility in Scotland from 8 to 12 years in 2011, offending by children aged 8 to 11 has to be conducted through the hearings system. Offenders aged 16 to 17 are referred by the police to the Procurator Fiscal who decides whether to refer the matter to the criminal courts. The case may, however, alternatively be referred to the Children's Hearing which has the power to impose a range of penalties including fines, probation and custody.

The principles underpinning youth justice systems

Key idea

A tension exists as to whether youth justice systems should place the welfare of the child or the need to protect society from crime at the top of their agenda.

Youth justice systems face a key dilemma as to whose interests should be uppermost in their concerns. In other words, should the welfare of the child who has either committed crime or is deemed at risk of doing so be the main concern of the system, or should the key role of a youth justice system be to protect society from the harmful effects of juvenile crime?

A juvenile justice system will cater for both of these considerations, but the existence of these competing aims is responsible for creating tensions within the process.

Determining which of these two principles should dominate the operations of the juvenile justice system is influenced by a number of key parties that include professionals working in this area of justice, pressure groups that embrace the concerns of juvenile offending behaviour and the political preferences of politicians. The latter are frequently informed by public opinion, the mood of which is subject to change that affects whether the juvenile justice system caters for the welfare or the punishment of the young offender.

Historical periods in which sympathy for the plight of young offenders dominated the philosophy of the youth justice system are typically characterized by approaches that seek to divert young offenders from custodial regimes in the belief that this will simply place them on the road to a future criminal career. The alternatives include community penalties, treatment programmes and formal warnings issued by agencies such as the police that do not constitute a criminal conviction. In England and Wales the 1969 Children and Young Persons Act was underpinned by this approach and sought to place the welfare principle as the main concern of the juvenile justice system. One justification for doing this was a belief that much juvenile crime was of a temporary (or transient) nature, part of the process of growing up and which would not develop into a permanent way of life.

An emphasis on the welfare of the young offender may result in perceptions that the juvenile justice system is overly lenient towards crime committed by young people and be used to argue that more punitive approaches should be directed at this problem. Concerns of this nature are often orchestrated by media-inspired moral panics in which a serious episode of juvenile crime is highlighted and used to justify a perception that the behaviour of some young people (especially those at the lower end of the social ladder) is out of control and needs to be firmly regulated by the use of punitive sanctions.

The murder by two youths of the toddler Jamie Bulger in England in 1993 is one example of a moral panic that inspired a much harsher response to juvenile crime that was underpinned by the penal populist concern of 'getting tough with criminals'. It gave rise to developments that included reduced use of cautioning, an increase in the period that a young offender could spend in a Youth Offender Institution and the introduction of 'high intensity training' regimes (that were popularly, albeit erroneously, referred to as 'boot camps') in two Youth Offender Institutions in which persistent offenders aged 18 to 21 were offered a last chance to mend their criminal ways. Punitive approaches towards juvenile crime were continued under post-1997 Labour governments, one aspect of which was an attempt to regulate the behaviour of young people by clamping down on antisocial behaviour.

Spotlight

'Boot camps' entail highly disciplined environments that were modelled on training regimes used by the American military and were subsequently applied to correctional facilities for young offenders. Today the term is used to refer to any demanding form of requirements imposed on subjects, including those who succeed in progressing through the early rounds of *X-Factor*.

The regulation of antisocial behaviour in England and Wales

Key idea

Tackling antisocial behaviour, especially that committed by young people, has been high on the agenda of governments since the latter years of the twentieth century.

Most aspects of antisocial behaviour constituted a nuisance rather than a crime and could thus not be dealt with by the formal mechanisms of the criminal justice system. It was, however, viewed as a serious problem by members of the general public and was an important factor in explaining why, after the mid 1990s, the *fear* of crime failed to reduce at the same rate as the occurrence of it.

The response to this problem that was put forward by the Labour government was the introduction of curfew notices and antisocial behaviour orders (usually referred to as ASBOs) in the 1998 Crime and Disorder Act.

ASBOs were issued by magistrates' courts following a successful application that was initially made by the police or a local authority, although subsequently other agencies such as social landlords could make similar requests – in the form of antisocial behaviour injunctions – to deal with problem tenants. They could be directed at individuals or groups (such as families) whose actions caused, or were likely to cause, *harassment, alarm or distress to one or more persons not of the same household* but which fell short of a criminal act. An ASBO contained provisions that were designed to halt these activities, for example by imposing a curfew or prohibiting a person from specific locations. Failure to observe these requirements could result in a prison sentence.

ASBOs were not confined to juveniles and could be applied to any person over ten years of age, although young people were often targeted by them. However, other developments of a similar nature exclusively applied to juveniles. Curfew notices were introduced by the 1998 Crime and Disorder Act and enabled children under ten years of age (an age limit that was extended to under 16 years of age by the 2001 Criminal Justice and Police Act) to be banned from being out on the streets in a stipulated geographic area after a designated time within the period 9 p.m. to 6 a.m. unless in the control of a responsible person aged 18 or over. Those who ignored such an order could be returned to their homes by a police officer and could be the subject of further interventions such as a child safety order. These provisions were repealed in 2009, but new initiatives associated with combating antisocial behaviour (such as dispersal orders that were provided for in the 2003 Anti-social Behaviour Act) were also exclusively directed at young persons below the age of 16.

Although data on the number of ASBOs issued could be used to provide evidence that the government was taking the problem of antisocial behaviour seriously, they contained several weaknesses. They made no attempt to get to the root causes of antisocial behaviour (especially when this was committed by young people) and seemed to assume that a punitive approach would solve the problem. However, the conditions contained in ASBOs were frequently ignored by those who were subject to them and there was also a danger that, far from coercing younger people into correct behaviour, they might instead be regarded as a 'badge of honour' that secured prestige within a peer group.

> The emphasis that has been placed on combating antisocial behaviour derives 'from the philosophy underpinning the "broken windows" approach to dealing with "incivilities"' in the US in the 1980s' (Wain, 2007: 20).
>
> This approach argued that 'The citizen who fears the ill-smelling drunk, the rowdy teenager, or the importuning beggar is not merely expressing his distaste for unseemly behavior; he is also giving voice to a bit of folk wisdom that happens to be a correct generalization – namely, that serious street crime flourishes in areas in which disorderly behavior goes unchecked. [...] Muggers and robbers, whether opportunistic or professional, believe they reduce their chances of being caught or even identified if they operate on streets where potential victims are already intimidated by prevailing conditions' (Kelling and Wilson, 1982).
>
> Kelling, G. and Wilson, J. (1982). 'Broken Windows: The Police and Neighbourhood Safety', *Atlantic Monthly*, 1982 (available online at http://www.theatlantic.com/magazine/archive/1982/03/broken-windows/4465/1/e) [accessed 22 June 2012].
>
> Wain, N. with Burney, E. (2007). *The ASBO: Wrong Turning, Dead End*. London: The Howard League for Penal Reform.

Problems such as these made the 2010 Coalition government sceptical of this approach towards antisocial behaviour. Their intention is to replace ASBOs with a new raft of measures that include criminal behaviour orders and crime prevention injunctions. The August 2011 riots, however, delayed the implementation of this reform.

Dig deeper

Champion, D., Merlo, and Benekos, P. (2012). *The Juvenile Justice System: Delinquency, Processing and the Law*, 7th edn. Upper Saddle River, NJ: Prentice Hall.

Muncie, J. (2009). *Youth and Crime*, 3rd edn. London: Sage.

Smith, R. (2007). *Youth Justice: Ideas, Policy, Practice*. London: Routledge.

Squires, P. and Stephen, D. (2005). *Rougher Justice: Anti-social Behaviour and Young People*. Cullompton, Devon: Willan Publishing.

Fact-check

1 In England and Wales, which custodial institution was set up by the 1908 Crime Prevention Act?
   A Bortsals
   B Boot camps
   C Young Offenders' Institutions
   D Correction centres

2 Whose interests does the welfare principle seek to place at the forefront of youth justice systems?
   A The general public
   B The state
   C The offender
   D The victim

3 In England and Wales the age of criminal responsibility is:
   A 8 years
   B 10 years
   C 12 years
   D 15 years

4 Which multi-agency initiative was created to deal with juvenile offenders in England and Wales by the 1998 Crime and Disorder Act?
   A Multi-agency Public Protection Arrangements
   B Neighbourhood policing teams
   C Youth Offending Teams
   D Youth Offender Panels

5 Which intervention to deal with juvenile offending is unique to Scotland?
   A The Sheriff's Court
   B The Hearings System
   C The High Court of Justiciary
   D Restorative justice

6 In England and Wales the reform of the youth justice system in the 1990s was inspired by a report entitled *Misspent Youth*. The agency that produced this report was:

A The Prisons Inspectorate

B The Youth Justice Board

C The Home Office

D The Audit Commission

17

Punishment in the community

Those who break the law will (if caught) be punished for their actions. However, there is a wide range of options that can be used as responses to crime. In particular, there exists a distinction between serious offences that require the offender to be removed from society and placed in prison and less serious crimes for which the lawbreaker can serve a penalty while remaining a member of his or her community. This chapter examines penalties that are imposed on offenders which are served in the community as opposed to custodial regimes. It examines the nature of community-based sentences and the issues that are raised by the use of these as a response to crime.

Community sentences

Key idea

Sentences served in the community may impose a wide range of demands upon an offender. These may include performing unpaid work within the community or taking part in treatment programmes.

There are various ways whereby those who commit criminal offences can be punished for their crimes. For example, an offender may be fined for his or her offence. This penalty was traditionally a sentence of a court, but in England and Wales low-level crime and disorder may be punished by an on-the-spot fine handed out by a police officer. This procedure is often referred to as summary justice.

In this chapter, however, we will focus on sentences which are served in the community but which have an element of supervision attached to them. In England and Wales this supervision was traditionally provided by the National Probation Service, although in recent years some aspects of this work have been carried out by private sector companies. Electronic monitoring (or tagging) is also used to monitor an offender's compliance with the terms of a community sentence.

In England and Wales community-based sentences for adult offenders that contain an element of supervision are governed by the 2003 Criminal Justice Act. This legislation replaced earlier forms of community-based sentences (such as probation orders and community service orders) with a new penalty termed a community order. This comprises a wide range of components (which are termed 'requirements'), consisting of:

▶ the unpaid work requirement (which since 2008 has been called Community Payback)

▶ the activity requirement

▶ the programme requirement

▶ the prohibited activity requirement

▶ the curfew requirement

- the exclusion requirement

- the residence requirement

- the mental health treatment requirement

- the drug rehabilitation requirement

- the alcohol treatment requirement

- the supervision requirement

- the attendance centre requirement.

A magistrate or judge who imposes a community order on an offender identifies which requirements from this list the offender will have to complete. There is no limit on the number of requirements that an offender is obliged to complete, and the duration varies (for example the unpaid work requirement is between 40 and 300 hours).

The community order may be applied to adult offenders, aged 18 years and above. A similar sentence (the Youth Rehabilitation Order) applies to offenders below the age of 18.

Case study: Community Payback in England and Wales

Community Payback is an example of a sentence served in the community rather than in custody. Its origins lie in community service orders that were introduced into England and Wales by the 1972 Criminal Justice Act and which became incorporated into the generic community order as the unpaid work requirement.

The aim of a sentence of this nature was to ensure that the penalty inflicted upon an offender provided a tangible benefit to the community. Unlike probation orders that were used in the latter decades of the twentieth century, this sentence was seen as a punishment rather than a mechanism to reform the habits of the offender and this philosophy underpinned the introduction of the community order by the 2003 Criminal Justice Act.

However, in common with other forms of community sentences, the unpaid work requirement of the community order was not viewed as being sufficiently punitive in an era dominated by the 'get tough with criminals' approach of punitive populism. This was important, since the unpaid work requirement was the most commonly used requirement imposed on offenders under the 2003 legislation. Accordingly, following a recommendation arising from a review conducted by Louise Casey in 2008, the unpaid work requirement order was renamed 'community payback'. In order to make this form of punishment more visible to the community (and thus enhance their confidence in it as a response to crime), those subject to it were required to wear fluorescent jackets which clearly identified the offender who was making amends for his or her crime.

It remains debateable whether community payback is viewed by the public or by the magistrates and judges who impose it as a sufficiently robust response to crime. The nature of the work, the vigour with which it is performed and concerns about the completion rate of sentences of this nature may lead to conclusions that this is too soft a response to crime.

The supervision of community sentences in England and Wales

Key idea

Community sentences are supervised by an agency such as the National Probation Service in England and Wales.

In England and Wales approximately 180,000 community sentences were handed out by the courts in 2011. These sentences are supervised by the Probation Service. This agency (which since 2001 has become the National Probation Service) was set up in 1907 by the Probation of Offenders Act. This legislation placed probation work on a statutory footing and allowed courts to appoint and pay probation officers whose role was to advise, assist and befriend offenders within their communities. The role of probation officers was to supervise offenders who were given non-custodial sentences that required supervision (historically, in the form of probation orders and community service orders but, since the enactment of the 2003 Criminal Justice Act, in the form of requirements derived from the community order) and also to supervise those who had been released from custody on licence.

The supervision that was provided by probation officers sought to bring about changes in an offender's habits and behaviour. Initially, they did this through individualized treatment that entailed regular one-to-one meetings between themselves and offenders who had been placed in their care.

However, this form of intervention became questioned in the latter decades of the twentieth century. The Probation Service and the community penalties that it administered seemed overly lenient towards offenders in an era that was dominated by the 'get tough with criminals' approach that underpinned penal populism. Increasingly, therefore, the role performed by the Probation Service was redefined to emphasize the punishment as opposed to the treatment aspects of community sentences. One aspect of this new approach was that community services orders were renamed community punishment orders by the 2000 Criminal Justice and Court Services Act. This new approach also involved probation officers engaging in risk-assessment techniques which emphasized a new role for the Probation Service of ensuring that society was protected from crime.

A second factor that affected the historic role of the Probation Service was a form of pessimism that queried the effectiveness of traditional forms of probation work to prevent reoffending. The solution to this was the development of a range of programmes that were designed to alter behaviour patterns and whose effectiveness could be evaluated. These programmes were piloted and, if deemed effective, were rolled out nationally in the form of accredited programmes. This meant that the role of probation officers shifted from individualized casework to that of placing offenders on standardized programmes that were deemed to be appropriate to their offending behaviour and monitoring their progress on these programmes. This development introduced a considerable degree of centralization into the work of the Probation Service and was at the expense of the discretion traditionally exercised by probation officers.

The strengths and weaknesses of community sentences

Community sentences possess a number of advantages. They reduce the burden placed on prisons, thus enabling these institutions to devote more attention to reforming the habits of serious offenders. Their success rate in reforming the habits of the criminal are generally judged to be more successful than short-term prison sentences of below one year. Further, they bring about this outcome at considerably less expense than is occasioned by custodial sentences. It has been estimated that around 15 persons can be supervised by the Probation Service at the same cost as imprisoning one offender for a year.

However, community sentences do possess weaknesses. The most important of these are that the public do not view them as a sufficiently harsh response to crime: they regard offenders who walk away from a court with a community penalty as opposed to a custodial sentence as having 'got off lightly' – a view that is often shared by offenders. One aspect of this problem in England and Wales concerned the historic reluctance of probation officers to initiate sanctions (we refer to these as 'breach proceedings') against those offenders who failed to comply with the requirements that were placed upon them by community sentences. This situation tended to erode the trust that magistrates and judges had in community penalties and encouraged them to use custodial sentences instead.

Advocates of community penalties believe that they possess many advantages over imprisonment: 'Given what we know [...] about other advantages of punishment in the community, such as its lower costs, its general tendency to be less dehumanising than custody and to drive fewer of those who endure it to self-harm and suicide, the lack of any demonstrable superiority on the part of institutional sentencing in controlling recidivism should mean that it is the use of custody not community sentencing that has to be justified and defended' (Brownlee, 1998: 180).

Brownlee, I. (1998). *Community Punishment*. Harlow: Longman.

One further difficulty with community sentences is that penalties of this nature may be applied to those who have committed relatively minor offences that might not merit official intervention but which might, for example, be dealt with informally, perhaps by a police officer warning a person against repeating an action and threatening to take formal proceedings should this advice be ignored.

It is in this respect, therefore, that community penalties can be used to draw increased numbers of low-level offenders into the formal machinery of the criminal justice system whose actions could be responded to by unofficial methods. We refer to this as 'net widening', which means the increased ability that community penalties provide to the state for exercising punitive sanctions against its citizens who commit minor transgressions of the law (and which also increase its capacity to exercise surveillance over increased numbers of the population).

A further problem with net widening is that an offender who is sucked into the formal machinery of justice at a relatively early stage in his or her criminal career may be unable to break away from lawbreaking. Such a person becomes known to the police who may subsequently be on the lookout for him or her. The person may also suffer from a sense of social exclusion and be encouraged to mix socially with others who have also acquired the label of 'criminal'. This situation may result in the development of more serious forms of offending behaviour.

> *Community penalties may promote the use of formal responses to minor criminal acts, thereby extending the scope of the criminal justice system: 'far from reducing the restrictions on criminals who might otherwise have been sent to prison community penalties create a new clientele of criminals who are controlled by other mechanisms. The boundaries between freedom and confinement become blurred. The "net" of social control is thus thrown even wider into the community, its thinner mesh designed to entrap even smaller "fish". Once caught in the net, the penetration of disciplinary intervention is even deeper, reaching every aspect of the criminal's life (Worrall, 1997: 25).*
> Worrall, A. (1997), *Punishment in the Community: The Future of Criminal Justice.* Harlow: Longman.

Community penalties are also widely used in the US. Around 4.9 million persons were under community supervision in 2010 (compared to a prison population of 2.25 million), the great bulk of whom were on probation (the remainder being on parole having served a portion of their custodial sentence). More than 90,000 probation officers and specialists in correctional treatment are employed to administer these sentences. Probation officers serve at state, county and city level.

Restorative justice

Key idea

Restorative justice is a community-based response to crime whose main aim is to secure the reintegration of offenders into their communities.

A further form of a community-oriented response to crime is provided by restorative justice. A number of other terms are used to describe this approach including 'positive justice', 're-integrative justice', 'relational justice', 'reparative justice' and 'restitutive justice'. It is carried out through a wide range of activities: initially it was 'virtually synonymous with a specific model of practice called Victim–Offender Reconciliation Program (VORP) or Victim–Offender Mediation (VOM)' which entailed a one-to-one mediation meeting facilitated by a neutral mediator but latterly has been identified with other models, including community mediation and conferencing.

Family group conferencing as an option for dealing with young offenders was first developed in New Zealand under the 1989 Children and Young People and Their Families Act. It was based upon the traditional Maori methods of conflict resolution.

Conferencing was subsequently adopted in Australia, North America and Europe. It takes several forms that include family group conferencing, community group conferencing and peace-making circles which are convened by a person termed a 'facilitator'. All forms of conferencing seek to bring people together in order to enter into a dialogue which seeks to enable the victim to explain the impact of the crime on him or her and for the perpetrator to explain his or her actions and to agree to undertake actions designed to repair the harm caused by a crime. This frequently entails the offender making reparation to the victim or the community.

The formal mechanisms of the criminal justice system are thus dispensed with in favour of an approach to crime that is fashioned within the framework of neighbourhood or community involvement. This decentralized form of justice aims to make it easier for offenders to be reintegrated into their communities: in England and Wales this approach is frequently used in connection with low-level juvenile crime, the mechanism through which it is applied being the Youth Offender Panel that was initiated by the 1999 Youth Justice and Criminal Evidence Act. In other countries, restorative justice is used to deal with a wider range of criminal actions.

Restorative justice can be conducted through a wide range of mechanisms and was initially developed from a model that was called Victim-Offender Reconciliation Programme (VORM). This was based upon a one-to-one mediation meeting between offender and victim that was organized (the technical word is 'facilitated') by a neutral mediator. Restorative justice has subsequently been based on different models that include community mediation and conferencing but all entail some form of meeting in which a dialogue can be entered into between those who are affected by a crime. These may include the victim, offender, the victim's and offender's family members, community representatives and criminal justice practitioners.

> Restorative justice 'refers to a process that brings people together in dialogue to gain understanding and repair the damage caused by a crime or conflict' (Roberts, 2004: 245). It has been defined as consisting of 'values, aims and processes that have as their common factor attempts to repair the harm caused by criminal behaviour' (Young and Hoyle, 2003: 200).
>
> The message is that 'restorative justice deserves, and is achieving, a rightful place within the mainstream of criminological discourse. More than this perhaps, it offers the opportunity to abandon entirely punitive methods of dealing with those who break the law, to make offenders more accountable, and to give appropriate recognition to the legitimate needs of the victims of crime' (Cameron, 2008: xviii).

Cameron, T. (2008). *Criminal Punishment & Restorative Justice.* Winchester: Waterside Press.

Roberts, A. (2004). 'Is Restorative Justice Tied to Specific Models of Practice?', in H. Zerr and B. Toews (eds), *Critical Issues in Restorative Justice.* New York: Criminal Justice Press.

Young, R. and Hoyle, C. (2003). 'Restorative Justice and Punishment', in S. McConville (ed.), *The Use of Punishment.* Cullompton, Devon: Willan Publishing.

WHAT ARE THE KEY PRINCIPLES OF RESTORATIVE JUSTICE?

Restorative justice is not concerned with exacting retribution on criminals – indeed, some advocates of restorative justice view it as a response to crime as opposed to a form of punishment. Instead, it seeks to focus on the damage or harm that a crime has caused to a member of the community as the basis for the offender seeking to put wrongs to rights by making adequate amends for the criminal action – amends that will also enable his or her reintegration into the community. 'Adequate amends' are likely to go beyond saying 'sorry' and entail some form of financial – or equivalent – recompense that demonstrates that offenders have acknowledged their wrongdoing and wish to do something positive to remedy the harm they have caused. One advantage of restorative justice is that, whereas in criminal trials in a court of law the main actors are lawyers hired by the defence and prosecution, magistrates, judges and juries, within restorative justice the key players are those most affected by a criminal act who (especially victims of crime) are often marginalized within formalized legal procedures.

A key issue affecting restorative justice is how offenders react to the process. One way whereby they can be persuaded to take personal responsibility for what they have done and acknowledge the wrongfulness of their actions is through shaming – the processes involved in restorative justice make them feel ashamed of what they have done. The process of shaming is used as a mechanism to secure the reconciliation of members of the community whom crime has brought into conflict. It is thus termed 're-integrative shaming'.

> *Restorative justice may operate by making a criminal feel ashamed of their actions and form the basis of the offender's reintegration into society: 'reintegrative shaming means that expressions of community disapproval, which may range from a mild rebuke to degradation ceremonies (serious denunciation) are followed by gestures of reacceptance into the community of law-abiding citizens' (Braithwaite and Roche, 2001: 74).*
> Braithwaite, J. and Roche, D. (2001). 'Responsibility and Restorative Justice', in G. Bazemore and M. Schiff (eds), *Restorative Community Justice: Repairing Harm and Transforming Communities*. Cincinnati, OH: Anderson Publishing.

However, the role of shaming within restorative justice is not universally acknowledged. Although it is not designed as a means of punishment to embarrass or humiliate an offender, there is no guarantee that those on the receiving end of the process will not view it in this light and react negatively towards the process. It has also been argued that shaming will work more effectively in societies that are underpinned by group-oriented values (such as Japan) than those rooted in individualism (such as the US) and that some offenders – for whatever reasons – may feel no sense of guilt for the actions they have carried out.

There are also other difficulties associated with restorative justice. The dialogue between offender and victim which lies at the heart of restorative justice may not always be readily forthcoming. The offender may unable to express him- or herself in any meaningful manner and victims may not wish to be involved in face-to-face meetings with those who have caused them harm. Further, the general public may regard this approach as overly lenient towards offenders if they regard the process as one whereby offenders merely have to apologize for their actions (whether they mean it or not) and be let off.

Dig deeper

Johnstone, G. (2012). *A Restorative Justice Reader.* London: Routledge.

Raynor, P. and Vanstone, M. (2002). *Understanding Community Penalties: Probation, Policy and Social Change*. Buckingham: Open University Press.

Winstone, J. and Pakes, F. (eds) (2005). *Community Justice: Issues for Probation and Criminal Justice.* Cullompton, Devon: Willan Publishing.

Worrall, A. and Hoy, C. (1997). *Punishment in the Community: Managing Offenders, Making Choices.* Cullompton, Devon: Willan Publishing.

Young, R. and Hoyle, C. (2003). 'Restorative Justice and Punishment', in S. McConville (ed.), *The Use of Punishment.* Cullompton, Devon: Willan Publishing.

Fact-check

1 In England and Wales, what new initiative concerning community penalties was introduced by the 2003 Criminal Justice Act?
   A The Community Order
   B The Probation Order
   C The Community Sentence Order
   D The Community Rehabilitation Order

2 In terms of preventing reoffending, community penalties are:
   A Less effective than short-term custodial sentences
   B More effective than short-term custodial sentences
   C More or less the same in terms of effectiveness as short-term custodial sentences
   D Incapable of being evaluated to judge their success or otherwise

3 In England and Wales in 2011, approximately how many sentences passed by the courts were in the form of a community penalty?
   A 180,000
   B 250,000
   C 300,000
   D 500,000

4 The public are often sceptical about the use of community penalties as a response to crime as:
   A They are very expensive to administer
   B They are viewed as unnecessarily harsh on offenders
   C They are seen as being too soft on offenders
   D They are complex and nobody understands what exactly they involve

5 In England and Wales, following the publication of the Casey Report in 2008, the unpaid work requirement of the community order was replaced by:
   A The chain gang
   B The Welfare to Work programme
   C The New Deal for Offenders programme
   D Community Payback

6 In England and Wales which agency has the main responsibility for implementing community sentences?

A The Ministry of Justice

B The National Probation Service

C The police service

D The National Criminal Justice Board

18

Recidivism – what is it and how can we prevent it?

A considerable proportion of persons who break the law and are punished for their actions subsequently commit further criminal acts. We refer to this reoffending behaviour as 'recidivism'. This chapter focuses on those who, having committed a crime and served the sentence imposed on them by the courts, subsequently commit a further criminal act for which they are again convicted. In particular, we will examine the various methods that have been put forward in an attempt to prevent reoffending behaviour.

The nature of the problem

'Reoffending' is the term applied to those who, having committed a crime for which they are convicted, go on to commit a further crime. However, this crime (and others subsequently committed) may not be detected and thus they are not punished for it. There is thus little reliable data available to gauge the extent of reoffending behaviour since some of it is not subject to any form of penalty.

'Reconviction' refers to a criminal who, having completed a sentence that was imposed on him or her for a crime they committed, commits a further criminal offence and is convicted for it. Statistics related to reconviction can easily be collected and form the basis of our information regarding recidivism.

Recidivism is a serious problem. In England and Wales around 60 to 65 per cent of prisoners are reconvicted within two years of their release. Figures released by the Ministry of Justice in 2010 indicated that in 14 prisons reconviction rates exceeded 70 per cent. This problem was especially acute among those given short-term prison sentences. The same set of figures indicated that recidivism among those who were given a community sentence rather than a brief spell of imprisonment was slightly lower.

Problems of a similar nature occur in the US. A study published by the Pew Center on the States in 2011 revealed that overall 45.4 per cent of people released from prison in 1999 and 43.3 per cent of those sent home in 2004 were re-incarcerated within three years, either for committing a new crime or for violating conditions governing their release.

Figures of this nature give rise to the suggestion that a considerable proportion of crime is committed by a relatively small group of hardened persistent offenders for whom crime is a way of life and punishment is viewed as an occupational hazard. Figures released by the Ministry of Justice in 2011 for England and Wales indicated that a total of 510,000 offences were committed in one year by 180,000 offenders who had been convicted in 2009.

How do we explain recidivism?

Key idea

Recidivism can be explained by a range of factors that include the background of prisoners and the inability of punishments to reform the habits of offenders.

There are a number of reasons that explain why convicted offenders carry out subsequent criminal acts.

An offender's background may make it difficult to find employment. Factors that include poor educational attainment and low levels of vocational skills make it hard to obtain work. The stigma of having been convicted of a crime (especially if the punishment was served in prison) may aggravate an already difficult situation and drive the ex-offender into committing further criminal acts in order to survive economically.

An offender who has served a prison sentence may encounter a wide range of problems when released. Family ties may have broken down while in prison and a released offender may experience homelessness. An offender may lack adequate practical and emotional support following release, the absence of which may encourage the return of past bad habits.

One difficulty faced by initiatives seeking to combat reoffending is that of continuity: a treatment programme started in prison, for example, might no longer be available when an offender is released back into the community. In England and Wales concerns of this nature (especially the tendency of the Probation Service and the Prison Service to operate as totally distinct agencies) resulted in the creation in 2004 of the National Offender Management Service (NOMS). This brought together the headquarters of the Probation and Prison Services whose aim was to provide end-to-end offender management which was designed to ensure that the support, guidance and treatment provided to offenders when in prison was maintained upon their release.

In 2003 a report by Patrick Carter argued that the Probation and Prison Services 'remain largely detached from one another and the structure of the system encourages concentration on the day-to-day operation of the services. A more strategic approach to the end-to-end management of offenders across their sentence is needed' (Carter, 2003: 23). This new approach was designed to ensure that both agencies could work together effectively to reduce reoffending.

Carter, P. (2003). *Managing Offenders, Reducing Crime: A New Approach.* London: Home Office Strategy Unit.

Reoffending may also occur when sentences are oriented towards punishment rather than the reform and rehabilitation of offenders. This focus may especially affect the environment of prisons whereby educational and vocational facilities are inadequately provided and in which factors such as prison overcrowding in England and Wales have resulted in security concerns dominating all aspects of prison life.

However, the desire to punish may also underpin sentences served in the community: in England and Wales, for example, offenders subjected to the unpaid work requirement of the community order (now referred to as 'Community Payback') are required to wear distinct clothing. Although this is designed to increase public confidence in the severity of community punishments, it may increase an offender's determination to commit crime in order to get his own back on society for the shame and humiliation that has been imposed on him or her.

Programmes to combat recidivism

Key idea

Treatment programmes, including those based on cognitive behavioural therapy, have been used in an attempt to stop those who have been convicted of a crime (offenders) from subsequently reoffending.

There are a number of ways through which recidivism might be tackled.

Various forms of treatment programmes may be delivered in conjunction with a punishment, whether this is served in the community or a prison. These may be designed to tackle a specific factor that influences criminal behaviour such as alcohol abuse or drug taking. Alternatively, initiatives to combat reoffending may also be delivered through programmes based upon the principles of cognitive behavioural therapy (CBT). Programmes of this nature include the Reasoning and Rehabilitation Programme that was pioneered in Ottawa, Canada, and subsequently introduced in prisons in England and Wales in 1992. The aim of these programmes is to focus on the thinking patterns and thought processes of offenders and address issues that include self-control, impulse management and critical and moral reasoning.

Cognitive behavioural therapy (CBT) is an approach that seeks to alter the thought processes which may result in criminal behaviour – this approach is 'directed toward changing distorted or dysfunctional cognitions (cognitive restructuring) or teaching new cognitive skills, and involves therapeutic techniques typically associated with CBT, i.e., structured learning experiences designed to affect such cognitive processes

as interpreting social cues, monitoring one's own thought processes, identifying and compensating for distortions and errors in thinking, reasoning about right and wrong behavior, generating alternative solutions, and making decisions about appropriate behavior' (Landenberger and Lipsey, 2005).

Landenberger, N. and Lipsey, M. (2005). 'The Positive Effects of Cognitive-Behavioral Programs for Offenders: A Meta-analysis of Factors Associated with Effective Treatment', *Journal of Experimental Criminology* 1: 451–76.

In England and Wales the partnership approach (which entails the co-operation of a number of agencies) underpins other initiatives that seek to prevent reoffending. One of these is integrated offender management. This focuses on offenders whose crimes have caused serious damage to their communities and requires a number of local agencies (within and outside of the criminal justice sector and including the voluntary sector) to co-ordinate activities that are designed to prevent a repetition of such behaviour. In doing this, integrated offender management approaches may make use of existing programmes including the Drug Interventions Programme and schemes that are based upon Prolific and other Priority Offender approaches which focus on a hard core of the most persistent offenders.

Multi-agency initiatives can also be directed at those whose actions threaten to cause serious harm in a locality, even if they have not previously offended. This raises the issue as to whether the main purpose of these schemes is to provide for the welfare of the offender (or those deemed to be potential offenders) or to serve the needs of society by interventions that seek to protect communities from the risk of criminal behaviour occurring. An example of partnership programmes whose main aim is to protect the public is Multi-Agency Public Protection Arrangements (MAPPAs), which have been developed in England and Wales to assess and manage the risk to the public posed by violent, dangerous or sex offenders when they are released from custody and placed back into the community. Considerations as to whether the offender's or society's interests should be paramount in multi-agency interventions affect the manner in which they are delivered – either sympathetically or coercively. This will heavily influence the way in which those on the receiving end react to them.

The resettlement of offenders

Key idea

The intention of programmes designed to combat recidivism is to enable offenders to reform their criminal habits and become resettled within communities.

The resettlement of offenders back into communities is a difficult objective to accomplish. This is so for a number of reasons.

Offenders may suffer from a range of social problems that include homelessness, unemployment, lack of education and vocational skills, health / mental health issues, debt, family breakdown, alcohol and drug dependence and behavioural difficulties. Although some of these problems can be addressed by programmes that have been referred to earlier in this chapter, it may be necessary to pursue a wide range of interventions at the same time in order to address offending behaviour. Concerted interventions of this nature carry considerable financial implications, which may not be readily forthcoming when offenders are in competition with law-abiding members of society for finite resources such as housing.

Case study

The background of prisoners may make reform, rehabilitation and resettlement into communities difficult to accomplish.

An examination of the backgrounds of prisoners in England and Wales revealed that they were a socially excluded group according to a wide range of indicators:

▶ 47% of male prisoners and 50% of female prisoners ran away from home as a child (compared with 11% of the general population);

▶ 27% of all prisoners had been taken into care as a child (compared to 2% of the general population);

- 43% of all prisoners had a family member convicted of a criminal offence (compared to 16% of the general population);

- 81% of all prisoners were unmarried prior to being imprisoned (compared to 39% of the general population who were unmarried);

- 30% of all prisoners regularly truanted from school (compared to 3% of the general population);

- 49% of male and 33% of female prisoners had been excluded from school (compared to 2% of the general population);

- 52% of male and 71% of female prisoners had no academic qualifications (compared to 15% of the general population);

- 65% of all prisoners had numeracy skills at or below Level 1 (compared to 23% of the general population);

- 48% of all prisoners had reading ability at or below Level 1 (compared to 21–23% of the general population);

- 82% of all prisoners had writing ability at or below Level 1 (there was no direct comparison available for the general population);

- 67% of all prisoners were unemployed in the four weeks prior to imprisonment (compared to 5% of the general population);

- 72% of male prisoners and 70% of female prisoners suffered from two or more mental disorders (compared to 5% of men and 2% of women in the general population);

- 44% of male prisoners and 62% of female prisoners suffered from three or more mental disorders (compared to 1% of men and 0% of women in the general population);

- 40% of male prisoners and 63% of female prisoners suffered from a neurotic disorder (compared to 12% of men and 18% of women in the general population);

- 64% of male prisoners and 50% of female prisoners suffered from a personality disorder (compared to 5.4% of men and 3.4% of women in the general population);

- 72% of all prisoners were in receipt of benefits immediately before entry into prison (compared to 13.7% of the working-age population);

▶ 32% of all prisoners were not living in permanent accommodation prior to imprisonment (compared to 0.9% of the general population).

These statistics may lead to the conclusion that prisons serve as warehouses of the unwanted.

Social Exclusion Unit (2002). *Reducing Re-offending by Ex-prisoners.* London: Office of the Deputy Prime Minister.

A further difficulty is that programmes designed to combat recidivism will not produce standardized responses from those who take part in them and, to work effectively, may require additional interventions and the resources with which to provide them.

An individual's transition from prison to the community is discussed in literature whose focus in desistance. This emphasizes the importance of factors such as motivation and argue that this needs to be sustained (often in the face of setbacks) in order for an offender to be successfully resettled in a community. Mentoring delivered on a one-to-one basis in the community is one way to overcome difficulties of this nature, but this also requires additional financial outlay.

Desistance is not an easy term to define: 'One of the key problems that has plagued desistance research has been how "desistance" can be defined and operationalized. [...] In theory, the concept is clear: to "cease and desist" means to abstain from committing further offending behavior. Yet, in practice, operationalizing this process has not been as easy. After all, even the highest rate offender surely takes a rest between committing crimes. As such, researchers have struggled with how exactly to distinguish "real" desistance from these predictable lulls between offences' (Maruna et al., 2004: 271–2).

Maruna, S., Lebel, T., Mitchell, N., and Napples, M. (2004). 'Pygmalion in the Reintegration Process: Desistance from Crime through the Looking Glass', *Psychology, Crime & Law* 10: 271–81.

Payment by results

Key idea

An important initiative of the UK's 2010 Coalition government designed to combat recidivism is to introduce the system of payment by results as a mechanism to improve the performance of prisons in attaining the reform of prisoners.

One incentive for prisons to effectively tackle the root causes of offending behaviour is being introduced in England and Wales by the policy of payment by results. This means that the rates of recidivism for individual prisons will be monitored. Those institutions which fail to achieve a satisfactory level of desistance will suffer a financial penalty whereas those which succeed in securing low rates of reoffending will be financially rewarded. This reform is underpinned by initiatives such as Social Impact Bonds whereby prisons secure finance from investors in the private sector who seek to make substantial profits from their outlay. This arrangement is designed to exert considerable pressure on prisons to reduce reoffending rates.

Dig deeper

Immarigeon, R. and Maruna, S, (eds) (2004). *After Crime and Punishment: Ex-offenders' Reintegration and Desistance from Crime.* Cullompton, Devon: Willan Publishing.

Mulheirn, I., Gough, B. and Menne, V. (2010*). Prison Break: Tackling Recidivism, Tackling Costs.* London: Social Market Foundation.

Ward, T. and Maruna, S. (2007). *Rehabilitation: Beyond the Risk Paradigm.* London: Taylor and Francis.

Fact-check

1 The term 'recidivism' means:
   A The rate at which convicted offenders reoffend on completion of the sentence imposed on them by the courts
   B The rate at which convicted offenders are able to find paid employment on completion of their sentence
   C The proportion of community penalties that offenders fail to complete
   D The comparative success rate of custodial and community sentences in preventing reoffending

2 In England and Wales a major initiative that was introduced in 2004 to reduce recidivism was:
   A The creation of the Ministry of Justice
   B The creation of the National Offender Management Service
   C The creation of the Office for Criminal Justice Reform
   D The creation of neighbourhood policing teams

3 In terms of reducing recidivism, which of the following is least effective?
   A A lengthy prison sentence
   B A community penalty
   C A fine
   D A short-term prison sentence

4 In England and Wales a major initiative of the 2010 Coalition government to encourage individual prisons to reduce the rate of recidivism was:
   A The appointment of Kenneth Clarke as Justice Secretary
   B The introduction of the system of best value into prison operations
   C The introduction of the principle of payment by results into prison funding
   D Increased expenditure on the Prison Service

5 The concept of 'desistance' refers to:
   A Programmes that seek to encourage offenders to give up alcohol
   B Programmes that seek to encourage offenders to give up drugs

C The elimination of all factors that may tempt an offender back into a life of crime

D Examinations that seek to provide an understanding of the factors that underpin an offender's decision to refrain from reoffending

6 In England and Wales, approximately what percentage of convicted offenders who receive custodial sentences reoffend within two years of their release?

A 20%

B 40%

C 60%

D 80%

19

The criminal justice system – is it fair?

It is important that the criminal justice system treats all members of society fairly and does not display prejudice towards any of its citizens. This chapter is concerned with examining the issue of racial and sexual discrimination within the criminal justice system. It focuses on contemporary events in England and Wales. In particular, it assesses whether all members of society are treated in the same manner by the main criminal justice agencies when they are suspected of having committed a crime and when they are victims of such actions.

Racial bias

Key idea

The criminal justice system has been accused of displaying bias towards minority ethnic groups so that race and colour of skin are regarded as factors that influence a person's treatment by the main criminal justice agencies.

Racial bias is based upon two factors – *racial prejudice* and *racial discrimination*. Racial prejudice denotes a person's irrational dislike of members of minority ethnic groups and racial discrimination refers to the acting out of those prejudices so that members of those groups suffer actual disadvantages. In this section we will examine two aspects of this in relation to the treatment given to members of minority ethnic groups when they are suspected of having committed a crime and when they are victims of crime.

MINORITY ETHNIC GROUPS AS SUSPECTS OF CRIME

Racial bias can be exhibited at various stages in the criminal justice system. The situation whereby excessive numbers of persons from minority ethnic groups enter the criminal justice system is sometimes referred to as 'disproportionality': this term denotes that a larger ratio of persons from these groups are arrested, prosecuted, sentenced and imprisoned than persons drawn from indigenous white groups.

The police service in a number of countries has been accused of bias against minority ethnic groups. In England and Wales an important manner in which this is reflected relates to the use of stop and search powers whereby police officers are authorized to search persons whom they encounter while performing patrol work. The routine use of this power requires the officer to have a justified (or reasonable) suspicion that the search will yield evidence relating to a criminal offence, although some legislation underpinning this power does not require this. It is frequently alleged that stop and search powers are used in a discriminatory way, underpinned by a stereotypical assumption that links black youths and crime.

What is perceived to be harassment of minority ethnic communities has long been a source of friction between themselves and the police service. This situation was argued to have been an important factor in explaining the riots that occurred in a number of English towns in 1981 and police–public relationships were argued to also have had a bearing on similar events that took place in 2011.

The powers of the police to stop and search may lead to a person being arrested, although arrests will also occur for reasons that are separate from stop and search powers, for example arising from a criminal act being observed by a police officer or being reported to the police by a member of the general public. In situations such as these, a police officer may decide to arrest a person or deal with the matter in another way (perhaps informally warning a person not to repeat the offence if it constitutes a minor act). The decision to arrest an offender may also be influenced by racial bias and result in a greater number of persons from minority ethnic communities being subject to this sanction.

The police serve as gatekeepers of the criminal justice system. Thus, if police officers display racial bias which results in large numbers of persons from minority ethnic groups being arrested, this bias will then affect the operations of other criminal justice agencies further down the line. Although these agencies may remedy the problem of police bias (for example, if the prosecuting authorities refuse to continue with a case referred to them by the police since they feel there is insufficient evidence to justify it being taken to court), this situation may be further aggravated if personnel employed by the courts and prisons also exhibit discriminatory behaviour.

A further series of injustices may therefore arise if persons from minority ethnic groups are more likely to be prosecuted for offences referred to them by the police service, are less likely to be granted bail pending a trial in a Crown Court, are more likely to be convicted by the courts and, if found guilty, are more likely to receive custodial sentences for their crimes.

Key idea

In England and Wales statistics are regularly produced by the Ministry of Justice in an annual publication entitled *Race and the Criminal Justice System*. This provides information that relates to the treatment of minority ethnic groups by the police service. These suggest that discrimination is a problem.

Allegations that discrimination exists towards members of minority ethnic groups who are suspected of having committed crime may be derived from statistics relating to outcomes at key stages of the criminal justice system:

► **Stop and search and arrest:** Figures released in 2010 suggested that black people were seven times more likely to be stopped by the police than were white people. Statistics for that year (based on a per one thousand population figure) also revealed that black people were three times more likely to be arrested than white people;

► **Crown Prosecution Service (CPS):** The existence of discriminatory action by the CPS is harder to establish. In 2003 a report that examined CPS decision-making entitled *Race for Justice* found some evidence of discriminatory treatment of African Caribbean defendants in relation to opposing the granting of bail and engaging in plea bargaining. The report also stated that a greater proportion of cases involving African Caribbean and Asian defendants failed when they reached court, perhaps suggesting an element of racial bias in discontinuance decisions that were perhaps taken with greater care and thought in the case of white defendants;

► **Imprisonment:** A report by the Ministry of Justice in 2008 stated that, in June 2007, there were five times more black British national prisoners in prison compared with their white British counterparts (the proportion of black prisoners relative to the population was 7.4 per 1,000 compared with 1.4 per 1,000 for white prisoners). In 2011 more than 25 per cent of the prison population in England and Wales whose ethnicity was recorded were from a minority ethnic group.

Statistics of this nature do not automatically prove that the criminal justice system in England and Wales is racially biased. There may be other interpretations – for example, higher rates of imprisonment experienced by minority ethnic groups may reflect a disproportionate tendency to commit more serious offences. Nonetheless, whether valid or not, statistics of this nature convey an image of bias that undermines the legitimacy of the criminal justice system in the eyes of many members of minority ethnic communities.

MINORITY ETHNIC GROUPS AS VICTIMS OF CRIME

Key idea

Members of minority ethnic groups frequently suffer from inadequate responses from the criminal justice system when they are victims of crime, especially in connection with crime that is racially motivated.

Discrimination towards members of minority ethnic groups can also be displayed in the manner in which the criminal justice system responds to their needs when they are victims of crime, in particular crime that is racially motivated – that is, a criminal act is directed against a person simply because of the colour of his or her skin. This is an aspect of what we refer to as *hate crime*.

Traditionally, the police service in England and Wales did not treat hate crime with the seriousness that it deserved. The racial motive was also downplayed, the act being viewed as a dispute between neighbours that did not require official intervention. When called upon to assist the victim of a racially motivated crime, there was a tendency to interview the alleged perpetrator of the offence rather than the victim. If, during the course of an attack, the victim took measures of self-defence, there was also a possibility that the police would view this action as a crime, especially if the victim picked up any sort of weapon during the attack. For reasons such as this, many instances of racially motivated violence failed to be reported to the police.

However, the scale of the problem began to be appreciated within official circles towards the end of the twentieth century. A report by the Home Affairs Committee of the House of Commons in 1981 estimated that around 7,000 racial attacks took place each year. This information was derived from incidents reported to the police; other data, derived from victimization surveys, suggested that the problem was significantly more serious than this – one study suggested that around 130,000 racial attacks had occurred in 1991.

If the police decided to charge a person with a racially motivated offence, there was no guarantee that this matter would be fairly handled by other criminal justice agencies. The Crown Prosecution Service might decide not to continue with the case or to remove the racial underpinning from the offence that they decided to prosecute; and even if the decision was made to prosecute an offender for a racially motivated crime, there was no guarantee that the courts would treat it fairly. Biases of magistrates, judges and (where used) juries might deny the victim justice. Nor was this problem confined to England and Wales. In the US, for example, the decision in 1991 by an all-white jury to acquit white Los Angeles police officers who had been filmed on video beating a black motorist, Rodney King, resulted in large-scale riots taking place as people reacted to this obvious display of racial bias.

In England and Wales concerns that the criminal justice system, and especially the police service, failed to deliver justice to members of minority ethnic groups when they were victims of crime came to a head in 1993 with the murder of a young black teenager, Stephen Lawrence, in South London. The Metropolitan Police Service failed to secure a conviction for this crime and public perceptions that the investigation had not been properly conducted eventually led to intervention by the Labour government that was elected in 1997. Home Secretary Jack Straw appointed a retired High Court judge, Sir William Macpherson, to examine the police investigation of this murder and issue a report.

Case study: Stephen Lawrence – the murder that shook a nation

In 1993 a young black teenager, Stephen Lawrence, was stabbed to death while waiting at a bus stop in Eltham, South London. His attackers were a gang of white youths and the murder was unambiguously racially motivated.

Unfortunately, the investigation conducted by the Metropolitan Police Service (MPS) was unable to bring the attackers to justice. Nor was a racial motive discerned. Stephen's parents attempted a private prosecution of those deemed responsible for the attack but the case was thrown out of court in 1994.

In 1997 a newly elected Labour government agreed to an investigation into the conduct of the MPS in this matter and a retired High Court judge, Sir William Macpherson, was chosen to conduct it.

Macpherson's report was published in 1999 and constituted a damning indictment of the conduct of the MPS in this matter. He concluded that the investigation was professionally incompetent and believed that institutional racism was a significant contributor to the botched investigation.

His report contained 70 recommendations that required action, most of which applied in whole or in part to the police service. His first recommendation was that Home Secretary Jack Straw should formulate a ministerial priority to rebuild the confidence between minority ethnic communities and the police service that would be measured by indicators such as the recruitment, promotion and retention of members of minority ethnic communities to the police service.

Macpherson also suggested that the definition of 'racist incident' should be amended to ensure that the police service became more victim-oriented when dealing with these matters, that the police service should be brought under the scope of the 1976 Race Relations Act (thus opening its actions to outside scrutiny) and that stop and search procedures should be subjected to stringent recording procedures.

However, perhaps his most important suggestion was that the double jeopardy rule should be changed to allow a person who had been acquitted of a crime to be prosecuted for it again should new and compelling evidence subsequently emerge. This change was incorporated into the 2003 Criminal Justice Act and in 2012 two persons (one of whom had been acquitted of Stephen Lawrence's murder in 1994) were convicted and received sentences of life imprisonment. The new evidence arose from the analysis of samples that were collected at the time, which advances in forensic science made possible to analyse and pin to the pair who were subsequently convicted.

In a report written in 1999, retired High Court judge Sir William Macpherson branded the police service in England and Wales as 'institutionally racist'. His definition of this term was 'the collective failure of an organization to provide an appropriate and professional service to people because of their colour, culture or ethnic origin. It can be detected in processes, attitudes and behaviour which amount to discrimination through unwitting prejudice, ignorance, thoughtlessness and racist stereotyping which disadvantage minority ethnic people' (Macpherson, 1999: para. 6.34, p. 28).

Macpherson, Sir W. (1999). *The Stephen Lawrence Inquiry. Report of an Inquiry by Sir William Macpherson of Cluny.* London: TSO, Cm. 4262.

Gender discrimination

Women have traditionally experienced discrimination in employment within the criminal justice system. In the police service, for example, in 1971 only 3,884 female police officers were employed in the 43 police forces in England and Wales. Reforms that included the 1970 Equal Pay Act and the 1975 Sex Discrimination Act improved the status of women in the police service and in other criminal justice agencies, but much remained to be accomplished to provide for equality of opportunity. Currently around 26 per cent of police officers in England and Wales are female.

> *A particular problem faced by women is the culture of agencies within the criminal justice system. In connection with the police service in England and Wales, it has been observed that 'the role of policewomen is ambiguous in that they are not fully accepted as equals by their male colleagues. [...] At the heart of all these issues is the question of what kind of impact the Sex Discrimination Act has had on the career prospects of women in an organization which is characterized by its predominantly male-oriented culture in which physical strength and prowess are prized attributes' (Jones, 1986: 21–2).*
>
> Jones, S.(1986). *Policewomen and Equality: Formal Policy versus Informal Practice.* Basingstoke: Macmillan.

Further reforms were embodied in the 2006 and 2010 Equality Acts. However, a report by the Fawcett Society in 2009 (*Women and the Criminal Justice System*) stated that in 2008:

▶ Only 12% of police officers at chief inspector rank and above were female;

▶ Only 15.9% of partners in the UK's ten largest law firms were women;

▶ Only 42 females compared to 479 males were QCs in the top 30 sets of the UK bar. The number of female applicants for QC in this year stood at its lowest level for ten years;

▶ Below one-quarter of prison governors were female and below one-quarter of prison offices were women;

▶ Around 10% of High Court judges and around 8% of Court of Appeal judges were women. There was only one female Law Lord (who had been appointed in 2004).

In 2010 the National Police Improvement Agency estimated that on current rates of progression (without wastage) it would take 57 years for there to be 35 per cent of women at the rank of chief superintendent.

THE CRIMINAL JUSTICE SYSTEM AND WOMEN WHO COMMIT CRIME

Key idea

There is debate as to whether the criminal justice system is more lenient towards women offenders or adopts a harsher attitude towards them.

The main issue relating to women who committed crime was whether they were treated fairly. There are two views relating to this.

The first of these suggested that women who committed crime were treated more leniently than male offenders. Criminal justice professions were dominated by males who adopted a protective attitude towards females and did not rigorously enforce the law when they had committed a crime. This especially affected the way in which police criminal justice practitioners used their discretion – a police officer might decide to warn or officially caution a female offender and a magistrate or judge might impose a community penalty rather than a custodial sentence on a woman who came before the courts. We refer to this lenient attitude as 'male chivalry'.

However, the view that women offenders received more lenient treatment within the criminal justice system was not universally accepted. A counter argument was that of 'double deviance'.

This suggested that women offenders received discriminatory treatment within the criminal justice system since the attitude that was adopted by criminal justice practitioners reflected both the seriousness of the crime and the extent to which the crime constituted a departure from the role that society expected of women, in particular in relation to being a housewife and bringing up children. Thus, a female whose crime was one of violence, especially when children were the victims of it, would expect to receive a harsher penalty than a male for whom violence was seen as a socially acceptable attribute. We refer to this form of discriminatory treatment as 'double deviance', and in England and Wales it was historically reflected in charging decisions where a female who under extreme provocation killed an abusive male partner would be charged with murder rather than manslaughter.

Criminologists hold different opinions as to whether male chivalry or double deviance accurately describes the treatment typically received by women in the criminal justice system. One problem in coming down on one side rather than another is the difficulty of obtaining a sample of male and female offenders who have committed a similar crime in identical circumstances.

THE CRIMINAL JUSTICE SYSTEM AND WOMEN AS VICTIMS OF CRIME

Women may suffer from a further form of discrimination within the criminal justice system relating to their treatment when they are victims of crime. This problem especially affects the attitude adopted towards women who are victims of crime including sexual abuse, domestic violence and rape.

Practitioners within the criminal justice system may adopt a discriminatory attitude towards females who have been the victim of male violence. In England and Wales this attitude was evidenced by a tendency of police forces not to intervene in cases of domestic violence and by the procedure adopted by the courts when dealing with serious crimes such as rape. Issues that included the absence of evidence to corroborate a woman's accusation coupled with trial procedures which generally permitted a woman to be cross-examined regarding her lifestyle and sexual history contributed towards an extremely low conviction rate that, even with changes in the law brought about by the 2003 Sexual Offences Act, is considerably less than 10 per cent.

This situation has led some criminologists to argue that violence displayed by men towards women is designed to ensure that women are placed in a position of social subordination to men and this aspect of a patriarchal society is reflected in the way in which the criminal justice system may excuse or mitigate male violence towards women. This attitude was starkly displayed in England in 1982 when a judge (male) stated that a women hitchhiker who was raped by the male who offered her a lift was herself guilty of contributory negligence – in other words, she had provoked the male's natural sexual urges.

> *Male violence towards women and the response to this by the criminal justice system has provoked considerable criminological attention. This violence has been attributed to 'a conscious and systematic attempt by men to maintain women's social subordination' (Eardley, 1995: 137) and viewed as an aspect of 'a patriarchal culture' (Kennedy, 2005).*
>
> Eardley, T. (1995). 'Violence and Sexuality', in S. Caffrey and G. Mundy (eds), *The Sociology of Crime and Deviance: Selected Issues*. Dartford: Greenwich University Press.
>
> Kennedy, H. (2005). 'Why is the Criminal Justice System Still against Women?' *The Guardian*, 10 March.

Reforms to combat racial and gender discrimination

The above sections have referred to a range of problems that relate to racial and gender discrimination within the criminal justice system. This final section examines the way in which this problem may be addressed.

Key idea

Gender and racial discrimination can be tackled by reforms to the criminal justice system that affect recruitment and training. There are also more coercive approaches that can be adopted whereby those on the receiving end of discrimination can seek redress from official machinery and the law.

RECRUITMENT

One way to tackle discrimination experienced by minority ethnic groups and women in the criminal justice system (whether as offenders or as victims of crime) is to make the criminal justice professions more representative of the society in which they operate. This entails recruiting more members of minority ethnic groups and women in the key criminal justice professions. The rationale for doing this is that minority ethnic and female criminal justice practitioners would deal more fairly with members of the social groups from which they derive in connection with both offending behaviour and when they were victims of crime.

> Lord Scarman's investigation into the urban disorders that occurred in 1981 emphasized that diversity should underpin recruitment policies. His comments are as valid today as when they were first made. 'There is widespread agreement that the composition of our police forces must reflect the make-up of the society they serve. In one important respect [...] it does not do so: in the police [...] the ethnic minorities are very significantly under-represented. [...] The real problem is not that too many members of the ethnic minorities fail to meet the standards of appointment, but that too few apply' (Scarman, 1081: para. 5.6, p. 76).

> However, reforms to enhance the level of diversity in the police service have had a limited impact on its composition:

> In 2011, there were a total number of 135,838 police officers. Of these:

> ▶ 95,962 (69%) were white male
> ▶ 36,532 (26%) were female
> ▶ 6,615 (5%) were Black and Minority Ethnic (Berman, 2012).

Scarman, Lord (1981). *The Brixton Disorders 10–12 April 1981. Report of an Inquiry by the Rt. Hon. The Lord Scarman, OBE.* London: HMSO, Cmnd. 8427.

Berman, G., (2012). *Police Numbers.* London: House of Commons Library (available online – www.parliament.uk/briefing-papers/SN02615.pdf).

In the US the quota system can be used to achieve this objective – thus, if a city had an Hispanic population of around 30 per cent, this ratio ought to be reflected in key criminal justice agencies such as the police force. If, instead of 30 per cent, only 3 per cent of the city's police force were Hispanic, discrimination might be assumed as the explanation which could lead to a costly class action being brought against the offending institution.

UK law does not permit a quota system and instead equal opportunities policies have been put forward to address racial or gender discrimination in the criminal justice professions. This has succeeded in increasing the number of minority ethnic and female criminal justice practitioners but has not totally resolved historic imbalances in recruitment trends.

Recruitment is only one aspect of reforms designed to make the criminal justice system more socially representative. It also entails ensuring that members from minority ethnic groups and women do not experience racial or sexual harassment at work and do not suffer from discrimination in issues that include promotion and internal disciplinary procedures. The monitoring of wastage rates is one indicator of the extent to which harassment and discrimination have been successfully tackled within the criminal justice professions.

TRAINING

Training is a further way through which to combat racial and gender discrimination within the criminal justice system. It is primarily directed at those who are members of the social groups who dominate the criminal justice professions and is designed to make them more sensitive to the needs and concerns of minority ethnic groups and women both as suspected criminal offenders and as victims of crime.

A particular problem affects how training of this nature should be delivered and the extent to which it succeeds in altering the attitudes of criminal justice practitioners in their everyday work. Racism, for example, might be tackled through programmes that have a multicultural or an antiracist focus. The former suggests that racial prejudice and discrimination arise from misunderstandings between races that can be addressed by providing a greater awareness of the background and culture of minority ethnic groups. Antiracist training, however, seeks to make participants aware that they may harbour racist sentiments (even if they are not immediately aware of this) and the aim of the training is to bring this to the surface as a starting point for individuals to seek to alter their beliefs and actions. This is more challenging than multicultural training and, if delivered insensitively, may result in an atmosphere of aggression between trainers and participants which fails to remedy the problem.

FORMAL COMPLAINTS MACHINERY

Those who have suffered from what they regard as discriminatory treatment by criminal justice agencies may have the ability to address their concerns to a formal complaints machinery. This may examine complaints made by members of the general public about the conduct of professionals working within specific agencies, In England and Wales examples of this include the Independent Police Complaints Commission that was set up in 2004 to deal with complaints regarding the conduct of police officers.

Additionally, other agencies may exercise a superintending role over the operations of public bodies including agencies within the criminal justice system. In England and Wales the Equalities and Human Rights Commission can fulfil this role and intervene if it feels that sections of the public are being subjected to discriminatory behaviour.

LEGAL RECOURSE

Persons who feel that they have suffered discriminatory actions by the criminal justice system may also refer the matter to the courts. In England and Wales those who felt that they had been treated unfairly by members of the police service might take out a civil suit against the officer's chief constable.

The European Convention on Human Rights also offers the hope of redress in those countries that have signed up to it. Article 14 specifically outlaws discrimination and this can be applied both by the personnel working within criminal justice agencies and members of the general public who have experienced what they regard as discriminatory treatment in their dealings with these bodies.

Dig deeper

Bowling, B. and Phillips, C. (2002). *Racism, Crime and Justice.* Harlow: Longman.

Hall, N., Grieve, J. and Savage, S. (2009). *Policing and the Legacy of Lawrence.* Cullompton, Devon: Willan Publishing.

Kennedy, H. (1993). *Eve Was Framed.* London: Vintage.

Walklate, S. (2004). *Gender, Crime and Criminal Justice*, 2nd edn. Cullompton, Devon: Willan Publishing.

Fact-check

1 The term 'institutional racism' refers to:
  A Racial prejudice exhibited by members of an organization
  B The culture and working practices of an organization that result in discriminatory outcomes, whether intended or not
  C Racism that is embedded within society
  D Racist views held by senior members of an organization that they insist are adopted throughout the organization

2 In England and Wales there were approximately 135,000 police officers in 2011. What percentage of these were female?
  A 56%
  B 46%
  C 36%
  D 26%

3 In England and Wales the report into the investigation conducted by the Metropolitan Police Service into the murder of Stephen Lawrence was written by:
  A Lord Scarman
  B Lord Bradley
  C Sir William Macpherson
  D Sir Patrick Carter

4 In the UK the first female Law Lord (who would now be titled Justice of the Supreme Court) was appointed in:
  A 1945
  B 1963
  C 1975
  D 2004

5 In England and Wales the 1984 Police and Criminal Evidence Act authorized police officers to stop and search members of the general public:
  A Whenever they felt like doing so
  B When there were reasonable grounds to suspect that the search would produce evidence relating to a criminal act
  C When they didn't like the look of them
  D When a group of six or more persons had gathered between the hours of midnight and 6 a.m.

6 In connection with policing in England and Wales, the term 'disproportionality' refers to:

A The over-recruitment of members from minority ethnic groups into police forces

B The under-recruitment of members from minority ethnic groups into police forces

C The targeting of members of minority ethnic groups in activities such as stop and search

D The high rate at which minority ethnic police officers leave the police service

20

Studying criminology

Gathering information is a crucial aspect of criminological study. This enables us to put forward ideas that are supported by evidence. There are, however, a number of ways that we may use to gather information. This chapter is concerned with study methods. It seeks to provide a brief discussion of the main approaches that we use to study criminology and criminal justice policies and also aims to give a brief account of the way in which material should be researched and presented by those in the early stages of studying criminology in an academic institution.

Approaches to criminological research

Detailed investigations related to criminological study require the researcher to produce original findings that are based on material that has not been previously published. There are two approaches that may be used to do this – *quantitative* and *qualitative* research methodologies.

Key idea

There are two main approaches that may be used to provide new and original insights into a criminological problem. These approaches can be based on either *quantitative* or *qualitative* methodologies (or a combination of both).

Quantitative methodologies are based upon the gathering of data that is capable of being analysed through the use of statistical methods. The findings that are produced in this manner form the basis of conclusions regarding the subject matter that is under consideration. Quantitative methodologies are often used in connection with new approaches to criminological or criminal justice issues to ascertain, for example, whether a programme that is designed to prevent offending behaviour succeeds in this objective. For this reason, quantitative approaches are an important tool in the evaluation of criminal justice policy and the findings that are produced are designed to have wide application across the criminal justice system.

Qualitative methodologies seek to provide an understanding of a criminological or a criminal justice issue from the perspective of those who have first-hand experience of the problem and seek to enable them to 'tell their own tale'. For example, if a criminologist wishes to find out the realities of prison life, one way to approach this issue would be to interview prisoners and those who work in custodial institutions. Although the findings derived from qualitative methodologies may apply only to the person who provides the information, this approach does enable tentative conclusions to be drawn which could provide the basis of further study, perhaps using quantitative methodologies.

Ethical issues in research

Ethical considerations underpin the conduct of all criminological research. This means that legal and moral obligations are placed upon the researcher to ensure his or her personal safety and to uphold the rights and sensibilities of those who are the subjects of the research.

Spotlight

It is important that ethical considerations are fully considered when conducting criminological research. For example, one aspect of field research that could be relevant to investigating paedophilia is examining images posted on Internet sites. However, neither the police nor the courts might be willing to accept that your rationale for doing this was academic and your research could land you with a prison sentence.

The key ethical considerations that underpin criminological research are:

▶ The researcher must comply with the law – they should not, for example, participate in criminal actions in order to gather material or to secure credibility with those who are the subjects of the research;

▶ The methods used to gather research must be morally defensible. When researching into sensitive areas, consideration should be given as to how the information required can be gathered using ways that minimize any potential legal risk or accusation of moral impropriety;

▶ Those who are the subjects of research should be provided with guarantees of anonymity and confidentiality. These guarantees have implications for the safe storage of the data collected during the research study;

▶ The purpose of the research should normally be fully explained to participants, who should also be given the assurance that they can opt out of the study at any time and that any information that they have contributed to it will be removed. Those who opt out must not be placed under any subsequent pressure to become involved again in the project;

▶ Participants should normally have given their express consent to be involved in the research project. There may be exceptions to this, typically in connection with covert research (which we will consider below) when the researcher may decide that the end result of the study justifies withholding information of this nature from those who have been studied;

▶ Where samples are used, the researcher should ensure that the size of the group is appropriate for the investigation in hand – in particular, unnecessarily large samples should be avoided;

▶ All risks to the researcher and to his or her subjects should be fully assessed before any research is commenced. The key objective is to ensure that the researcher and the subjects of research are not placed in any danger arising from the project;

▶ Care must be taken to avoid any course of action that causes unnecessary distress to those who are the subjects of research.

Key research methods

There are a number of ways through which we can conduct quantitative and qualitative research. One of these entails the use of surveys.

SURVEYS AND SAMPLING

Key idea

Surveys are directed at a small section of the population and are designed to provide us with information on a criminological problem whose findings can be applied to a broader section of the population.

Surveys are an important tool of quantitative research methodology and seek to gather information on a criminological issue from a number of people whose views can be used as the basis of formulating conclusions which may shape the future direction of criminological and criminal justice approaches.

There are various ways through which surveys may be conducted. These include questionnaires, interviews and the use of focus groups. The key issue that underpins surveys is the way in which participants are chosen.

The starting point is to identify all persons whose opinions are potentially relevant to the issue that is being investigated. We refer to this as the 'sampling frame'. However, unless the issue being investigated is relevant to only a small number of people, it would not be feasible to survey all of those whose views are relevant to it. We need, therefore, to address our survey to a smaller section of the overall sampling frame. The process that we use to reduce the sampling frame down to a manageable number that can be surveyed is known as 'sampling'.

There are various forms of sampling that may be used in criminological investigation. The sample may be randomly selected from the sampling frame in a manner that is similar to drawing names out of a hat. Alternatively, what is termed *stratified sampling* may be employed. This entails breaking the sampling frame into a number of subgroups or categories, defined, perhaps, in terms of factors that are relevant to the issue being investigated. This may include social class, race, gender, age or disability. Persons from each subgroup are then chosen to complete the survey using the same approach as is used in random sampling except that names are pulled out of several 'hats' rather than one.

Another widely used form of sampling is known as *quota sampling*. This is employed in market research and may also be employed during election contests to discover the level of support for political parties in the run-up to polling day. Typically, the sampling frame used is the general population and this is then broken down into a number of subgroups in order to try to ensure that all key sections of the general population are represented. Those conducting the survey will then be asked to select a specified number of persons drawn from each of the designated categories.

Other forms of sampling include *convenience sampling* and *snowball sampling*. In the former, the survey is addressed to an audience that is convenient for the researcher to approach. Thus, an undergraduate student conducting research into student experiences of crime might survey all the persons in his or her hall of residence. Snowball sampling entails an approach whereby a researcher addresses a survey to a person or small group of persons who then provide him or her with further contacts who can be surveyed, thus enabling the researcher to gain access to an audience that might otherwise not have been accessible. Both methods suffer from a similar problem in that there is no guarantee that the information that is obtained is truly representative of the broader sampling frame.

ETHNOGRAPHIC STUDIES

Surveys, whatever methods are used and sampling techniques employed, are primarily associated with quantitative research methodology. Qualitative research, however, is commonly identified with the use of what are termed 'ethnographic studies'.

Key idea

Ethnographic studies focus on the views and opinions of those whose experiences or conduct is being investigated. This approach is associated with qualitative research methodology and is conducted through the mechanism of field research.

Ethnographic studies seek to obtain secure information regarding a criminological issue through a prolonged period of face-to-face contact between the researcher and the person (or persons) who are the subject of research. We refer to this as *field research*. The participant's perspective is placed centre stage of the research and the aim of the researcher is to gain an insight into the social world of the subject(s) and discover information on issues such as why they act the way they do, the meanings that they attach to their actions, and their perceptions and emotions regarding a particular situation in which they are placed.

Information of this nature may be gained in a prolonged interview conducted between a researcher and subject. The nature of this interview may resemble a lengthy conversation (or series of conversations) and is technically referred to as an unstructured interview (which, unlike a structured interview associated with quantitative research, is not capable of being subjected to statistical analysis). Alternatively, a researcher may become a member of a group or a community that he or she wishes to investigate. This may involve observing the actions of the group with their full consent and knowledge, in which case the researcher acts in the manner of a 'fly on the wall'. Alternatively, a researcher may infiltrate a group and observe their actions without them giving their permission to be the subject of criminological examination. We refer to this as *covert research* in which the subjects are not aware that they are the subject of observation.

> Covert research is defined as: 'Research that is undertaken without the consent or knowledge of respondents. This type of social research is most strongly associated with participant observational work where a researcher joins a group or organization assuming a covert role in order to observe first-hand the functioning and daily life of the group' (Davidson, 2006: 48).
> Davidson, J. (2006), in V. Jupp (ed.). *The Sage Dictionary of Social Research Methods.* London: Sage.

COVERT RESEARCH

Covert research raises ethical concerns relating to subjects being studied without their permission being sought and also may affect the reliability of research if a researcher studying the actions of a group begins to sympathize with their actions and the sentiments that underpin them. This is sometimes referred to as going native and in extreme cases may result in a researcher who has joined a group to observe its actions becoming a fully fledged member of it and participating in its activities.

Case study: Covert research and ethical issues

Criminological research needs to adhere to ethical guidelines – but are there times when they can legitimately be broken? Let us consider the following case.

In 2003 television reporter Mark Daly joined the Greater Manchester Police as a probationer constable. However, his aim was not to pursue a career in policing but, rather, to examine the extent to which racism within policing had been eradicated following the publication of the Macpherson Report in 1999 which had branded the police service institutionally racist.

In the early weeks of his training he secretly filmed his fellow recruits at a training centre in Bruche, Warrington, some of whom articulated extreme racist sentiments and behaviour. The findings of the undercover journalist formed the basis of a television programme, *The Secret Policeman*, which was screened in 2003.

The programme was important in that it raised the question as to how persons harbouring extreme racist views were able to secure entry into the police service. In this sense, the research provided valuable evidence that more needed to be done to tackle racism in the police service and in particular to prevent racists from gaining entry.

However, gathering information from subjects without their express knowledge or consent and then making their views public knowledge has considerable ethical implications. The justification for doing this might be that this was a serious matter that needed to be addressed, that this was the only course of action that could be used to secure such information and that the end justified the means.

Do you agree?

All research (whether performed by overt or covert methods) requires a constant evaluation of ethical considerations: 'engagement with the ethics of research is not a ritualistic tick box that once done at the beginning of the project can then be obviated, but runs throughout the lifetime of a project. Although such ethical reflexivity is more pronounced in covert research, it applies clearly to overt research contexts as well. A proportion of covert practices are routinely glossed over in sanitized overt accounts. [...] In certain research contexts it is difficult to maintain a strict either/or division between overt and covert hence the messy reality is more akin to a continuum' (Calvey, 2008: 909).

Calvey, D. (2008). 'The Art and Politics of Covert Research: Doing "Situated Ethics"' in the Field', *Sociology* 42: 905–18.

Studying criminology

The above section has briefly considered the main approaches that may be conducted by professional criminologists who seek to advance the discipline through original research into an issue. The following section discusses how to study criminology at university. It examines the manner in which students in their early stages of studying criminology at universities are taught and how they should research and present written material.

THE TEACHING OF CRIMINOLOGY

Students who study criminology within universities are provided with information by their course tutors. This is commonly delivered in the format of a lecture in which a tutor imparts knowledge of a particular topic. This is typically delivered verbally, although technology such as podcasts may also be employed instead of, or as a supplement to, a traditional lecture. Lectures may also be supplemented by other sources that include providing links to various forms of electronic sources.

University teaching also makes use of seminars or tutorials in which small groups of students meet to discuss a topic under the guidance of a tutor. This method of teaching typically entails students being provided with a question or a topic for discussion and a range of sources that they should consult in order to discuss the issue. Classes of this nature are designed as opportunities for students to air their views and opinions: they are interactive in nature and seek to ensure that everybody who attends can learn from each other.

Assessment forms an important aspect of university teaching and learning experiences. It aims to examine how well students have understood the subjects that they have been studying. Assessment used within universities falls into two broad categories – *formative* and *summative* assessment.

Formative assessment consists of work that is submitted to a tutor but does not count towards the final grade that is given to a piece of work. It seeks to enable a tutor to identify a student's knowledge and understanding of a topic, identify strengths and weaknesses in his or her approach to it and eliminate bad practices before the work is submitted for formal assessment.

Summative assessment comprises material that is formally submitted and graded by a tutor. This may take many forms that include presentations, examinations or assessed written work. In the following section we will consider a number of issues that relate to researching for and presenting written work.

PREPARING AND PRESENTING WRITTEN WORK

Key idea

One way to study criminology is to consult material that has been published by others. We refer to this as *documentary* (or *library-based*) *research*.

Some of the methods used by professional criminologists will also be used by students to gather material in relation to an issue they are examining. Methods such as interviews and questionnaires are often used (especially in final-year undergraduate dissertations). However, the aim of this research is usually to supplement existing published material with information that the student has gathered rather than making the original research the prime focus of the study.

In the early stages of studying criminology, much of our knowledge will be gained from reading material that has already been published. In doing this, we are aiming to make sense of a wide range of literature and perhaps write up our findings in a format such as an essay or a case study. This is referred to as *documentary research*. The material that we consult may consist of books and journal articles written by professional criminologists (which are termed secondary sources) or it may comprise material that is published by official criminal justice agencies (such as the Home Office or Ministry of Justice in England and Wales) or written by those with first-hand knowledge of crime and the operations of the criminal justice system (which we refer to as *primary sources*).

Key idea

In the early stages of studying criminology, students will be asked to present material in a variety of written formats. There are important rules that need to be observed when presenting this material.

Students who study criminology for an academic qualification will periodically be required to present work on topics which are often chosen for them by their tutors. This may entail delivering material verbally (for example, in the form of a presentation to a class of fellow students) but will also include some form of written work. This may take various forms such as a traditional essay, a report, a case study or a book review. In the final year of undergraduate study it is common for students to write an elongated piece of work in the form of a project or a dissertation that enables them to study in depth a topic which is of interest to them.

There are a number of matters that must be considered when presenting written work, regardless of the format which it takes.

▶ **Analysis:** Although written work needs to be based upon factual material, it is important that it should also contain analysis based upon a detailed consideration of the issues that are related to the factual content of the work. It is further important that the analysis should consider all sides of the argument even if, having considered all relevant aspects, you come down of one side of an argument rather than another;

▶ **Use of sources:** Written work that is presented during the course of academic study must be based on published literature and, further, material that has been consulted must appear as references in the text of the work itself and also at the end in the bibliography. There are a number of approved ways to reference sources and prepare bibliographies, the most widely used of which are the Harvard and the Chicago (or numeric) referencing systems;

▶ **Plagiarism:** In its basic form, plagiarism is cheating – it entails an attempt to pass off someone else's work as your own. This commonly entails taking material from something that you have read and putting this in your written work without acknowledging the source from which it was taken. Plagiarism is relatively easily detected using devices such as the JISC 'Turnitin' plagiarism detection software and in academic institutions the penalties for doing this can be severe;

▶ **Use of the Internet:** The Internet provides a range of material that is relevant to the study of criminology. However, one problem with the Internet is that anyone with the technical know-how can post material in this format and there is no form of quality control that will weed out material that is based upon inadequate research or which imparts information which is completely inaccurate. This criticism does not, however, apply to books or journals which are available in electronic format or to material available on the Internet that is published by official bodies such as government departments.

Dig deeper

Bryman, A. (2008). *Social Research Methods*, 3rd edn. Oxford: Oxford University Press.

Calvey, D. (2013). *Undercover: Art, Politics and Ethics.* London: Sage.

Joyce, P. (2009). *Criminology and Criminal Justice: A Study Guide.* Cullompton, Devon: Willan Publishing.

May. T. (2004). *Social Research: Issues, Methods and Process,* 3rd edn. Buckingham: Open University Press.

Fact-check

1 The gathering of data that is capable of being analysed through the use of statistical methods in connection with criminological research is known as:

A Field research

B Quantitative methodology

C Qualitative methodology

D Convenience sampling

2 An example of covert research conducted in England and Wales formed the basis for a television programme, *The Secret Policeman*, which was screened in 2003. What issue did this programme seek to raise?

A The operations of the Security Service (MI5)

B The work performed by members of the Special Constabulary

C The prevalence of racism in the police service

D The operations of the Secret Service (MI6)

3 The term 'snowball sampling' refers to research that is gathered:

A In the winter months

B In connection with cold case review

C On the basis of respondents providing further contacts who can be approached by the researcher

D From those whom it is convenient for the researcher to approach

4 The term given to research that seeks to obtain information through a prolonged period of face-to-face contact between a researcher and a person who is the subject of research is known as:

A Ethnographic study

B Convenience sampling

C Quota sampling

D An interview

5 Documentary research is conducted on the basis of:

A Factual television programmes

B A discussion and analysis of material that has been previously published

Index

Answers

CHAPTER 1

1 B

2 C

3 A

4 B

5 A

6 B

CHAPTER 2

1 B

2 A

3 D

4 D

5 A

6 A

CHAPTER 3

1 A

2 B

3 C

4 C

5 D

6 C

CHAPTER 4

1 D

2 A

3 D

4 C

5 C

6 B

CHAPTER 5

1 A

2 B

3 B

4 C

5 C

6 C

CHAPTER 6

1 A

2 D

3 B

4 C

5 D

6 B

CHAPTER 7

1 A

2 A

3 D

4 C

5 C

6 D

CHAPTER 8

1 C

2 B

3 C

4 D

5 B

6 B

CHAPTER 9

1 B

2 A

3 C

4 A

5 B

6 C

CHAPTER 10

1 B

2 C

3 B

4 D

5 B

6 C

CHAPTER 11

1 C

2 A

3 D

4 C

5 B

6 A

CHAPTER 12

1 B

2 A

3 D

4 C

5 D

6 B

CHAPTER 13

1 B

2 B

3 D

4 B

5 A

6 C

CHAPTER 14

1 C

2 A

3 C

4 D

5 B

6 D

CHAPTER 15

1 B

2 A

3 C

4 C

5 B

6 C

CHAPTER 16

1 A

2 C

3 B

4 C

5 B

6 D

CHAPTER 17

1 C

2 B

3 A

4 C

5 D

6 B

CHAPTER 18

1 A

2 B

3 D

4 C

5 D

6 C

CHAPTER 19

1 B

2 D

3 C

4 D

5 B

6 B

CHAPTER 20

1 B

2 C

3 C

4 A

5 B

6 D